Well-Ordered License

APPLICATIONS OF POLITICAL THEORY

Series Editors: Harvey Mansfield, Harvard University, and Daniel J. Mahoney, Assumption College

This series encourages analysis of the applications of political theory to various domains of thought and action. Such analysis will include works on political thought and literature, statesmanship, American political thought, and contemporary political theory. The editors also anticipate and welcome examinations of the place of religion in public life and commentary on classic works of political philosophy.

Early Modern Skepticism and the Origins of Toleration, edited by Alan Levine

Machiavelli's Romans: Liberty and Greatness in the Discourses on Livy, by J. Patrick Coby

Privilege and Liberty and Other Essays in Political Philosophy, by Aurel Kolnai, edited by Daniel J. Mahoney

Tyranny in Shakespeare, by Mary Ann McGrail

The Liberal Tradition in Focus: Problems and New Perspectives, edited by João Carlos Espada, Mark F. Plattner, and Adam Wolfson

Lincoln's Sacred Effort: Defining Religion's Role in American Self-Government, by Lucas E. Morel

The Moral of the Story: Literature and Public Ethics, edited by Henry T. Edmondson III

Well-Ordered License: On the Unity of Machiavelli's Thought, by Markus Fischer

Well-Ordered License

On the Unity of Machiavelli's Thought

Markus Fischer

LEXINGTON BOOKS
Lanham • Boulder • New York • Oxford

LEXINGTON BOOKS

Published in the United States of America
by Lexington Books
4720 Boston Way, Lanham, Maryland 20706

12 Hid's Copse Road
Cumnor Hill, Oxford OX2 9JJ, England

Cover illustration by M. Jules Duvaux. In *La Colonne Trajane* by W. Froehner (Paris, 1865). The Roman republic approximates Machiavelli's best regime. Relying on superior organization, its soldiers conquered most of the Western world.

British Library Cataloguing in Publication Information Available

Library of Congress Cataloging-in-Publication Data

Fischer, Markus, 1957–
    Well-ordered license : on the unity of Machiavelli's thought / Markus Fischer.
      p.   cm.
    Includes bibliographical references and index.
    ISBN 0-7391-0107-2 (alk. paper) — ISBN 0-7391-0108-0 (pbk. : alk. paper)
    1. Machiavelli, Niccolò, 1469–1527. I. Title.
B785.M24 F57 2000
320.1′092—dc21   99-052998

Printed in the United States of America

♾™ The paper used in this publication meets the minimum requirements of American National Standard for Information Sciences—Permanence of Paper for Printed Library Materials, ANSI/NISO Z39.48–1992.

Contents

Abbreviations

A.[p]   Niccolò Machiavelli, *Dell' Ambizione* [On ambition], in TO.983-987, mt

AS.[ch].[p]   Niccolò Machiavelli, *L'Asino* [The ass], in TO.954-976, mt

AG.[bk].[p]   Niccolò Machiavelli, *Dell'Arte della Guerra* [On the art of war], in TO.299-398, mt

C.[act].[scene]   Niccolò Machiavelli, *Clizia,* in TO.891-913, mt

CC.[p]   Niccolò Machiavelli, *La vita di Castruccio Castracani da Lucca* [The life of Castruccio Castracani of Lucca], in TO.613-28

CW.[vol].[p]   Niccolò Machiavelli, *Machiavelli: The Chief Works and Others,* trans. Allan Gilbert (Durham: Duke University Press, 1958)

D.[bk].[ch].[§]   Niccolò Machiavelli, *Discourses on Livy,* trans. Harvey C. Mansfield and Nathan Tarcov (Chicago: University of Chicago Press, 1996)

Ded   Dedication or dedicatory letter

DF.[p]   Niccolò Machiavelli, *Discursus Florentinarum Rerum post Mortem Iunioris Laurentii Medices* [Discourse on Florentine affairs after the death of Lorenzo de' Medici the Younger], in TO.24-31, mt

ea	emphasis added
F.[p]	Niccolò Machiavelli, *Di Fortuna* [On Fortune], in TO.976-979, mt
FH.[bk].[§]	Niccolò Machiavelli, *Florentine Histories,* trans. Laura F. Banfield and Harvey C. Mansfield, Jr. (Princeton: Princeton University Press, 1988)
L.[no].[p]	Niccolò Machiavelli, *Lettere* [Letters], in TO.1007-1256, mt
M.[act].[scene]	Niccolò Machiavelli, *Mandragola,* in TO.868-890, mt
mt	my translation
P.[ch].[p]	Niccolò Machiavelli, *The Prince,* trans. Harvey C. Mansfield, Jr. (Chicago: University of Chicago Press, 1985)
Pref	preface, prologue, or proem
T	Title or chapter heading
TO.[p]	Niccolò Machiavelli, *Tutte le Opere* [Complete works], ed. Mario Martelli (Florence: Sansoni, 1992)
W.[vol].[p]	Niccolò Machiavelli, *The Historical, Political, and Diplomatic Writings of Niccolò Machiavelli,* trans. Christian E. Detmold (Boston: Houghton, Mifflin, 1891)

Chapter 1

Introduction

The Problem with Machiavelli

Ever since Machiavelli's writings began to circulate in manuscript form at the beginning of the sixteenth century, they have posed a challenge to the Western tradition. For centuries, this problem consisted mainly of his counsel to break the rules of morality in order to succeed in politics, which could not but shock Christians who upheld St. Paul's principle that *"evil must not be done that good may come* (Rom.iii.8) or that evil may be avoided."[1] Now that expedient wickedness no longer upsets us so readily, the problem with Machiavelli has shifted to the true meaning of his diverse and seemingly inconsistent writings. Was he a cynic who showed individuals how to pursue their advantage with ruthless efficacy? Was he a political realist who declared openly that the security and prosperity of states rest on regrettable but necessary injuries to innocents? Was he the first political scientist, teaching us to inquire into what rulers really do rather than what they ought to do? Was he a classical republican, a kind of hard-nosed Aristotelian, who sought civic virtue and liberty with unconventional means? Was he a preacher of paganism, hoping to overthrow Christianity? Or was he a rhetorician who emulated classical oratory and, perhaps, assumed that political phenomena are fundamentally discursive?

1

These questions are not merely of academic interest, for Machiavelli's writings had a lasting effect on political and moral thought in the West and influenced the ideas and sensibilities of generations to come. Indeed, the fact that reading him no longer startles many of us shows how much his ideas have become part of our unspoken premises. For instance, when we defend a morally dubious policy by referring to the national interest or argue for late-term abortion on grounds of its benefits to the parents, we show ourselves disciples of Machiavelli's consequentialist ethic. When we feel no shame in asserting that the good life consists of wealth, power, fame, and sexual pleasure, we owe the initial exculpation of these ends to Machiavelli. When we believe that nonviolent competition among interest groups makes for a vigorous democracy, we apply a conception that the founders of the American republic inherited from Machiavelli. Indeed, even when we turn away from politics as something inherently dirty and seek solace in private life, we follow a counsel given by Machiavelli.

Studying Machiavelli thus reenacts the discovery of beliefs we take for granted and therefore no longer fully understand. It returns us to the watershed in the history of ideas that led us from seeing the world as it *ought* to be to knowing what it *is,* from relying on scriptural authority to requiring empirical corroboration of all knowledge, from believing in absolute prohibitions to calculating the utility of all actions, from striving to transcend our passions to wholeheartedly devoting ourselves to their enjoyment, from understanding ourselves as members of communities to thinking and acting as individuals, from distinguishing the few from the many to asserting that they are created equal, and from believing that we become virtuous by serving in public office to viewing the state as a means to the satisfaction of our desires.

But anyone who seriously seeks to understand Machiavelli cannot help being daunted by a secondary literature that is best known for its disagreements over even the most basic aspects of his thought. The primary reason for this lack of consensus rests undoubtedly with the way Machiavelli wrote: Bent on achieving the greatest effect, he took little care to clarify his premises and propositions, let alone arrange them in orderly fashion, but, instead, confronted the reader with a manifold of assumptions, claims, and maxims that not infrequently seem to contradict each other. Nonetheless, a number of his major interpreters, most of them were students of philosophy, once had the clear sense that his scattered utterances were undergirded by an unified scheme of thought. Ernst Cassirer (1946) thus found that "the whole argument of Machiavelli is clear and coherent," making him "the great constructive thinker whose conceptions and theories revolutionized the modern world."[2] In the mind of Isaiah Berlin (1953), Machiavelli aimed at "systematic knowledge" and had a "clear vision of the society which he wishes to see realised on earth," a vision that remained "central and constant."[3] According to Leo Strauss (1958), Machiavelli was a "philosopher," whose two books that contain everything he knows present "substantially the same teaching from two different points of view."[4] Felix Gilbert (1965) thought that the "inconsistencies" that stem from Machiavelli's effort at "making an impressive argument" appear "only in his subsidiary argumentations" and that "unity is provided by his general vision of politics."[5] Anthony Parel (1972), finally, voiced the claim that Machiavelli was an "unsystematic political writer who nevertheless cannot be understood correctly except in light of the system implicit in his theory."[6]

While acknowledging the rational unity of Machiavelli's thought, these and other distinguished scholars nonetheless remained divided over its content and meaning, with their interpretations tending to fall on either side of the various tensions in Machiavelli's writings. The first of these tensions concerns Machiavelli's method. On the one hand, Machiavelli seems to have paved the way for the scientific study of humain affairs by "going directly to the effectual truth of the thing," that is, "what is done" rather than "what should be done" (P.XV.61), and by supporting his claims with empirical evidence rather than quotations from authoritative texts. Thus, according to Ernst Cassirer, he "studied and analyzed political movements in the same spirit as Galileo, a century later, did the movement of falling bodies," and thus "became the founder of a new type of science."[7] But Machiavelli also stated that "one cannot give certain rules because the modes vary according to circumstances" (P.IX.40-41), and that "one cannot give a definitive judgment on all these things unless one comes to the particulars . . . where any such decision has to be made," and thus decided to "speak in that broad mode which the matter permits in itself" (P.XX.83). Accordingly, Eugene Garver (1987) would later count Machiavelli's writings as a milestone in the history of prudential reasoning, which originated with Aristotle.[8]

In a related tension, it can be argued that Machiavelli analyzed politics in a purely instrumental manner, working out the methods for becoming tyrant as much as those for preserving liberty, for he claimed to write "something useful to whoever understands it" (P.XV.61), indeed, to discuss "those parts that are notable . . . as well

for those who wish to maintain a republic free as for those who plan
to subject it" (D.I.40.1). Thus, Benedetto Croce (1924) argued that
Machiavelli had discovered the "autonomy of politics" from ethics,
and Ernst Cassirer maintained that Machiavelli's "*Prince* is neither a
moral nor an immoral book: it is simply a technical book."[9] Yet,
Machiavelli also described the founders of republics and kingdoms as
"praiseworthy" and tyrants as "worthy of reproach" (D.I.10.T),
professed to have written the *Discourses* because "it is the duty of a
good man to teach others the good that [he] could not work" himself
(D.II.Pr.3), and censured Christianity for having "rendered the world
weak" while praising Greco-Roman religion for "having placed the
highest good in [the honor of the world]" (D.II.2.2). According to
Isaiah Berlin, Machiavelli's men are thus "choosing not a realm of
means (called politics) as opposed to a realm of ends (called morals),
but opt for . . . an alternative realm of ends. In other words, the
conflict is between two moralities, Christian and pagan."[10] In the
words of Leo Strauss (1958), Machiavelli opposed "to a wrong
normative teaching the true normative teaching."[11]

With regard to human nature, Machiavelli deplored in the *Prince*
that "men are wicked," calling them "ungrateful, fickle, pretenders
and dissemblers, evaders of danger, eager for gain" (P.XVII. 66), but in
the *Discourses* he praised the "goodness" of the Roman people
(D.I.55.1) and of those princes who "wish to help not [themselves]
but the common good" (D.I.9.2). Further, Machiavelli clearly assumed
that human beings have a constant nature, since "in all peoples there
are the same desires and the same humors, and there always have
been" (D.I.39.1), but, at the same time, seemed to believe that
individuals can be molded for the good by their princes, for instance,
when he wrote that "in every country drill can produce good soldiers,
because where nature fails, the lack can be supplied by industry, which
is in this case more important than nature" (AG.I.309). On the
political level, this tension in Machiavelli's view of human nature
manifests itself mainly in the contrast between the autocratic order of
principalities and the institutional and lawful life of republics. In the
Prince, Machiavelli thus advised rulers to "enter into evil, when
forced by necessity" (P.XVIII.70), on the grounds that "a man who
makes a profession of good in all regards must come to ruin among so
many who are not good" (P.XV.61). According to Friedrich Meinecke
(1924), Machiavelli was thus "the man, with whom the history of the
idea of *raison d'état* in the modern Western world begins."[12] But in
the *Discourses,* Machiavelli argued that "in a republic, one would not
wish anything ever to happen that has to be governed with

extraordinary [i.e., unlawful] modes . . . for if one sets up a habit of breaking the orders for the sake of good, then later, under that coloring, they are broken for ill" (D.I.34.3), and showed how "towns and provinces that life freely in every part" make it possible for the individual not to "fear that his patrimony will be taken away" and to know that his children "are born free and not slaves" (D.II.2.3). Assimilating the *Prince* to the *Discourses,* Rudolf von Albertini (1955) thus concluded that "Machiavelli is a republican" who advocated nothing less than a "constitutional state [Rechtsstaat]."[13] In contrast, finding the spirit of the *Prince* in the *Discourses,* Leo Strauss (1958) argued that Machiavelli's republic is really a tyranny of its leading men over the masses.[14]

Finally, the question has arisen whether Machiavelli's thought was so innovative that it ushered in modernity, or whether he sought to revive antiquity and belonged to the classical tradition. Machiavelli appears modern in his inquiry into what is rather than what ought to be, his rejection of Christianity, his consequentialism, his assumption that human beings are self-seeking individuals who are ethically the same, and his conception of politics as a struggle of interests. According to Leo Strauss (1975), it thus was Machiavelli who discovered "the continent on which all specifically modern political thought, and hence especially present-day political science, is at home."[15] But Machiavelli also looks in important ways like a pre-modern, especially when he assumes that history occurs in cycles, asserts the superiority of the ancients, elevates glory to the highest good, and accepts that the occult forces of the heavens and Fortune govern human affairs. Thus, Mark Hulliung (1983) argued that Machiavelli espoused the "heroic ethic" that had come down from pre-Socratic times and valued violent greatness as an end in itself, and Anthony Parel (1992) concluded that "a pre-modern cosmology and a pre-modern anthropology underlie Machiavelli's political theory."[16]

Faced with these and other tensions, a number of scholars have considered it a mistake to seek logical consistency in Machiavelli's writings. According to Sidney Anglo (1969), Machiavelli simply had a "tendency to set down ideas as they occur to him regardless of the logic which their context demands."[17] In the eyes of a number of historians, on the other hand, the tensions in his work are due to differences of context. Herbert Butterfield (1940) thus asserted that

> it is important that we come to his work as historians, not as theorists who hanker after synthesis. . . . It was always a particular policy or expedient that he was commending for adoption by the practical statesman. . . . His teaching is a collection of concrete maxims—

warnings and injunctions in regard to certain points of policy, rules of
conduct for specific emergencies, and expositions of tactical moves.[18]

According to Hans Baron's seminal article (1961), the central
contrast between the tyrannical teaching of the *Prince* and the
doctrine of republican liberty in the *Discourses* results from a decisive
change in Machiavelli's professional and intellectual development:

> The closer the comparison of the two works, the more absurd seems the
> idea that these should be two harmonious parts of one and the same
> political philosophy . . . between the creation of two so deeply
> divergent views of the political world some crisis or development must
> have occurred in the author's mind . . . instead of so many efforts to
> harmonize Machiavelli's thought, we ought to face the obvious
> differences and explore whether their secret may, after all, yield to a
> genetic approach.[19]

More precisely, Baron argued that the *Prince* reflects
Machiavelli's personal involvement in the power politics of
Renaissance Italy during his tenure as Secretary of the Second
Florentine Chancery from 1498 to 1512, whereas the *Discourses* were
shaped by his immersion in the intellectual tradition of "civic
humanism" from 1515 onwards, when he attended the literary and
republican circle at the Oricellari Gardens in Florence.[20]
Since Machiavelli's republican writings can thus be taken to
represent his mature thought, a growing number of interpreters have
placed him squarely in the context of civic humanism and its effort to
recover the classical republicanism of Aristotle and Cicero. In a highly
influential study of the modern revival of classical republicanism,
which understands the American founding as the last great act of civic
humanism and bears the telling title *The Machiavellian Moment,* J. G.
A. Pocock (1975) thus defined Machiavelli's republic as a "structure
of virtue" in the Aristotelian sense, where *vivere civile*–the humanist
ideal of an ethical life–attains stability not just by habituation, but
more importantly by the enduring actualization of our natural
potential for virtue:

> The experience of citizenship . . . had changed their natures in a way
> that mere custom could not. Custom at most could affect men's second
> or acquired natures, but if it was the end of man to be a citizen or
> political animal, it was his original nature or *prima forma* that was
> developed, and developed irreversibly, by the experience of a *vivere
> civile.*[21]

This image of Machiavelli as a civic humanist and classical republican became truly predominant through the programmatically contextual work of Quentin Skinner, especially in his *Foundations of Modern Political Thought* (1978), where he sought to show in detail how "the format, the presuppositions and many of the central arguments of *The Prince* make it a recognisable contribution to a well-established tradition," namely the humanist "mirror-for-princes genre," and to illustrate the "extent to which Machiavelli's *Discourses* can be represented as a relatively orthodox contribution to a well-established tradition of Republican political thought," namely, that of the "so-called 'civic' humanists of early quattrocentro Florence."[22] In later research, Skinner (1990a) qualified this claim by tracing Machiavelli's "wholehearted defence of traditional republican values" to the prehumanist republican thought of twelfth-century Italy, which drew far more on the republican ideals of Cicero and Sallust than Aristotle.[23] The extent to which this classical Machiavelli has become received wisdom can be seen from a popular textbook, *Political Ideologies and the Democratic Ideal* by Terence Ball and Richard Dagger (1999), now in its third edition, which presents Machiavelli as the key exponent of "Renaissance republicans" who drew on the "writings of Aristotle and Polybius," and cites "mixed government, a virtuous citizenry, the rule of law" as "the republican ideals of Machiavelli's *Discourses*."[24]

Most recently, the consistency problem in Machiavelli's writings has found another important solution in what might be called the rhetorical approach. Machiavelli clearly had a practical purpose in writing his books: he sought to persuade his readers to overcome Italy's political and military crisis, which had been precipitated by the French invasion in 1494, by imitating the modes and orders of their Roman forebears. To be persuasive, Machiavelli availed himself of the classical rhetoric that Renaissance humanists had learned from such ancient works as Cicero's *De Oratore* and *De Partitione Oratoria,* as well as the pseudo-Ciceronian *Rhetorica ad Herennium* and Quintilian's *Institutio Oratoria*.[25] Now, the very endeavor of writing rhetorically tends to produce logical tensions in a text, for the writer who wants to impress tends to exaggerate those aspects of his argument that make it appear stronger and to play on the passions of his audience. Machiavelli thus gets himself into inconsistencies by inferring general rules from individual cases, as when he takes the case of Heraclea to show that the people "desire freedom so as to live secure" and are "easily satisfied by making orders and laws in which universal security is included" (D.I.16.5), but then finds that the struggle between the plebeians and patricians of Rome demonstrates that once the people have secured their freedom they begin "to engage in combat through ambition, and to wish to share honors and belongings with the nobility" (D.I.37.1). According to Maurizio Viroli (1998), therefore, Machiavelli's "truths will never attain the status of a scientific or philosophical truth; they will remain partial, probable, adorned, accommodated, and coloured truths, identified because they offer useful advice"; for "what would be contradictory for a philosopher . . . is perfectly permissible, indeed, praiseworthy, for an orator."[26]

Other interpreters having taken the presence of rhetorical devices in Machiavelli's writings to suggest that he understood human reality itself in rhetorical terms. According to Michael McCanles (1983), "historical events for Machiavelli are not transformed into discourse after the fact; rather, these events become possible only because they originate in and are constituted by human discourse"; thus, the logical tensions in Machiavelli's writings should be understood as manifestations of the fact that discourse and hence politics follow "dialectical laws that determine the interrelations and mutual causality between differential opposites."[27] For example, the tension between Machiavelli's initial advice that princes make themselves independent by commanding their own army and his later point that they need to gain the support of the people is really an artful way of showing that power is a dialectical synthesis of independence and dependence.[28] In Victoria Kahn's view (1994), Machiavelli did not write a "political theory with a coherent thematic coherent" and thus "should not be chiefly read as a theorist of republicanism but rather as a proponent of a rhetorical politics, one that proceeds topically and dialectically, and that can be used by tyrant and republican alike"–using "the term *rhetoric* . . . as the humanists did"; for instance, the fact that Machiavelli offers neither a substantive nor thematic definition of *virtù* is a device for teaching us that "only a destabilized *virtù* can be effective in the destabilizing world of political reality."[29]

Both the historical and rhetorical approach have made contributions to our understanding of Machiavelli. To cite but two examples, we now know that much of the semantic shift that Machiavelli imparted to his central concept of *virtù*–from moral virtue to the ability to succeed under adverse and contingent circumstances–had already been effected by other Renaissance writers, who had sought to return the word to its Latin root *virtus,* the glory-winning excellence of a man who performs his duties as patriarch, citizen, and soldier.[30] And, the recently demonstrated fact that

Machiavelli structured the *Prince* according to Cicero's oratorical rules implies that the patriotic exhortation of the last chapter is an integral part of the book[31]–rather than being at odds with the more factual character of the other chapters, as previously surmised by some.[32]

However, we must be careful not to confuse context with text and style with substance. In other words, the fact that an author drew on the concepts of an intellectual tradition does not imply that he had no seminal ideas of his own, and that he wrote rhetorically does not necessarily mean that his underlying thought lacked consistency. For, as the remainder of this book seeks to demonstrate, a careful excavation of Machiavelli's premises on nature and man allows us to account for most of his political maxims in a fairly straightfoward and consistent manner. And this can be done without lapsing into what Quentin Skinner called the "mythology of coherence," whereby the interpreter "gives the thoughts of various classical writers a coherence, and an air generally of a closed system, which they may never have attained or even been meant to attain."[33] Obviously, the key to avoiding such false coherence is to support one's interpretive claims with textual evidence that is weighty, explicit, and semantically accurate, which surely requires consideration of what the words meant to the author at the time. To this extent, Skinner's contextualist critique serves are a valuable guide. But once these caveats have been observed, the effort to detect coherent thought in scattered writings through philosophical analysis is neither hopeless nor frivolous. Indeed, if Skinner's version of Occam's razor–"that an apparent contradiction may simply *be* a contradiction"[34]–is applied prematurely, the most profound insights that an author has to offer may be lost; for there are writers who do not make their deepest reflections readily explicit, but let them emerge from the way their utterances hang together. In other words, there exists not only a danger of imposing logical coherence on an author who had none, but an equally grave possibility of missing the deeper truth of an author who thought coherently but wrote rhetorically.

The Substance of Machiavelli

But what is the evidence–textual as well as contextual–that such an analytical or philosophical approach to Machiavelli's writings is warranted? To begin with, it is clear that Machiavelli believed in the constancy of the world across times as well as places, rather than assuming every historical situation to be so different that no general propositions can be made; for his entire project of reviving the political and military greatness of the ancients rests on the belief that both the world and human beings have remained the same and that the lessons of the past can therefore be applied to present problems. Thus, he castigated his contemporaries for thinking "that imitation [of the ancients] is not only difficult but impossible–as if heaven, sun, elements, men have varied in motion order, and power from what they have been in antiquity" (D.I.Pr.2), whereas in truth "men are born, live, and die always in one and the same order" (D.I.11.5). In particular,

> whoever considers present and ancient things easily knows that in all cities and in all peoples there are the same desires and the same humors, and there always have been. So it is an easy thing for whoever examines past things diligently to foresee future things in every republic and to take the remedies for them that were used by the ancients. (D.I.39.1)[35]

Indeed, Machiavelli underscores the continuity of history by freely mixing ancient and contemporary events. In the *Prince,* for instance, he speaks in exactly the same manner of Moses (c. 1300 B.C.) and Fra Girolamo Savonarola (1452-98) in the chapter on founders (P.VI.22-24), of Agathocles the Sicilian (361-289 B.C.) and Liverotto da Fermo (1475-1502) in the chapter on becoming prince through crimes (P.VIII.34-38), of Alexander the Great (356-323 B.C.) and Franceso Sforza (1401-66) in the chapter on what a prince should do regarding the military (P.XIV.58-60), and so forth. In the *Discourses,* he not only continues this ahistorical mode of analysis, but deliberately commits the anachronism of calling the ancient Gauls "the French" and referring to the ancient Etruscans as "Tuscans," presumably to indicate that the natures of these peoples have remained the same.[36]

Further, Machiavelli was bound to believe in the uniformity of history on account of his intellectual context, for the sceptical claim that all knowledge is relative to historical and ever-changing circumstances had yet to be made for the modern age.[37] To the minds of the Renaissance, "history was the 'memory of human things' grasped according to . . . the 'Polybian norm' (*norma Polybiana*) of objective truth. If the task of the philosopher was to understand causes, that of the historian was to understand both causes and their effects and so have a better grasp of truth (*cognition del vero*)."[38] Indeed, according to Jean Bodin's celebrated motto (1566), "the best part of universal law resides in history."[39] In other words, Machiavelli's belief that history repeats itself because the world remains the same was commonplace among Renaissance thinkers, not the least because it provided them with the ontological premise for their project of reviving antiquity. Even Francesco Guicciardini–who had a strong penchant for the particular and reproached Machiavelli for his tendency to overgeneralize–thus accepted the fact that "past events throw light upon the future, because the world has always been the same as it now is, and all that is now, or shall be hereafter, has been in times past. Things accordingly repeat themselves."[40] True, the later Renaissance did witness the first critique of the idea of universal historical truth in the work of Flacius Illyricus, whose rules for historical hermeneutics would much later be taken up by such "historicists" as Schleiermacher, Dilthey, and Gadamer; but Flacius wrote his ground-breaking piece in 1556, and thus well after Machiavelli's death in 1527.[41]

Next, Machiavelli clearly considered the generation of knowledge a rational enterprise. While describing the study of ancient writers that prompted his composition of the *Prince,* he claims to have "delve[d] as deeply as I can into reflections [*cogitazioni*] on this subject" (L.216.1160), and "thought out [*escogitate*] and examined these things with great diligence" (P.Ded.3). Likewise, he speaks of his "reasoning [*ragionare*] on republics" (P.II.6), and writes in his major work on republics that he would "never judge it to be a defect to defend any opinion with reasons" (D.I.58.1), and concludes in the manner of a philosopher that "it is good to reason [*ragionare*] about everything" (D.I.18.1). Further, Machiavelli showed a definite respect for the principle of non-contradiction–the axiom of rational knowledge–when he tried to resolve apparent inconsistencies among his propositions. For instance, having argued that the office of Dictator was not detrimental to Roman liberty because it was given by free election, Machiavelli remembers what happened under the Decemvirate–the ten citizens who had been given absolute power to reform the laws and used it to tyrannize over their fellows–and readily admits that this case "appears contrary to what was discoursed of above"; to resolve this contradiction, he immediately suggests to "consider the modes of giving authority and the time for which it was given" and finds the following boundary criterion: great authority given by election will not endanger liberty, if it remains checked by other institutions, as the Dictator was reined in by the Senate and the Tribunes of the People; but it will threaten liberty if all other institutions are suspended, as in the case of the Decemvirate (D.I.35).

In another instance, Machiavelli resolves an apparent contradiction by recategorizing the evidence:

> I believe that the experience of the Venetian republic, in which none can have any rank except those who are gentlemen, will *appear contrary to this opinion of mine* that where there are gentlemen a republic cannot be ordered. To which it may be replied that this example does not impugn it because in that republic they are gentlemen more in name than in fact. (D.I.55.6, ea)

In yet another instance, Machiavelli discusses at length the fact that there seem to be two contrary modes by which leaders can make themselves obeyed, namely to proceed harshly in order to be feared and humanely in order to be loved. "Considering how one could save both of these opinions," Machiavelli first reasons that it depends on whether one leads equals or inferiors, implying that citizens should rule their fellows humanely whereas princes should make themselves feared by their subjects (D.III.19.1). Secondly, he asserts that "it is of little import to a captain whichever of these ways he walks in," provided that his *virtù* makes him reputed among men; for "when it is great . . . it cancels all those errors that are made so as to make oneself loved to much or to make oneself feared too much" (D.III.21.3). Finally, "so as not to leave this part undecided," he concludes in an apparent reversal of his first reasoning that citizens should be harsh so that they cannot gain partisans that would help them tyrannize over their fellows, whereas princes should be humane to make themselves loved because they need the support of their subjects (D.III.22.4-6). At any rate, Machiavelli endeavors to resolve the seeming contradiction in all three reasonings, twice with the boundary criterion of citizens versus subjects and once with the superior regulating principle of *virtù*.

That Machiavelli strove for coherence in his thought is also suggested by the way in which his major political works fit together. In the *Discourses,* he seeks to show his readers how to have "recourse to the examples of the ancients" in "ordering republics, maintaining [princely] states, governing kingdoms, ordering the military and administering war, judging subjects, and increasing empire" (D.I.Pr.2). Since "any republic or kingdom that is ordered well from the beginning . . . is ordered by one individual" who has "authority alone" (D.I.9.2), those eager to carry out such a founding should first consult the *Prince,* where Machiavelli analyzes the actions of the "most excellent" men that have introduced "new orders and modes" (P.VI.23) in detail. Since such a founding requires also a "regeneration of arms," as Machiavelli mentions at the end of the *Prince* (P.XXVI.105), his followers should further avail themselves of his *Art of War,* where he shows how "to bring the [militia] back to ancient modes and to restore some of the forms of past *virtù*" (AG.Pr.302). Machiavelli's *Florentine Histories,* finally, teach the citizens of the new state how to avoid the "hatreds and divisions" that ravaged Florence, so that, having "become wise through the dangers of others," they can maintain a law-bound way of life (FH.Pr). In short, all four of Machiavelli's major works are complementary parts of the same practical project, namely, to overcome Italy's crisis by founding a political order whose prudent mix of force, fraud, laws, and institutions would enable it to rival the great states of antiquity.

In addition to believing in the constancy of the world and the coherence of knowledge, Machiavelli clearly assumed that things exist objectively, that is, independently from their representation in the thought and speech of human beings. For his claim that "the generality of men feed on what appears as much as on what is; indeed, many times they are moved more by things that appear than by things that are" (D.I.25.1) implies not only that the few can easily deceive the many, but also that there is a reality behind appearances— which can be known by the few insofar as they are "are more prudent and more knowing of natural things" (D.I.12.1). This knowing takes the form of "general rules" that are derived from experience with previously existing facts. For instance, from the observation that "the greatness in Italy of the Church and of Spain has been caused by France, and France's ruin caused by them . . . one may draw a general rule that never or rarely fails: whoever is the cause of someone's becoming powerful is ruined" (P.III.16). However, "one cannot give certain rules because the modes vary according to circumstances" (P.IX.40-41). Accordingly, Machiavelli's general rules are prudential statements that hold true only most of the time. But this fact denies only that the correspondence between the world and its representation will ever be completely accurate, not that the world exists objectively or that its representation can be internally consistent. In other words, while prudential knowledge cannot aspire to the certainty of scientific truth, it can surely lay claim to philosophical truth; for otherwise, the ethical and political writings of Aristotle, who considered it "satisfactory if we can indicate the truth roughly and in outline, since we argue from and about what holds good usually," would no longer count as philosophical works.[42]

That Machiavelli believed in the objective existence of the world is further suggested by his use of the term "history" (*istoria*). For he did not understand history as an object of study–as we do when we claim "to study the history of Rome," as if what we studied were the accounts that have been given about what happened there–but merely as the act of study itself.[43] In other words, he believed history to consist of the "description" or "narrations" (FH.Ded) of something other than history, namely, past events that exist independently from the accounts that may be given of them, and, consequently, spoke of "actions that have greatness in themselves . . . however they are treated" by historians (FH.Pr). In short, there is clear evidence that Machiavelli believed that words *represent* facts rather than constitute them, and that knowledge *corresponds* to reality rather than constructs it.

Hence, the fact that Machiavelli used rhetorical devices to make his writings more persuasive does not imply that he considered all of human reality to be shaped by rhetoric or discourse. This can be seen most clearly from his claim that prophets need to be armed because "it is easy to persuade [peoples] of something, but difficult to keep them in that persuasion"; hence, "things must be ordered in such a mode that when they no longer believe, one can make them believe by force" (P.VI.24). Differently put, a prince should make himself feared rather than loved because "fear is held by a dread of punishment that never forsakes you," whereas a "prince who has founded himself entirely on [men's] words, stripped of other preparation, is ruined"; for "men love at their convenience and fear at the convenience of the prince" (P.XVII.66-68). And force must underwrite not only honest persuasion but also fraud, which is the ultimate weapon in the arsenal of rhetoric; for even the politically most effective form of fraud–the belief that the gods will punish those who disobey the ruler–is contingent upon the prior violence by which people are made religious. Thus, Numa, the second king of Rome, succeeded at introducing religion through persuasion only because his predecessor Romulus had used force to make the Romans believe in the words of their kings, and because Numa's successor Tullus Hostilius did so as well; in Machiavelli's words, "the *virtù* of Romulus was so much that it could give space to Numa Pompilius to enable him to rule Rome for many years with the arts of peace," and "after him succeeded Tullus, who by his ferocity regained the reputation of Romulus" (D.I.19.3). In short, force is the most "effectual truth" (P.XV.61) of political order because it enables its wielder to control others in an objective way, whereas persuasion is inescapably subjective and thus contingent.

This objectivity of force, in turn, is rooted in the fact that "no one is found who wishes to go to a certain death" (D.III.6.2), so that everyone rather submits to the wielder of deadly force. When advising generals to block their troops' escape route in order to make them fight harder, Machiavelli expresses this objectivity by stating that "necessities may be many, but that is strongest which constrains you either to win or die" (AG.IV.354). And the fact that Machiavelli himself used rhetoric to persuade others to implement his political ideas does not negate this necessity; for those who are swayed by his propositions must still use force to make them effective. Having exhorted the addressee of the *Prince* to found a powerful Italian state, Machiavelli thus admonishes him that "it is necessary before all other things, as the true foundation of every undertaking, to provide [yourself] with [your] own arms" (P.XXVI.104).

Moreover, we should not forget that Cicero–the master of classical rhetoric–staunchly defended the union of eloquence (*oratio*) and philosophical reason (*ratio*). For "to employ reason and speech rationally . . . and in everything to discern the truth and uphold it– that is proper."[44] More precisely, "the contents of philosophy are discovered by intellects of the keenest acumen in eliciting the probable answer to every problem, and the results are elaborated with practised eloquence."[45] Thus, the fact that "it is necessary to adapt one's discourse to conform not only with the truth but also with the opinions of one's hearers," that is, the "emotions and sense of the vulgar," implies that the truth of the wise underlies the rhetoric aimed at the unwise.[46] In sum, as one of Cicero's interlocutors put it, "you always thought matters relating to philosophy more important, [which] are the sources from which this oratorical fluency has been derived."[47] Hence, the rhetorical approach to Machiavelli, which takes his use of rhetoric to imply that he no longer believed in truth and understood reality to be discursively constructed, seems to rely on a "postmodern" understanding of rhetoric–inspired more by Foucault, Ricoeur, Derrida, Bourdieu, and Habermas than Cicero.[48] But to proceed in this manner is to see Machiavelli through one's own perspective rather than his, and thus to read him out of context.

Given the necessity emanating from force, Machiavelli advises princes to study war rather than literature: "a prince should have no other object, nor any other thought, nor take anything else as his art but the art of war . . . for that is the only art of concern to one who commands" (P.XIV.58); for "books and study do not suffice for the preservation of states."[49] And this maxim applies not only to princes, but also to the leading men of republics, who bring ruin to their state if they are trained in "letters" rather than "arms":

It has been observed by the prudent that letters come after arms and that, in provinces and cities, captains arise before philosophers. For, as good and ordered armies give birth to victories and victories to quiet, the strength of well-armed spirits cannot be corrupted by a more honorable leisure than that of letters, nor can leisure enter into well-instituted cities with a greater and more dangerous deceit than this one. This was best understood by Cato when the philosophers Diogenes and Carneades . . . came to Rome. When he saw how the Roman youth was beginning to follow them about with admiration, and since he recognized the evil that could result to his fatherland from this honorable leisure, he saw to it that no philosopher could be accepted in Rome. (FH.V.1)

Now, Machiavelli knew only too well that the leading spirits of his age received their education mostly from humanists–who had abandoned the scholastic concern with theology and metaphysics for the study of grammar, rhetoric, poetry, history, and morality in relation to public life. Hence, his critique of letters implies that the humanist reliance on moral suasion fails to prepare men for the harsh realities of politics.[50] Also, there is a conspicuous parallel between the coming of the Greek philosophers Carneades and Diogenes to Rome (156 B.C.) and the arrival of the Byzantine scholar Manuel Chrysoloras to Florence (1397), which enabled Florentine humanists to learn Greek from an authentic source and established the study of Greek authors as a major part of Western education.[51] Indeed, at least three of the chancellors of the Florentine republic during the period covered by Machiavelli's *Florentine Histories*–Collucio Salutati, who had invited Chrysoloras, as well as Leonardo Bruni and Poggio Bracciolini–were also leading humanist authors, whose careers were decisive in establishing the close association of rhetoric with political life in Florentine minds.[52]

Moreover, two of these men–Bruni and Poggio–had written well-known histories of Florence in accordance with the rhetorical practices of humanism, which served Machiavelli as a foil for composing his own historical work; in its preface, Machiavelli thus states that he had "read their writings diligently so as to see with what orders and modes they proceeded in their writing, so that by imitating them our history might be better approved by readers," but then goes on to criticize them on grounds of having been "altogether silent" about "civil discords and internal enmities" and so brief about "the effects arising from them" as to be of "no use to readers or pleasure to anyone," and suspects that "they did this either because these actions seemed to them so feeble that they judged them unworthy of being committed to memory by written word, or because they feared that they might offend the descendants of those they might have to slander in their narrations" (FH.Pr). In other words, Machiavelli adopted the style of the humanist historians—division into books, beginning each book with general reflections, inventing speeches to interpret the reasons of the actors, giving climactic battle scenes—while, at the same time, rejecting their rhetorical practice of omitting shameful events in order to preserve the reputation of their city, to educate the readers by presenting only wholesome example, and to secure the goodwill of their audience.[53] To Machiavelli, such an approach falls short of the effectual truth and thus cannot teach his readers how to maintain a republic; for "if no other lesson is useful to the citizens who govern republics, it is that which shows the causes of the hatreds and divisions in the city, so that when they have become wise through the dangers of others, they may be able to maintain themselves united" (FH.Pr). In other words, Machiavelli criticized his humanist forerunners for having been moralistic rather than realistic.[54]

Analogous claims can be made about Machiavelli's other major works. While composing the *Prince* in the traditional mirror-of-princes style, Machiavelli famously declared that "I depart from the orders of others . . . since my intent is to write something useful," rather than following the "many [who] have imagined republics and principalities that have never been seen or know to exist in truth" (P.XV.61)—that is, the medieval and humanist writers on princely government. While writing the *Discourses* in the fashion of a humanist commentary on a classical author, Machiavelli criticized his contemporaries for failing to imitate the ancients in politics and explained that "this arises" mostly "from not having a true knowledge of histories" (D.I.Pr.2), which, of course, had been recovered and commented on by the humanists; in particular, when Piero Soderini, the leader of the Florentine republic, who "proceeded in all his affairs with humanity and patience," should have summarily put to death the enemies of the republic, he "did not know how to do it, so that he together with his fatherland was ruined" (D.III.3, 9.3). While adopting the classical dialogue form for his *Art of War,* Machiavelli castigated his age for holding that "no two things are less suited to one another, or are as dissimilar as civil from military life" (AG.Pr.301)—a likely reference to the humanist ideal of a civic life devoted to the arts and letters—and blamed Italy's princes for "believing, before tasting the blows of the ultramontane war, that it was enough for a prince to think of a sharp riposte in his study, to write a beautiful letter, to show wit and readiness in sayings and words, to know how to weave a fraud, to adorn himself with gems and gold," from which "arose great fright, sudden flights, and miraculous losses in [the French invasion of] fourteen hundred ninety-four" (AG.VII.388).

There is significant contextual support for this claim to Machiavelli's criticism of humanist ideals on grounds of their incompatibility with political reality. As Felix Gilbert showed, the inability of the Florentine elite to defend the city led to a severe crisis in its political thinking; more precisely, whereas the leading men had previously "anchored their political claims to the concepts and teachings which the humanists had derived from their study of the classical world," which "were designed to demonstrate the necessity of following ethical rules in practical politics," a number of observers now thought that force was the really decisive factor.[55] For instance, Francesco Guicciardini wrote in response to the overthrow of the Florentine republic by Spanish troops in 1512, which returned the Medici princes to power, that "every government is nothing but violence over subjects, sometimes moderated by a form of honesty," and that we "must not look for an imagined government that appears more easily in books than in practice."[56] Likewise, Francesco Vettori stated that "speaking of the things of this world without respect and according to what is true, I say that if one of the republics written and imagined by Plato [and Thomas More] . . . were made, perhaps they could be said not to be tyrannical governments: but all the republics and princes of which I have knowledge from history, or that I have seen, appear to me to smell of tyranny."[57]

In sum, Machiavelli used humanist rhetoric as a literary tool to make his writings more persuasive, but at the same time rejected the humanist claim that moral suasion is the foundation of political order. Humanist rhetoric was Machiavelli's style, not his substance.

This fact was well understood by Felix Gilbert–one of the first major historians to interpret Machiavelli in his Renaissance context– when he wrote that "conformity to traditional patterns also strengthened his message: Machiavelli was conscious that his unconventional suggestions would appear even more striking if they were presented in a conventional manner."[58] But since this balanced judgment was made in 1965, the "contextualizing" of Machiavelli has reached such a degree that most of the radical novelty and substantial unity of his thought has been all but effaced in the popular interpretations of Pocock, Skinner, Viroli, McCanles, Kahn, and others. As we just saw, this effacement has happened in two major ways: First, Machiavelli has been submerged among the civic humanists by emphasizing the continuity of their themes, tropes, and terms, and overlooking or miminizing their deep disagreement concerning the cosmos, human nature, the purpose of the city, and necessary wickedness; second, Machiavelli has been assimilated to a constructivist reading of the rhetorical aspect of humanism, which equally mistakes his expedient use of humanist verbiage for the altogether different substance of his thought.

In a wider context, these developments can be understood as part of the revisionist vogue that has swept through the humanities and social sciences since the seventies. More precisely, there are at least four postmodern beliefs that inform the overly contextual interpretations of Machiavelli's writings: (1) Reason's quest to impose coherence on the chaos of existence is futile; hence, a radical like Machiavelli, who dwelled on strife and contingency, can be taken to express this fact by allowing inconsistent statements to stand. (2) All knowledge is perspectival; hence, there can be no universal propositions in Machiavelli's writings that might be accessible as such, but all of his utterances must be read in the light of his historical context; for that is the only available source of information about his perspective. (3) All consciousness is intersubjective; hence, Machiavelli's thought must have been shaped by his discourse with the predominant thinkers and writers of the age, that is, his humanist context. (4) All human reality is discursively constructed; hence, a writer like Machiavelli, who dwelled on fraud and appearances, must have organized his works rhetorically in order to convey the fact that politics is discursive as such.

But Machiavelli was not a postmodern before his age on any of these counts: (1) Rather than abandoning reason, he sought to eliminate contradictions from his thought in order to make it coherent. (2) Rather than believing every historical context to be *sui generis,* he believed in timeless truth and thus assumed that events in the past could be readily understood by observers in the present. (3) Rather than following his predecessors, he declared several times that he departed from the order of others, and thus asserted his ability to break out of his humanist context. (4) Rather than assuming human reality to be discursively constructed, he took it to exist independently from its representation by human beings, and thus argued that force succeeds where persuasion fails. Again, to interpret Machiavelli in light of these postmodern beliefs, is thus to impose an alien context on him.

To make sense of Machiavelli as he understood himself, we need an interpretive approach that can perform the following tasks: to ascertain in depth how far Machiavelli succeeded in his effort to think coherently (rather than consider such an endeavor to be futile a priori); to distill the universal propositions that his thought may have contained (rather than assume beforehand that such statements cannot exist); to fathom radical change in the history of ideas (rather than presuppose on methodological grounds that all change is incremental); and to distinguish theory from rhetoric (rather than assume as a matter of discipline that the former inevitably reduce to the latter). Obviously, the approach that works best on these counts is the analytical or philosophical one, for its way of disaggregating thought into its elementary components and determining their logical relations is geared to uncover coherence that is hidden at first sight; its capacity for abstraction enables us to ascertain universal propositions; and its ability to determine what is logically prior helps us to distinguish what is essential from what is incidental, and thus to decide not only whether an author belongs to a particular context or has fundamentally broken with it. If, in addition, we consider relevant contextual information–for instance, what Machiavelli's words meant insofar as he used them in the conventional sense–we should succeed at interpreting Machiavelli in accordance with his own perspective.

Among the major philosophical interpreters mentioned above, the most sustained claim to the rational unity of Machiavelli's thought has come from the work of Leo Strauss, as well as those who have been inspired by him.[59] Assuming this rational unity as well, the present study agrees with Strauss on a number of propositions, which, briefly listed, are as follows: Machiavelli broke with the classical tradition and rejected Christianity for having made the world weak; he assumed human beings to be inherently selfish, but also thought them capable of habituation to society; he considered the few to be ethically the same as the many; he believed political order to be founded on crime; he advised leaders to manipulate the people through religious fraud and to act for the common good in order to gain personal glory; he showed why cities cannot cultivate classical virtue if they are to remain safe from foreign threat; and he held that republics must make war abroad in order to keep peace at home.

But there are also fundamental points on which this inter-pretation disagrees with Strauss. Above all, it disputes his crucial claim that Machiavelli's republic is only a cover for the tyrannical rule of its leading men, by showing on precise textual grounds that the violent "returns to the beginnings," which republics need every day in order to forestall corruption, are really punishments handed out by public officials in defense of the laws against transgressors, rather than acts of despotism. In other words, Machiavelli was serious about institutionalized authority, even though he excused the injury of innocents for the sake of maintaining the institutions. Further, whereas Strauss seemed to think that Machiavelli had abandoned any traditional notions of good and evil because he no longer believed in God, this study asserts that he maintained them while at the same time excusing the use of evil means for good ends. Whereas Strauss believed that Machiavelli saw the world in completely contingent terms, this interpretation maintains that he believed in the astrological order of the heavens, which generates a measure of necessity by affecting the quality of the times in occult but natural ways. Finally, whereas Strauss thought that Machiavelli created modernity in a conscious act of revaluation, this reading argues that he intended to return to antiquity, but interpreted it in such a novel way that he made an important contribution to modernity nonetheless.

Machiavelli's Political Theory

To determine whether Machiavelli succeeded at making his thought coherent despite the tensions occasioned by his rhetoric, we now need to turn to the task of reconstructing his political theory. This reconstruction will proceed in two steps: first, we will ascertain Machiavelli's assumptions about the world at large, how it can be known, the qualities and propensities of human beings, and what is good, evil, and excusable; on this basis, we will then account for Machiavelli's maxims on republics, principalities, and their foreign relations. In other words, we will show the unity of Machiavelli's thought by demonstrating how his propositions on politics flow from his premises in natural philosophy, anthropology, and ethics. To make this flow more readily apparent, the remainder of this chapter gives a synopsis of the interpretive argument, to serve both as a guide to the remaining chapters and a convenient place from which to survey Machiavelli's thought as a whole.

Chapter 2 argues that Machiavelli embraced Renaissance astrology because he considered it an empirical science that challenged the Christian belief in divine providence, replacing it with the occult but natural effects which the heavenly bodies and Fortune have on human affairs. Importantly, this natural philosophy furnished Machiavelli's thought with two ontological categories: necessity, emanating from the regular motions of heavenly bodies, and contingency, caused by

Fortune and experienced by human beings as accidents.

How do we know this world? By subscribing to astrological naturalism, Machiavelli settled for a universe governed by merely efficient causes, rooted in the occult workings of the heavens and Fortune and the psychological propensities of human beings. To get at the "effectual truth" of human causation, Machiavelli broke with the classical tradition by considering what men do rather than what they ought to do–based on his experience with contemporary affairs and his knowledge of ancient history. Since Fortune's sway renders the world highly contingent, this empirical approach can only take a prudential form whose "general rules" hold usually but not always, requiring the practitioner to use judgment when applying them to concrete situations. Finally, since Machiavellian prudence counsels wicked deeds for the gratification of human ambition, it differs decisively from what Aristotle called "prudence" (*phronesis*) and equates to what he considered mere "cleverness" (*deinotike*).

With these ontological and epistemological premises in place, chapter 3 proceeds to analyze Machiavelli's assumptions on human nature and action. Accordingly, human beings have their qualities "either by nature or by accident," that is, they consist of necessary properties present from birth as well as contingent attributes that are acquired later and may form habits. Corresponding to the substance-accident distinction of the Aristotelian-Thomist tradition, this psychological duality obviously agrees with Machiavelli's ontological distinction between necessity and contingency. Further, it resolves the apparent contradiction in his thought between the constancy and mutability of human beings, who remain the same on account of their nature (also called first nature) and can be shaped by princes that make them acquire habits (forming a second nature).

In particular, nature consists of spirit, mind, desires, and humors. Taking the place of the rational soul, the spirit–an ethereal substance in brain and nerves, as postulated by premodern medicine–mediates perception, cognition, and bodily motion. While spirit animates us to act, the mind tells us how to proceed in order to satisfy our desires for self-preservation, glory, power, wealth, and sexual pleasure. Differing in their faculties of imagination and ingenuity, people fall into three categories: founders, ordinary princes, and the multitude. The humors are bodily fluids, occultly linked to the heavens, which endow everyone with a fixed and characteristic temperament, such as being cautious or tempestuous. While serving the desires, the mind at the same time expands them by imagining ever new satisfactions and inventing the corresponding means–a limitless process which

Machiavelli summarized in his concept of ambition. Overall, it is these natural and necessary properties that give rise to the rapacious side of Machiavelli's image of man.

On the brighter side, this image allows individuals to become loyal subjects and law-abiding citizens by habituation. However, since such cooperative behaviors are contrary to nature, the corresponding habits must be acquired by repeated performance under constraint: Complying initially from fear of the prince, individuals eventually act loyally and lawfully because they have done so before. However, being merely contingent attributes contrary to nature, such "good customs" are always threatened by ambition and begin to dissolve when people realize that punishment need no longer be feared. In this way, the central tension Machiavelli's thought between the wickedness and goodness of man has been resolved by the duality of first and second nature.

That Machiavelli assumed human beings to be self-seeking individuals can be seen from his keen awareness of collective-action problems, that is, situations where people fail to provide a common good because they expect the individual cost of coordination or cooperation to exceed their share in the benefits. To succeed in their actions nonetheless, individuals must know how to manipulate others by threatening them with injury, promising them benefits, or forcing them to form habits. Also, they need to know how to accommodate themselves to the variations of things that are wrought by the occult order; in particular, they have to wait until their characteristic mode of proceeding (which arises from their humors and habits) matches the changing quality of the times. To recognize such an opportunity for action takes prudence, and thus it is the prudent use of force and fraud under adverse circumstances that defines Machiavelli's concept of *virtù*.

This account of human nature and action breaks with the classical tradition in decisive ways. To begin with, Machiavelli leaves out the rational soul and thus denies free will—which Aristotelians, Christians, and humanists considered the essence of man. Accordingly, the mind no longer rules the passions, but merely serves them instrumentally and, in so doing, stimulates them to grow into an insatiable ambition. Thus, while borrowing the idea of a first and second nature from tradition, Machiavelli radically inverts its meaning: first nature is no longer a capacity for virtue, which, according to Aristotle, is enduringly developed by rational activity and proper habituation, but a potential for vice that is actualized by the mind and can be mitigated only temporarily by the opposing habits of second nature. Further,

Machiavelli's negation of the soul leads him to deny that at least a few can attain higher goods, and to assume instead that all men have vulgar ends–namely, to stay alive and attain as much glory, power, wealth, and sexual pleasure as possible.

Chapter 4 accounts for Machiavelli's views on good and evil. Taking men as they are, Machiavelli elevates the desires of the multitude to the good, provided it is attained collectively. In particular, the good of political order consists of glory won by public ways, followed by security, empire, and public wealth. Republican liberty is valued as a means to these ends, while sexual success is relegated to the private sphere. To generate this good, Machiavelli constructs political order in such a way that individuals of great *virtù* have to provide for these ends in order to satisfy their own ambition; for instance, princes pacify provinces to make their own rule more secure, and founders establish laws and institutions to gain perpetual glory for themselves. Thus, the tension in Machiavelli's thought between giving technical advice and having a normative purpose has been resolved by making the former instrumental to the latter.

Machiavelli believed that the generation of the political good rests on the commission of evil deeds, infamously counseling princes to "enter into evil" and citizens to disregard any consideration of justice when the safety of the republic is at stake. This consequentialist approach shocked the West because it not only repudiated the Pauline injunction against doing evil so that good may come, but made the even more radical claim that necessary evil is a intrinsic feature of political (and sexual) life. Accordingly, human reality is fundamentally incoherent: one can either succeed or be a good man–but not both. Thus, the classical belief in a *cosmos* or ethically ordered world has been denied once more.

With Machiavelli's ontological, epistemological, anthropo-logical, and ethical premises ascertained, the book then turns to his account of political order. Chapter 5 first shows how man's natural propensity for license shape his original condition–akin to a Hobbesian state of war. In the absence of government, violent conflict thus arises for two reasons: ambition for greater satisfaction than hitherto attained and fear of losing what one possesses, which prompts one to preventive attack. To get out of this condition, individuals need to be coerced by a new prince who uses violence to impose the first political order. Once such a "new principality" has been secured by force, religion and benefits are usefully added as means of compliance. Religion is both a habit and a fraudulent means of coercion, since it makes people believe that the gods will punish them for disobeying the ruler. In contrast, benefits work through exchange: The subjects obey in return for living securely or receiving honors. A "hereditary principality" comes into being when subjects have become so habituated to the rule of their princely line that they take it for granted; its ordering principle thus consists of custom rather than princely will. And an "ecclesiastical principality" rests on customary orders that center on religion.

In addition to princely will and custom, political order can also be based on a "civil way of life" (*vivere civile*), which centers on institutions and supports two kinds of regime: republics and law-governed kingdoms or "civil" principalities. Such a civil way of life has to be created by a founder, that is, a new prince who knows that leaving behind lasting institutions earns the greatest glory and thus lays down laws and orders and habituates the subjects to them. However, a civil way of life does not eliminate domestic conflict, but merely substitutes laws for arms as the means of fighting, which, according to Machiavelli, keeps a republic free and makes it powerful; this represents another sharp break with classical republicanism, which assumed that citizens had to live in true concord for their cities to prosper.

Machiavelli followed tradition by making his republic a mixed regime, where laws are proposed by magistrates and ratified by the popular assembly and where the magistrates are drawn mostly from the nobles or "the great," but elected by the people on account of their reputation. At the same time, the leading men ought to manipulate the common people through religious and electoral fraud in order to prevent them from ruining the city on account of their inability to grasp general ideas. In addition to punishments and benefits, citizens are made compliant by "good customs," which make them cooperate without calculating their individual costs and benefits. However, since such customs must be frequently renewed by exemplary punishments at the hand of the magistrates, it is really the compliance of the latter that habituation provides.

The essential function of Machiavelli's republic is to organize men's natural efforts at satisfying their desires in such a way that they collectively generate far more glory, dominion, and wealth than what they could have attained individually; instead of fighting each other, they combine to exploit foreigners. It is above all in this sense that Machiavelli's republic can be called a "well-ordered license." In Aristotle's terms, this republic is merely an alliance for mutual gain and protection, not a community of the good life, which seeks to make its members good and just.

In a civil principality, such as the kingdom of France or Florence under Cosimo de' Medici, the laws and orders of the civil way of life are executed by a prince instead of a number of magistrates. Such regimes may be established by a founder who intends to institutionalize authority, or they can arise from highly corrupt republics where either the great or the people feel so threatened by the other that they elevate one man to supreme power for their protection.

In chapter 6, we realize that the anthropological duality of first and second nature, which in turn rests on the ontological duality of necessity and contingency, structures Machiavelli's account of foreign relations as well: driven by ambition and fear, principalities and republics are forced to engage in a violent struggle for domination that tends to the formation of empires that encompass the international system; on the other hand, the cooperative habits acquired under such an empire may temporarily enable its successor states to maintain foreign institutions that mitigate conflict among them. Normally, however, cities cannot escape war and thus are constrained to secure themselves by acquiring empire over others, for they cannot maintain their power at such a level that it deters aggression without provoking preventive attack from fear. Another reason that security rests on imperial domination lies with the fact that alliances are easily split by aggressors who exploit the collective-action problem of allies by a strategy of divide and rule. Accordingly, cities should make war whenever victory seems likely, add to their empire in such a way that additional manpower can be drawn from conquered territories, and organize their domestic affairs for war. Since this organization implies opening the ranks to commoners and promoting immigration, it constitutes another critique of the classical tradition: for the ancients taught that cities should be aristocratic, small, and closed to support the cultivation of virtue.

Chapter 7 concludes with a critical assessment of Machiavelli's thought. His break with the classical tradition and concomitant contribution to modernity resulted from his peculiar way of reading the ancients: Whereas the humanists understood that the ancient writers had conceived politics as a branch of ethics, Machiavelli believed that their moral exhortations represented only the surface of their teaching and that they conveyed between the lines what he had already realized from his experience with Renaissance politics: that it is necessary to commit evil deeds in order to generate the good of political order.

One of the real insights that Machiavelli's thought has to offer lies on the psychological level: Endowed with the faculty of imagination, human beings are capable of projecting their awareness beyond the concrete moment and thus tend to become desirous of ever more pleasure and anxious about future pain–even though their bodies may presently feel satisfied. But Machiavelli's remedy for this predicament–to show us how to maximize glory, power, and wealth in the public sphere and sexual success in the private–only makes things worse; for pursuing these external goods implies drudgery in acquiring them, conflict with one's neighbors, and the continued dissatisfaction of not having more. And the fact that Machiavelli's assertion of the power of human action may have contributed to making autonomy a good of the modern soul hardly alters this negative conclusion; for his kind of action aims at nothing more than well-ordered license.

Then, the study sketches an answer to the crucial question whether Machiavelli's claim to necessary evil captures any enduring truth about politics. Historically, it can thus be argued that considerable good has come from unjust events, such as the renaissance in the arts and letters that followed the conquests of Charlemagne. But this argument is wrong insofar as the bad consequences of unjust events cancel the good ones and the good outcomes could have been attained by just means as well. Nonetheless, it seems plausible that humanity might still live on the tribal level if ambitious individuals had not used force to form larger entities, which made possible a more complex division of labor and the concomitant rise of civilization. However, this does not mean that Machiavelli was right about necessary evil; for no less a moralist than Kant has argued that force is just when used to create society out of the state of nature, because those who refuse to join commit a wrong by condemning the others to remain in their lawless condition. However, this coercive right of the founder ceases as soon as the units are large enough to allow for the development of the goods of the soul, as in an ancient city-state or medieval duchy.

But Machiavelli's more basic error was his failure to understand that political order is in fact grounded in moral relationships; for even if the people at large obeyed their ruler only from fear, he must at least have the consent of the policemen and soldiers who help him generate that fear; and even if the latter carry out his commands only because they expect benefits in return, such an exchange implies mutual trust that the bargain will be kept, and therefore constitutes a moral relation. In a less minimalist vein, Machiavelli failed to understand that the commission of unjust deeds for the sake of political order will eventually destroy it, because justice belongs to the essence of such order.

Nonetheless, was Machiavelli perhaps correct in claiming that wickedness is necessary outside of political order, that is, in foreign affairs? In other words, does security really rest on such unjust means as preventive war and imperial domination? Here, we must admit that Machiavelli may have had a point with regard to antiquity and the middle ages, when lack of information about the capabilites and intentions of others and the difficulty of forming alliances combined to make security by deterrence an uncertain prospect. But his argument fails in the modern era, when a number of major drives to domination–by Spain, France, Germany, and Soviet Russia–have been repeatedly checked by countervailing coalitions. Further, the argument for preventive war on the grounds that it eliminates the risk of an adverse shift in the balance of power overlooks the risk that resides in war itself; for a preventive attack launched in expectation of victory may well end in defeat. Further, it overlooks that the use of wicked means abroad tends to corrupt the civic habits needed at home, as leaders that routinely attack other countries will not shrink for long from injuring fellow citizens. Hence, security rests more reliably on deterrence, singly or in alliance with others.

Finally, the remarkable fact that liberal states have not gone to war with each other during the last two centuries suggests the fundamental possibility of transforming the foreign state of license into an institutional realm, where nonviolence and respect for the rights of others are the norm, as prophesied by Immanuel Kant.

Notes

1. Thomas Aquinas, *Summa Theologiae,* trans. Fathers of the English Dominican Province (New York: Benziger Brothers, 1947), Pt. II-II, Q. 64, A. 5.

2. Ernst Cassirer, *The Myth of the State* (New Haven: Yale University Press, 1946), 140, 128.

3. Isaiah Berlin, "The Originality of Machiavelli" [1953], in *Studies on Machiavelli,* ed. Myron P. Gilmore (Florence: Sansoni, 1972), 147-206, at 165, 166, 181.

4. Leo Strauss, *Thoughts on Machiavelli* (Chicago: University of Chicago Press, 1958), 10, 17, 29.

5. Felix Gilbert, *Machiavelli and Guicciardini: Politics and History in Sixteenth Century Florence* [1965] (New York: Norton, 1984), 164, 167.

6. Anthony J. Parel, "Introduction: Machiavelli's Method and His Interpreters," in *The Political Calculus,* ed. Anthony Parel (Toronto: University

of Toronto Press, 1972), 3-32, at 5.

7. Cassirer, *Myth of the State,* 136. Cf. Leonardo Olschki, *Machiavelli the Scientist* (Berkeley, Calif.: Gillick, 1945).

8. Eugene Garver, *Machiavelli and the History of Prudence* (Madison, Wisc.: University of Wisconsin Press, 1987).

9. Benedetto Croce, "Machiavelli and Vico" [1924], in *Poetry, History: An Anthology of Essays by Benedetto Croce,* trans. Cecil Sprigge (London: Oxford University Press, 1966), 665-60, at 655; Cassirer, *Myth of the State,* 153.

10. Berlin, "Originality of Machiavelli," 179.

11. Strauss, *Thoughts on Machiavelli,* 233.

12. Friedrich Meinecke, *Machiavellism: The Doctrine of Raison d'Etat and Its Place in Modern History* [1924], trans. Douglas Scott (Boulder: Westview, 1984), 29.

13. Rudolf von Albertini, *Das Florentinische Staatsbewußtsein im Übergang von der Republik zum Prinzipat* (Bern: Francke, 1955), 60, 62.

14. To see this argument, which Strauss makes in oblique fashion, combine the relevant statements on pages 44, 134, 166-68, 228-31, 269, 274, 278-79 of *Thoughts on Machiavelli;* for a more explicit rendering of this view, see Harvey C. Mansfield and Nathan Tarcov, "Introduction," in Niccolò Machiavelli, *Discourses on Livy,* trans. Harvey C. Mansfield and Nathan Tarcov (Chicago: University of Chicago Press, 1996), xvii-xliv, esp. xxv-xxvii.

15. Leo Strauss, *On Tyranny* (Chicago: University of Chicago Press, 1975), 22-23.

16. Mark Hulliung, *Citizen Machiavelli* (Princeton: Princeton University Press, 1983), 221-28; Anthony J. Parel, *The Machiavellian Cosmos* (New Haven: Yale University Press, 1992), 153.

17. Sidney Anglo, *Machiavelli: A Dissection* (London: Victor Gollancz, 1969), 170-71.

18. Herbert Butterfield, *The Statecraft of Machiavelli* (London: G. Bell, 1940), 19-20.

19. Hans Baron, "Machiavelli: the Republican Citizen and the Author of 'The Prince,'" *English Historical Review* 76 (April 1961): 217-53, at 228.

20. Baron, "Machiavelli," 248-50.

21. J. G. A. Pocock, *The Machiavellian Moment: Florentine Political Thought and the Atlantic Republican Tradition* (Princeton: Princeton University Press, 1975), 184.

22. Quentin Skinner, *The Foundations of Modern Political Thought,* vol. 1, *The Renaissance* (Cambridge: Cambridge University Press, 1978), 128-29, 152, 180; cf. Quentin Skinner, *Machiavelli* (New York: Hill and Wang, 1981), v.

23. Quentin Skinner, "Machiavelli's *Discorsi* and the Pre-humanist Origins of Republican Ideas," in *Machiavelli and Republicanism,* ed. Gisela Bock, Quentin Skinner, and Maurizio Viroli (Cambridge: Cambridge University Press, 1990a), 121-41.

24. Terence Ball and Richard Dagger, *Political Ideologies and the Democratic Ideal,* 3rd ed. (New York: Longman, 1999), 28, 30.

25. See Brian Vickers, "Rhetoric and Poetics," in *The Cambridge History of*

Renaissance Philosophy, ed. Charles B. Schmitt and Quentin Skinner (Cambridge: Cambridge University Press, 1988), 715-45, esp. 720-21.

26. Maurizio Viroli, *Machiavelli* (Oxford: Oxford University Press, 1998), 82, 112.

27. Michael McCanles, *The Discourse of* Il Principe (Malibu, Calif.: Undena, 1983), xvi-xvii, xiii.

28. McCanles, *Discourse of* Il Principe, ch. 2.

29. Victoria Kahn, *Machiavellian Rhetoric: From the Counter-Reformation to Milton* (Princeton: Princeton University Press, 1994), 4, 5,11, 25.

30. Russell Price, "The Senses of *Virtù* in Machiavelli," *European Studies Review* 3, no. 4 (October 1973): 315-45, at 319-25, 335-37, 344. On Roman *virtus,* see Karl Büchner, "Altrömische und Horazische virtus," in *Römische Wertbegriffe,* ed. Hans Oppermann, 376-401, Wege der Forschung, vol. 34 (Darmstadt: Wissenschaftliche Buchgesellschaft, 1967), 376-401; Ludwig Curtius, "Virtus und Constantia," in *Römische Wertbegriffe,* 370-75; Donald C. Earl, *The Moral and Political Tradition of Rome* (Ithaca: Cornell University Press, 1967), 21.

Note that throughout this study, Machiavelli's largely untranslatable term *virtù* will be rendered in the Italian and reinstated in translations that give English equivalents–except for the few places where it really means "virtue" in the moral sense; the same practice will be followed with *virtuoso,* the adjective to *virtù,* and *virtuosamente,* the adverb.

31. Viroli, *Machiavelli,* 73-74, 79-80.

32. Fredi Chiapelli, *Studi sul linguaggio di Machiavelli* (Florence: Le Monnier, 1952), 244; Giuseppe Prezzolini, *Machiavelli,* trans. Gioconda Savini (New York: Farrar, Straus & Giroux, 1967), 117; Nancy S. Struever, *Theory as Practice: Ethical Inquiry in the Renaissance* (Chicago: University of Chicago Press, 1992), 151.

33. Quentin Skinner, "Meaning and Understanding in the History of Ideas," *History and Theory* 8, no. 1 (1969): 3-53, at 16-17. For critiques, see Nathan Tarcov, "Quentin Skinner's Method and Machiavelli's *Prince,*" *Ethics* 92 (July 1982): 692-709; Michael P. Zuckert, "Appropriation and Understanding in the History of Political Philosophy: On Quentin Skinner's Method," *Interpretation* 13 (1985): 403-24.

34. Skinner, "Meaning and Understanding," 20.

35. Cf. D.III.43; C.Pr; *Del modo di trattare i popoli della Valdichiana ribellati* [On the mode of treating the people of the Valdichiana who have rebelled], in TO.13-16, at 14.

36. On "French" and "France" in place of the ancient Gauls and Gaul, see D.I.7.5, 8.1, 15, 23.3, 24.2, 29.2, 56, 57; D.II.1.1, 1.3, 4.1-2, 8.1, 10.1, 12.4, 19.2, 28.1, 29.1-2, 30.1; D.III.10.1, 10.3, 14.3, 18.1, 22.1, 33.1, 36.T, 36.1-2, 37.1, 37.3-4, 43, 48.2. On "Tuscans" and "Tuscany" in the sense of the ancient Etruscans and Ertruria, see D.I.7.5, 15, 21.1, 23.3, 24.2, 31.2; D. II.1.1-3, 2.1, 4.1-2, 5.2, 6.1, 8.1, 12.4, 25.2, 28.1, 33; D.III. 30.1, 31.4, 33.2, 43, 44.1, 44.3, 45, 47, 48.1.

37. Cf. Cassirer, *Myth of the State,* 124-25.

38. Donald R. Kelley, "The Theory of History," in *The Cambridge History of Renaissance Philosophy*, ed. Charles B. Schmitt and Quentin Skinner (Cambridge: Cambridge University Press, 1988), 746-61, at 754.

39. Jean Bodin, *Methodus ad facilem historiarum cognitionem* [1566] (Paris: P. Mesnard, 1951), 108, mt.

40. Francesco Guicciardini, *Ricordi* [1528-30] (Florence: R. Spongano, 1951), 87, mt.

41. Kelley, "Theory of History," 755. On Renaissance scepticism, see Richard H. Popkin, "Theories of Knowledge, in *The Cambridge History of Renaissance Philosophy*, ed. Charles B. Schmitt and Quentin Skinner (Cambridge: Cambridge University Press, 1988), 668-84, esp. 678-84.

42. Aristotle, *Nicomachean Ethics*, trans. Terence Irwin (Indianapolis: Hackett, 1985), 1094b20-22, cf. 1126b3.

43. Harvey C. Mansfield, Jr., "Translators' Introduction," in Niccolò Machiavelli, *Florentine Histories*, trans. Laura F. Banfield and Harvey C. Mansfield, Jr. (Princeton: Princeton University Press, 1988), vii-xv, at vii.

44. Cicero, *On Duties*, trans. Walter Miller, Loeb Classical Library 30 (Cambridge, Mass.: Harvard University Press, 1913), I.xxvii.94.

45. Cicero, *De Oratore*, trans. E. W. Sutton and H. Rackham, Loeb Classical Library 348-49 (Cambridge, Mass.: Harvard University Press, 1942), III.xxi.79; cf. I.iv.16-vi.20, I.xxviii.128, III.xiv.54, III.xvi.60, III.xix.72.

46. Cicero, *De Partitione Oratoria*, trans. H. Rackham, Loeb Classical Library 349 (Cambridge, Mass.: Harvard University Press, 1942), xxv.90, xxiii.79.

47. Cicero, *De Oratore*, III.xxii.82.

48. See Victoria Kahn, "Habermas, Machiavelli, and the Humanist Critique of Ideology," *PMLA* 105 (1990): 464-76; Kahn, *Machiavellian Rhetoric*, 238-41; Barbara Spackman, "Politics on the Warpath: Machiavelli's *Art of War*," in *Machiavelli and the Discourse of Literature*, ed. Albert Russell Ascoli and Victoria Kahn (Ithaca: Cornell University Press, 1993), 179-94, at 180-81; McCanles, *Discourse of* Il Principe, xvii-xviii, 102-103, 110, 128.

49. "Mission to Mantua on Business With the Emperor of Germany," in W.IV.195-219, at 214; cf. A.986.

50. See Gilbert, *Machiavelli and Guicciardini*, 166.

51. On the importance of Chrysoloras, see Paul Oskar Kristeller, "Humanism," in *The Cambridge History of Renaissance Philosophy*, ed. Charles B. Schmitt and Quentin Skinner (Cambridge: Cambridge University Press, 1988), 113-37, at 130.

52. On the significance of these men for humanist rhetoric, see Vickers, "Rhetoric and Poetics," 728. Salutati was chancellor from 1375 to 1406, Bruni from 1427 to 1444, and Poggio Bracciolini from 1453 to 1458; Machiavelli's history of Florence covers the years 1215 to 1492 (see FH, II, 2; FH, VIII, 36).

53. On the moralizing character of humanist historiography and Machiavelli's critique, see Gilbert, *Machiavelli and Guicciardini*, 216-17, 224-25, 236-38.

54. Machiavelli also ridiculed them by first describing the celebrated battle of

Anghiari in the ornate style of humanist historiography and then stating that "in such a defeat and in so long a a battle that lasted from twenty to twenty-four hors, only one man died, and he not from wounds or any *virtuoso* blow, but, falling off his horse, he was trampled on and expired"; see FH.V.33.

55. Gilbert, *Machiavelli and Guicciardini,* 79-80, 89; see also 117-39, 150-52, 243-54.

56. Francesco Giucciardini, *Dialogo e Discorsi del Reggimento di Firenze* [1521-23], ed. R. Palmarocchi (Bari, 1932), 222, 99, mt; cited in Gilbert, *Machiavelli and Guicciardini,* 117-18, 137.

57. Francesco Vettori, *Sommario della Storia d'Italia dal 1511 al 1527,* in *Archivio Storico Italiano* VI, 1848, 283-382, at 293, mt; cited in Gilbert, *Machiavelli and Guicciardini,* 249.

58. Gilbert, *Machiavelli and Guicciardini,* 164. See also Felix Gilbert, "The Humanist Concept of the Prince and *The Prince* of Machiavelli," *Journal of Modern History* 11, no. 4 (December 1939): 449-83.

59. See Strauss, *Thoughts on Machiavelli;* Leo Strauss, "Machiavelli and Classical Literature," *Review of National Literatures* 1, no. 1 (spring 1970): 7-25; Leo Strauss, "Niccolò Machiavelli: 1469–1527," in *History of Political Philosophy,* 3rd ed., ed. Leo Strauss and Joseph Cropsey (Chicago: University of Chicago Press, 1987), 296-317; Harvey C. Mansfield, Jr., *Machiavelli's New Modes and Orders: A Study of the* Discourses on Livy (Ithaca: Cornell University Press, 1979); Harvey C. Mansfield, *Machiavelli's Virtue* (Chicago: University of Chicago Press, 1996); Harvey C. Mansfield and Nathan Tarcov, "Introduction," in Niccolò Machiavelli, *Discourses on Livy,* trans. Harvey C. Mansfield and Nathan Tarcov (Chicago: University of Chicago Press, 1996), xvii-xliv; Vickie B. Sullivan, *Machiavelli's Three Romes: Religion, Human Liberty, and Politics Reformed* (De Kalb, Ill.: Northern Illinois University Press, 1996).

Chapter 2

The World and How We Know It

Heaven's Necessity and Fortune's Contingency

As Anthony Parel has recently shown, Machiavelli believed in Renaissance astrology, which had grown out of the cosmological speculations of Babylonians, Greeks, and Arabs, and had been recorded in such occult classics as Ptolemy's *Tetrabiblos* and Abu Ma'shar's *De Magnis Conjunctionibus.*[1] According to this ancient doctrine, the destinies and characteristics of nations, religions, and individuals are influenced by the motions of heavenly bodies and the personalized agency of Fortune. That Machiavelli believed in such ideas can be seen most directly from the fact that when lightning struck the seat of the Florentine government, destroying three golden lilies over a door, he took this event as a bad portent for the king of France (whose coat of arms bore three lilies), the Florentine republic (which depended heavily on French support), as well as himself who held the office of Secretary–and immediately composed his will.[2] Indeed, his interpretation was borne out when the Florentine republic, led by Piero Soderini, fell shortly afterwards due to a military defeat sustained by the French, and Machiavelli not only lost his post but was imprisoned and put to the torture by the new rulers. In his own words, the fact that "soon before Piero Soderini, who had been made gonfalonier for life by the Florentine people, was expelled and deprived of his rank, the very palace itself was struck by a thunderbolt" (D.I.56.1) can thus be subsumed under the maxim that "before great accidents occur in a city or in a province, signs come that forecast them" (D.I.56.T). Machiavelli was in good company with such beliefs, for a number of advanced thinkers of the age–Marsilio Ficino, Pietro Pomponazzi, Agostino Nifo, and even Johannes Kepler–found it more rational to explain puzzling phenomena by the motions of stars and planets than by demons or miracles.[3] Indeed, they considered astrology to be a natural science, closely related to astronomy, which explained the visible aspects of phenomena in the sky, whereas astrology accounted for their hidden or "occult" ones. Thus, Machiavelli equated the occult heaven with nature when he made one of Circe's animals state that "our species does not care for other food than the product of heaven without art; you wish that which nature cannot make" (AS.VIII.975). Overall, the natural and therefore immanent science of astrology posed a serious challenge to the transcendental teachings of the Church. In the Renaissance, to profess astrological belief was thus to make a statement on behalf of secular modernity.

With this in mind, we realize that Machiavelli blasphemously associated the Creator with Fortune, the pagan goddess of chance, when he took the belief that "worldly things are so governed by [F]ortune *and* by God" to imply that one should "let oneself be governed by chance" (P.XXV.98, ea). His claim that a certain prince "had been ordered by God for [Italy's] redemption, yet later it was seen that in the highest course of his actions, he was repulsed by [F]ortune" (P.XXVI.102) suggested either that God is the same as Fortune or that he has less power than her. Drawing on contemporary astrological speculation, Machiavelli also declared that religions are limited in their life span to a few thousand years (D.II.5), which allowed him to declare with regard to Christianity "that its ruin or its scourging is near" (D.I.12.1).[4] Add to this that Machiavelli not once mentioned natural law–which his age considered as the divinely willed ordering principle of the world[5]–and it becomes clear that his espousal of astrological naturalism was coterminous with a denial of the transcendent religion of Christ.

The occult powers work their effects above all by influencing the psychological attributes of human beings, such as their ambition, humor, and spirit. According to Machiavelli, ambition and avarice were thus sent to dwell on earth by Fortune in order to cause the "variation of every mortal condition" (A.984). Individuals obtain their humors or temperaments from the constellation of heavenly bodies present at time of birth, giving everbody an inner "order that heaven bestows on you" (F.978).[6] Fortune "blinds the spirits of men when [she] does not wish them to oppose [her] plans" (D.II.29.T), and "the heavens . . . *inspired* in the breasts of the Roman Senate the choosing of Numa Pompilius as successor to Romulus" (D.I.11.1, ea).[7] As a result, the rise and decline of political order, which is caused immediately by the fact that "the powerful are never sated with their power" and the cyclical alteration of *virtù* that "makes the regions tranquil" and leisure that "burns countries and towns," is more remotely occasioned by the occult influence of Fortune, as "this order permits and wills she who governs us, so that nothing beneath the sun ever will or can stay firm" (AS.V.966-7). In short, there is a hierarchy of psychological and occult causes.[8]

While Machiavelli's astrological belief thus helps us understand a number of particular aspects of his thought, its deeper significance rests with its ontological implications. Accordingly, the world is most generally structured by (1) necessity, which emanates from the regular motions of heavenly bodies, and (2) contingency, which issues from the arbitrary doings of Fortune.

More precisely, since the heavenly bodies–sun, planets, stars– seem to move in unchanging circles, astrological thought assumed that their occult influence made earthly affairs unfold in a cyclical pattern. In particular, the annually recurrent movements of the planets through the zodiac determine the "quality of the times"; for instance, the ascendancy of Mars brings war, whereas the conjunction of Jupiter with the contemplative Mercury portends peace.[9] Unable to affect these heavenly events, human beings are forced to "follow the things that the revolutions of the heavens, the conditions of the times and of men bring" (L.221.1168) and, if in distress, must wait for a turn of fate:

> Not yet has heaven changed opinion, nor will it change while the fates keep their hard intention toward you. And those humors which have been so adverse and so inimical to you, not yet, not yet are purged; but when their roots are dry and the heavens show themselves benign, times will turn out more happy than before. (AS.III.962)[10]

Similarly, mankind as a whole cannot advance beyond a certain point because there are "causes that come from heaven . . . that eliminate the human race and reduce the inhabitants of the world to a few," which, on the visible level, "comes about either through plague or through famine or through an inundation of waters" (D.II.5.2).

This belief in the "necessity of fate"[11] can readily be understood as an astrological descendant of the ancient cosmological concept of *moira* or *fatum*, which signified to the Greeks and Romans a universal necessity that allots to every being a particular domain and inexorably punishes its transgression.[12] By subscribing to astrology, Machiavelli thus reversed the Christian substitution of divine providence for the pagan notion of fateful necessity, and thus suggested again that the world is immanently rather than transcendentally ordered.[13]

Whereas the heavens constitute an impersonal mechanism, Fortune is an agent that wills in erratic ways. Descended from the ancient goddess *tyche* or *fortuna*, she is an "occult power which sustains itself in the heaven, among the stars which heaven, as it turns, encloses" (A.984). Drawing on the ancient description of chaos as a river or ocean, Machiavelli thus likens her to "one of these violent rivers which, when they become enraged, flood the plains, ruin the trees and the buildings, lift earth from this part, drop it in another" (P.XXV.98), and makes one of his characters lament that "Fortune throws me once more into the midst of the sea, and among the most turbid and tempestuous waves" (C.V.5).[14] With chaos being ontologically related to incessant change, Fortune also represents the coming into being and passing away of earthly things: "not a thing in the world is eternal: Fortune wills it so" (F.978).[15] And with becoming taking place in the temporal dimension, Fortune also "disposes of time in her mode" (F.746),[16] and thus decides when humans are born and when they die. For instance, when Castruccio Castracani fell mortally ill from standing sweat-soaked in cold wind, it was actually "Fortune, inimical to his glory, [who,] when it was time to give him life, took it from him" (CC.625). The same holds true for "mixed bodies," that is, collectives like republics, which come into being when "by the good fortune of a city there rises in it a wise, good, and powerful citizen" who acts as a founder (FH.IV.1).

To the uninitiated, Fortune's interventions in human affairs appear as "accidents," unexpected events that sometimes come to their aid but mostly lead to chaos. Thus, Machiavelli speaks of "accidents" mostly in reference to disturbances of order, such as the "confusions, noises, and dangers of scandals that arose between the plebs and the nobility" (D.I.3.2), or the conspiracy of the Roman matrons who plotted to poison their senatorial husbands (D.III.49.1). Although random, certain accidents can nonetheless be foreseen by those who know to interpret their occult portents; for "one sees by ancient and modern examples that no grave accident . . . ever comes unless it has been foretold either by diviners or by revelations or by prodigies or by other heavenly signs" (D.I.56).

Machiavelli's evaluation of Fortune wavered between ancient optimism and medieval pessimism. On the one hand, he held that Fortune bestows favors on those who please her–in contrast to the inexorable heavens; in particular, she "lets herself be won more by the impetuous than by those who proceed coldly," since, "like a woman, she is the friend of the young, because they are less cautious, more ferocious, and command her with more audacity" (P.XXV.101). Indeed, from Caesar's and Alexander's example, one realizes "how much he pleases Fortune and how acceptable he is who pushes her, who shoves her, who jostles her" (TF.979). Here Machiavelli followed the Romans who spoke of Fortune as the good goddess (bona dea), who brings health, glory, power, and riches.[17] But, on the other hand, he lapsed into the medieval association of Fortune with the transitoriness of worldly success, when he called her a "cruel goddess" that "keeps the good under her feet" and "raises up the wicked" (F.976), and avered that "Fortune carries one up high not to remain there, but that she may delight when, ruining him, she brings him to fall" (F.979).

As mentioned above, Machiavelli's astrological utterances imply a dual ontology of necessity emanating from the heavens and contingency caused by Fortune. But, according to Leo Strauss, Machiavelli reduced the heavens to Fortune in order to portray the universe as wholly contingent, for he elaborated the chapter title "Fortune blinds the spirits of men when [she] does not wish them to oppose [her] plans" with the phrase "accidents come about which the heavens altogether have not wished to be provided against" (D.II.29.1), and named the heavens as the origin of "grave accidents" when claiming that they are foretold "by heavenly signs" (D.I.56.1).[18] Indeed, there is further evidence for such a conflation: Machiavelli at times described the heavens as a personal agent capable of judging, knowing, wishing, and intending,[19] he cited both Fortune and the heavens as sources of the opportunity that founders need,[20] and he ascribed to Fortune the historical cycles that appear in the rise and fall of empires as well as the changing quality of the times, which, according to astrological doctrine, are caused by the heavens.[21]

However, as Anthony Parel has argued, this conflation of the heavens and Fortune represents only the popular strand of Renaissance astrology, in contrast to the philosophical strand which maintained their distinctness.[22] But it is difficult to see how Machiavelli could have subscribed to this popular view, since he considered the common people to be very much deceived in "general things" (D.I.47)–such as the question whether the world is ordered or chaotic–and since his project of restoring the greatness of the ancient Romans becomes much more plausible by assuming that the lowly condition of Italy–whose "travails" occurred "under stars inimical to her good"[23]–was ordered by the heavens to give way to another peak. This supposition is corroborated by the fact that Machiavelli reproved an "infinite number," that is, the common people, for being mesmerized by Fortune's accidents and failing to realize that the larger order of the heavens has remained the same:

> The infinite number who read [the histories] take pleasure in hearing of the variety of accidents contained in them without thinking of imitating them, judging that imitation is not only difficult but impossible: as if, heaven, sun, elements, men were changed in motion, order and power from what they were in antiquity. (D.I.Pr.2)

In other words, it is "by many this [goddess] is said to be omnipotent" (F.976), whereas Machiavelli knows that "fortune is arbiter of [only] half of our actions" (P.XXV.98).

True, Machiavelli was far too impressed with the element of chance to assume in fatalistic fashion that heavenly necessity determined history in detail, thereby obviating the need for *virtuoso* action on the part of men. But he did assume that history unfolds in cycles and ascribed this fact to a duality of psychological and occult causes, that is, the constancy of human nature and the circular motions of the heavenly bodies. To explain to the audience of his comedy *Clizia,* which imitates Plautus's *Casina,* how the same farce could have occurred in ancient Athens and contemporary Florence, he thus argues that "if into the world the same men should come back, as the same happenstances return, never would a hundred years go by where we would not find for another time the same things done as now" (C.891).

Overall then, Machiavelli presents us with a world that is bereft of transcendental order, but where immanent necessity, arising from the heavens and human nature, brings about a recurrence of events that limits Fortune's contingency to some extent.

Prudential Empiricism

How do we know such a world? Insofar as events are occultly caused, we obviously need to turn to astrology and divination: For "he who were so wise that he knew the times and the order of things and accommodated himself to them, would always have good fortune or always guard himself against the bad, and it would come to be true that the wise would command the stars and the fates" (L.116.1083).[24] On the other hand, to the extent that events are psychologically caused, we need to understand how the passions, humors, spirits, minds, and habits of human beings give rise to recurrent patterns of action:

> Whoever wishes to see what has to be considers what has been; for all worldly things in every time have their own counterpart in ancient times. That arises because these are the work of men, who have and always had the same passions, and they must of necessity result in the same effect. . . . To see a nation keep the same customs for a long time . . . also makes it easy to know future things by past. (D.III.43.1)

A similarly historical approach to human affairs had already been practiced by the humanists. However, whereas they followed the ancients in turning history into moral lessons, Machiavelli aimed his inquiry at what human beings really do rather than what they ought to do:

> I depart from the orders of others. But since my intent is to write something useful to whoever understands it, it has appeared to me more fitting to go directly to the effectual truth of the thing than to the imagination of it. And many have imagined republics and principalities that have never been seen or known to exist in truth; for it is so far from how one lives to how one should live that he who lets go of what is done for what should be done learns his ruin rather than preservation. (P.XV.61)

Striving to "take the world as it really is" (A.983), Machiavelli here breaks with nothing less than nineteen centuries of philosophical inquiry in the West, which had heeded Socrates's injunction to equate the True with the Good and thus to orient our study of the human condition by the best man and the best regime. In other words, Machiavelli inaugurated the modern tradition that denies "man-as-could-be-if-he-realized-his-essential-nature" and constructs society on the basis of "man-as-he-happens-to-be," which, according to Alasdair MacIntyre, constituted the central paradigm shift informing the Enlightenment.[25] From Plato to Aristotle, Augustine, and Aquinas, classical thinkers had considered it realistic to study what men ought to do because they had a teleological view of human nature, which took the development of a virtuous character to be our natural task and thus accepted moral purposes as valid explanations of human action. In contrast, Machiavelli assumed human beings to be incapable of virtue (as shown in chapter 3), and thus denied that moral judgments are adequate descriptions of human reality; from now on, the study of man was to assume what once had been seen as his primitive and untutored nature, and theories based on man at his best became "idealistic" and "utopian."[26]

In other words, Machiavelli repudiated the teleological view to the world, which assumed final causes as the primary articulations of being, and, instead, elevated efficient causes or the "effectual truth" to supreme significance. Thus, he gave an important impulse to the scientific method, which was acknowledged by its first founder Francis Bacon, who wrote that "we are much beholden to Machiavelli and other writers of that class who openly and unfeignedly declare or describe what men do, and not what they ought to do."[27] Thus, it was indeed Machiavelli who originated the separation of facts and values that was to become the hallmark of social science, as argued by Leo Strauss.[28] In this repudiation, Machiavelli was driven not only by his anthropological pessimism, which denied that man had a capacity for virtue, but also by his astrological naturalism, which rejected the transcendental (or metaphysical) level of reality and thus eliminated the place where the classical *telos*–the supreme final cause that gives being to all others–could exist; whence also Machiavelli's silence on natural law, which articulates this *telos* into precepts of human conduct.

Before Nietzsche, it was generally assumed that knowledge needs to be anchored in something continuous and constant. Since Machiavelli's world lacks the supreme final cause which used to serve this function, he takes as his anchor the necessity that exists on account of the regular motions of the heavens and the constancy of human nature and that manifests itself in the recurrent pattern of historical events. He grasps these patterns by generalizing the necessary relations between actions and their consequences into "general rules," "maxims," or "precepts." For instance,

> it may be seen from experience that the greatness in Italy of the Church and of Spain has been caused by France, and France's ruin caused by them. From this one may draw a general rule that never or rarely fails: whoever is the cause of someone's becoming powerful is ruined. (P.III.16)[29]

Indeed, Machiavelli professes an explicit preference for such an inductive approach to knowledge when he demands that a maxim "should be demonstrated through particulars, with ancient and modern examples, since it cannot be demonstrated so distinctly through reasons," that is, deductively (D.II.27.1). By ancient examples, he means the study of ancient historians, such as Livy, Sallust, Thucydides, Polybius, and Tacitus; by modern ones, he refers to contemporary affairs, which he knew in large measure from his personal experience as Secretary of the Second Chancery, which brought him into contact with such potentates as Cesare Borgia, Pope Julius II, Charles VIII of France, and Emperor Maximilian of Germany.[30] In the *Prince,* Machiavelli thus offers all the "knowledge of the actions of great men, learned by me from long experience with modern things and a continuous reading of ancient ones" (P.Ded.3), and in the *Discourses,* he gives expression to "as much as I know and have learned through long practice and a continual reading in worldly things" (D.Ded).

Machiavelli's empiricism is perhaps most evident when he revises his maxims because they come up against facts that contradict them. For instance, having postulated that dictatorial authority will not harm republics when given by free vote, he faces the fact that the dictatorial authority of the Decemviri did diminish the freedom of the Romans even though they had voted on it, and resolves the problem by qualifying his thesis: For dictatorial authority to be harmless, it must not only be given by free vote, but also be granted for less than a year and the other offices must remain in place as a check.[31] Or, when Machiavelli's maxim that one cannot make a republic were there are gentlemen seems falsified by the Venetian republic, which functioned well despite the fact that only gentlemen could hold office, he clarifies his thesis by making it refer only to gentlemen who possess castles and have jurisdiction over subjects.[32]

Although preferring induction, Machiavelli actually generates his knowledge in a deductive way as well; for he often derives his maxims directly from premises about the world at large and the nature of human beings. For instance, his claim that individuals ought to, but cannot, adapt their "mode of proceeding to the quality of the times" (P.XXV.99) rests on the twin assumption that the heavens impart defining characteristics to historical ages and that human beings have fixed dispositions. In the same vein, he declares that "it is much safer to be feared than loved" on the grounds that "one can say this generally of men: that they are ungrateful, fickle, pretenders and dissemblers, evaders of danger, eager for gain" (P.XVII.66). At the same time, however, Machiavelli clearly breaks with the medieval practice of deducing statements from authority, such as Scripture, ancient writers, and Church fathers; for instance, when challenging Livy he argues that "I do not judge nor shall I ever judge it to be a defect to defend any opinion with reasons, without wishing to use either authority or force" (D.I.58.1).[33] Hence, Machiavelli's use of deduction is limited to what he assumed to be empirically true statements about reality.

This empirical derivation of cause-and-effect relationships has led a number of commentators to argue that Machiavelli was the first modern scientist–the "Galileo of politics."[34] But this ascription is only half true. As shown above, Machiavelli can surely be credited with giving an important impulse to the empiricism and fact-value separation of modern science, but he decidely did not take the equally crucial step from *prudentia* (prudence) to *scientia* (science), as later done in exemplary fashion by Hobbes.[35] In other words, whereas modern science assumes a fully determinate universe that allows for general statements or "laws" that hold regardless of circumstances, Machiavelli continued the Aristotelian tradition of assuming human reality to be such that we can know it only approximately.[36] Thus, as we saw already, Machiavelli stops short of ascribing full determinacy to his general rules, claiming instead that they "never or rarely" fail (P.III.16),[37] or, more precisely, that "one cannot give certain rules because the modes vary according to circumstances" (P.IX.40-41). Accordingly, one who writes about politics in general should "speak in that broad mode which the matter permits in itself," for "one cannot give a definitive judgment on all these things unless one comes to the particulars of those states where any such decision has to be made" (P.XX.83).[38] Indeed, Machiavelli gives a veritable definition of prudence as a matter of uncertainty and trade-off:

> Nor should any state ever believe that it can always adopt safe courses; on the contrary, it should think it has to take them all as doubtful. For in the order of things it is found that one never seeks to avoid one inconvenience without running into another; but prudence consists in knowing how to recognize the qualities of inconveniences, and in picking the less bad as good. (P.XXI.91)[39]

This reliance on a prudential approach to political knowledge is ultimately driven by the significant role that Fortune plays in the affairs of the world. While the necessity arising from the heavens and human nature would allow for rules that are certain, the contingency introduced by Fortune implies that they can only be heuristic statements, that is, guidelines for action that need to be adapted by the agent to the circumstances at hand.

More precisely, an act of prudential reasoning can be separated into four parts:[40] (i) a premise that states the desirability of what is problematic to attain, for example, that "the highest good" consists of the "honor of the world" (D.II.2.2); (ii) a maxim of action, that is, a probabilistic claim based on experience that shows how a particular action tends to solve this problem under a number of circumstances: For instance, men who "depend on their own and are able to use force" (P.VI.24) can "to their perpetual honor . . . make a republic or a kingdom" (D.I.10.1), under the condition that they have the same "opportunity" as Moses, Cyrus, and Theseus, namely, to find a people that is enslaved, servile, malcontent, or dispersed (P.VI.23); (iii) an comparison of the current situation with the circumstances assumed by the maxim: "thinking to myself whether in Italy at present the times have been tending to the honor of a new prince" (P.XXVI.101), Machiavelli thus finds that Italy is "more enslaved than the Hebrews, more servile than the Persians, more dispersed than the Athenians" (P.XXVI.103); (iv) a conclusion that subsumes the current problem under the above maxim and thereby suggests to a particular agent how to proceed: Lorenzo de' Medici, to whom Machiavelli's *Prince* is addressed, should thus "prepare such arms for [him]self so as to be able with Italian *virtù* to defend [him]self from the foreigners" (P.XXVI.104), in order to "seize Italy and . . . free her from the barbarians" (P.XXVI.T).

If this prudential labor is divided between a theorist and a practitioner of politics, as in Machiavelli's case, it falls to the theorist to generate the maxim and to the practitioner to judge whether it can be applied to the current situation. It is above all this judgment that requires the quality of prudence, for it opens maxims that were formulated under known circumstances to the full uncertainty and contingency of the practical world; in particular, as the agent deliberates and begins to act, unexpected events may change the circumstances, remote repercussions of the suggested action may only now become apparent, the response of others may fundamentally alter the problem, time for deliberation may run short, etc. After describing the ideal form of an army's order of battle, Machiavelli thus tells his readers that

> you have to vary the form of the army according to the quality of the site and the quality and quantity of the enemy. . . . But we give you this form . . . because from it you take a rule and an order for knowing

the modes for ordering the others; for every science has its generality,
on which it is founded in good part. (AG.III.343)

The prudent men of the Roman Senate thus authorized the
commanders of the legions to make independent decisions, because
they realized that they were "not on the spot and did not know
infinite particulars that are necessary to know for whoever wishes to
give counsel well" (D.II.33).

Further, whether a prudential inference is valid can only be
determined after the action and its consequences have run their
concrete course; for it belongs to the very definition of prudential
knowledge that neither the problem nor its solution are fully
understood beforehand. In the example on founding, we thus would
have to assess whether princes, who applied Machiavelli's maxims
under comparable circumstances, actually succeeded at creating lasting
orders and thereby gaining perpetual honor for themselves. This is the
ultimate sense in which prudential truth is "effectual truth."

Finally, although Machiavelli sides with the Aristotelian tradition
in rejecting a deterministic science of politics, his notion of prudence
is nonetheless very different from Aristotle's. For Aristotelian
phronesis always subordinates the practical use of reason to what is
right,[41] whereas Machiavellian prudence not only permits but actually
commands the violation of moral rules: A "prudent lord . . . cannot
observe faith, nor should he, when such observance turns against him,
and the causes that made him promise have been eliminated"
(P.XVIII.69), and a "prudent orderer of republics . . . should contrive
to have authority alone," even if that requires murdering one's
brother and partner in authority (D.I.9.2). Indeed, Machiavelli seems
to offer his maxims on republics both to defenders and usurpers of
liberty, as when he discusses what is of "great importance, as well as
for those who wish to maintain a free republic as for those who plan
to subject it" (D.I.40.1). Hence, Machiavelli's notion of prudence
really corresponds to what Aristotle denounced as mere cleverness
(*deinotike*), that is, the use of practical reason for any end.[42]

In sum, Machiavelli prepared the ground for a modern science of
politics by redirecting our attention from final to efficient causes,
from authority to reason, and from what men ought to do to what
they really do. Nonetheless, he was not a scientist himself because he
cast his propositions as situation-dependent maxims rather than
universal laws. Thus, he is best described as a prudential empiricist who
freed prudence from its classical subservience to ethics.

Notes

1. Anthony J. Parel, *The Machiavellian Cosmos* (New Haven: Yale University Press, 1992), esp. ch. 1.

2. Roberto Ridolfi, *The Life of Niccolò Machiavelli,* trans. Cecil Grayson (Chicago: University of Chicago Press, 1963), 127.

3. On medieval and Renaissance astrology, see: Ernst Cassirer, *Individuum und Kosmos in der Philosophie der Renaissance* (Darmstadt: Wissenschaftliche Buchgesellschaft, 1963), 103-29; Brian P. Copenhaver, "Astrology and Magic," in *The Cambridge History of Renaissance Philosophy,* ed. Charles B. Schmitt (Cambridge: Cambridge University Press, 1988), 264-300; Alfonso Ingegno, "The New Philosophy of Nature," in *The Cambridge History of Renaissance Philosophy,* ed. Charles B. Schmitt (Cambridge: Cambridge University Press, 1988), 236-63; Simon Kemp, *Medieval Psychology* (New York: Greenwood Press, 1990), 90-95.

4. For Renaissance speculation on the periodicity of Christianity and the coming of the anti-Christ, see Ingegno, "New Philosophy of Nature," 237, 243, 250; Parel, *Machiavellian Cosmos,* 50.

5. Cf. Isaiah Berlin, "The Originality of Machiavelli," in *Studies on Machiavelli,* ed. Myron P. Gilmore (Florence: Sansoni), 149-206, at 159-60.

6. Cf. Parel, *Machiavellian Cosmos,* 12, 79.

7. Cf. "Second Mission to Francesco Guicciardini," in W.IV.339-73, at 360.

8. Parel, *Machiavellian Cosmos,* 42.

9. Parel, *Machiavellian Cosmos,* 12-15, 42.

10. Cf. FH.V.1; "Mission to the Countess Catharine Sforza," in W.III.6-26, at 13.

11. *I Decennali* [Decennial chronicles], in TO.939-54, at 939, mt.

12. On *moira,* see Irving M. Zeitlin, *Plato's Vision: The Classical Origins of Social & Political Thought* (Englewood Cliffs, N.J.: Prentice Hall, 1993), 25-31.

13. Cf. Kurt Kluxen, *Politik und menschliche Existenz bei Machiavelli: Dargestellt am Begriff der Necessità* (Stuttgart: W. Kohlhammer, 1967), 22-23; Herfried Münkler, *Machiavelli: Die Begründung des politischen Denkens der Neuzeit aus der Krise der Republik Florenz* (Frankfurt: Europäische Verlagsanstalt, 1982), 246.

14. Cf. F.979.

15. Cf. FH.III.5.

16. On time and Fortune in Machiavelli's thought, see also Robert Orr, "The Time Motif in Machiavelli," in *Machiavelli and the Nature of Political Thought,* ed. Martin Fleisher (New York: Atheneum, 1972), 185-208.

17. Thomas Flanagan, "The Concept of *fortuna* in Machiavelli," in *The Political Calculus,* ed. Anthony Parel (Toronto: University of Toronto Press, 1972), 127-56, esp. 131-32.

18. Leo Strauss, *Thoughts on Machiavelli* (Chicago: University of Chicago Press, 1958), 209, 217. Cf. Hannah F. Pitkin, *Fortune Is a Woman: Gender*

and Politics in the Thought of Niccolò Machiavelli (Berkeley, Calif.: University of California Press, 1984), 162-65.

19. See D.I.11.1; D.II.29.1; FH.I.25; FH.II.33; *Dell' Ingratitudine* [On ingratitude], in TO.980-83, at 981; "Second Mission to Francesco Giucciardini, in W.IV.339-373, at 360.

20. See D.I.10.6; P.VI.23, 25; DF.31.

21. See P.XXV.99; D.III.9.3; L.116.1083; F.978-79; AS.V.966-67.

22. Parel, *Machiavellian Cosmos,* 7-8, 43-44, 63.

23. *I Decennali,* in TO.939-54, at 940, mt.

24. Cf. D.I.56.

25. Alasdair MacIntyre, *After Virtue: A Study in Moral Theory,* 2nd ed. (Notre Dame, Ind.: University of Notre Dame Press, 1984), 52-59. Note also MacIntyre's statement that "these conceptual changes . . . at the level of philosophical theory are articulated by Machiavelli and Hobbes, by Diderot and Condorcet, by Hume and Adam Smith and Kant" (61).

26. It may be of import here that the Greek word for "nature" (*physis*) derives from the verb "to grow" (*physein)* and thus takes the nature of a thing to consist of its growth toward the fully developed form, whereas the Latin and Italian words for "nature" (*natura),* which Machiavelli used, take their origin from "to be born" (*nascere*) and thus associate the natural with the undeveloped and primitive.

27. Francis Bacon, *Of the Advancement of Learning* (London: Oxford University Press, 1906), II, 21.9. On Machiavelli's influence on Bacon, see also Vincent Luciani, "Bacon and Machiavelli," *Italica* 24, no.1 (March 1947): 26-41.

28. Leo Strauss, *Natural Right and History* (Chicago: University of Chicago Press, 1950), 61, cf. 3-4, 177-79.

29. Cf. D.I.9.2; D.II.17.1; AG.III.342. On Machiavelli's historical inductivism, see also Herbert Butterfield, *The Statecraft of Machiavelli* (London: G. Bell, 1940), 26-41.

30. For Machiavelli's missions, see W.III-IV.

31. D.I.34-35.

32. D.I.56.3-6.

33. Cf. D.I.4.1.

34. Leonardo Olschki, *Machiavelli the Scientist* (Berkeley, Calif.: Gillick, 1945); Ernst Cassirer, *The Myth of the State* (New Haven: Yale University Press, 1946), 116-62; Leslie J. Walker, "Introduction by the Translator," in *The Discourses of Niccolò Machiavelli,* trans. Leslie J. Walker (New Haven: Yale University Press, 1950), vol. I, 1-164, esp. 63-99; Anthony J. Parel, "Introduction: Machiavelli's Method and His Interpreters," in *The Political Calculus,* ed. Anthony Parel (Toronto: University of Toronto Press, 1972), 3-32, esp. 3-14.

35. Thomas Hobbes, *Leviathan: With Selected Variants from the Latin Edition of 1688* [1651], ed. Edwin Curley (Indianapolis: Hackett, 1994), V.17-22.

36. Aristotle, *Nicomachean Ethics,* trans. Terence Irwin (Indianapolis:

Hackett, 1985), 1094b20-22, cf. 1126b3.

37. Cf. D.I.9.2.

38. Cf. D.I.18.1.

39. Cf. D.I.6.3; D.III.11.1, 37.1.

40. On prudential reasoning, see David P. Gauthier, *Practical Reasoning: The Structure and Foundations of Prudential and Moral Arguments and their Exemplification in Discourse* (Oxford: Oxford University Press, 1963); Yves R. Simon, *Practical Knowledge* (New York: Fordham University Press, 1991).

41. Aristotle, *Nicomachean Ethics,* 1140a-b.

42. Aristotle, *Nicomachean Ethics,* 1144a-b.

Chapter 3

Human Nature and Action

By Nature or by Accident

As several commentators have noted, Machiavelli's assumptions about human nature contain two related tensions, namely between the ruthless selfishness so evident in the *Prince* and the respect for laws found among good citizens in the *Discourses* and other republican writings, and between the constancy of men and the fact that they can be molded by princes.[1] As we shall see, these tensions can be resolved with the help of Machiavelli's central distinction between necessary and contingent characteristics: Inherently, human beings have certain properties that make them rapacious, but they can also be made to acquire habits that mitigate their rapacity and thus enable them to lead a civil way of life.[2] Machiavelli words this distinction above all in terms of "nature" and "accident": Princes have their qualities "either by nature or by accident" (L.214.1155); generals have authority over their troops "by nature" if they are born in the same place or "by accident" if their assignment has lasted long enough for the soldiers to become accustomed to their command (AG.I.316); the "natural fury" of the Gauls was no match for the "accidental order" of the Roman legions, with "accidental" obviously meaning acquired by training rather than occurring by chance during battle (D.III.36.2); and, there are "natural or accidental subterfuges."[3]

Hence, "accident" has two meanings in Machiavelli's writing: a chance event that originates in Fortune's whim and cannot be foreseen by human beings, and an acquired characteristic that comes into being and passes away. Ontologically, these two meanings find common ground in Aristotle's assumption that accidental attributes have causes that are themselves accidents.[4] In Machiavelli's context, this means that such attributes are generated by a founder who has risen by chance; thus, a region that "lives unbridled by its nature" may "by accident be instructed and ordered under good laws," that is, a naturally licentious multitude may acquire good habits by chancing upon a prince that turns founder (A.985).[5] Indeed, habits are the most important kind of accidental attributes because they turn them into relatively stable determinants of action, and thus provide a second warrant for the derivation of general rules, in addition to necessary properties. In Machiavelli's words, "is it easy to know future things by past" first of all because "worldly things . . . are the work of men who have and always have had the same [natural] passions, and they must of necessity result in the same effect," but also because we "see a nation keep the same customs for a long time" (D.III.43.1).

Such use of the nature-accident distinction was quite common in Machiavelli's time. Francesco Giucciardini, for instance, wrote that "everything, either by nature or by accident, ends at some time" and no one should "trust so much in natural prudence that he believes it to be sufficient without the accidental of experience."[6] In contemporary Italian dictionaries, we find the following attributions to Dante and Petrarca–authors well known to Machiavelli: A bad attribute can be "accidental vice or also sin in nature," just as there is "accidental or natural infirmity"; "a place [can be] naturally loved but by accident annoying"; "earth is naturally cold and dry, but changes accidentally from extrinsic things"; a person can "take more after his nature than after accident"; however, something can also be "as much by nature as by accident"; and "nature cannot withstand custom." There is even an entry that defines nature as both unchanging and necessary, that is, as a substance: "Sagacious nature. That which does not become less in necessary things."[7]

This definition of nature directs us once more to the ontological meaning of Machiavelli's distinction between nature and accident: In the Aristotelian-Thomist tradition, things maintain their identity as long as the changes they undergo remain "accidental" in the sense that they do not affect their "nature" or "substance"; for instance, even though a tree presents us a with different appearances over time–as it keeps growing, bears leaves and fruit in one season, becomes barren in another, etc.–we naturally consider it the same tree because we assume that these alterations do not affect what makes it a tree in substance, namely, that it consists of wooden matter which takes the form of branches emerging from a common trunk, which remains rooted in the same place.[8] Of course, this is not to say that Machiavelli wrote as a metaphysician, but merely that he availed himself of the nature-accident distinction to make sense of the fact that human nature is both constant and malleable.

In related distinctions, Machiavelli contrasts nature also with "art," "education," and "industry," in short, with diligently learned skill. Accordingly, those Roman emperors were ruined "who by nature or by art did not have a great reputation such that they could hold both [the people and the soldiers] in check" (P.XIX.76). The "nature" of the Gauls, who are ferocious at the beginning of combat but cowardly toward the end, can be "ordered with art" to remain ferocious throughout (D.III.36.1), for "where nature is lacking, it is made up by industry, which in this case counts more than nature" (AG.I.309); in other words, "education can supply what nature is lacking" (A.985).[9] Similarly, animals are satisfied with food that heaven provides "without art," whereas men want "what nature cannot make" (AS.VIII.975), just as the latter "naturally believe many things that are false, and from art add many more" (D.II.31.1). On the other hand, since even Dante assimilated foreign phrases to his native tongue, it also follows that "art can never repulse nature entirely."[10]

While it is clear that contingent attributes are acquired skills, thoughts, and habits, Machiavelli's idea of nature needs to be determined more closely. To begin with, "nature" quite common-sensically refers to the world at large[11] and the essential or ordinary aspects of anything.[12] More pertinent to our topic, "nature" stands for the universal properties of human beings as in "the nature of men is ambitious and suspicious" (D.I.29.1),[13] but also refers to the ingrained characteristics of particular individuals, groups, and animals: "to know well the nature of peoples one needs to be prince, and to know well the nature of princes one needs to be of the people" (P.Ded.4), and prince should imitate the "natures" of fox and lion (i.e., use fraud like a fox and force like a lion) (P.XIX.78).[14] The possibility of emulating such particular natures leads to the paradoxical idea of natures that change–as when Appius Claudius did not do "well to change nature of a sudden and from a friend of the plebs show himself an enemy; from human, proud; from agreeable, difficult" (D.I.41).[15] More coherently put, "nature" may thus refer to acquired characteristics that have become second nature–which Machiavelli must have had in mind when he argued that people can become so accustomed to their ruler that he becomes a "natural prince" (P.II.7), who enjoys the "natural affection" of his subjects (P.IV.17), and when he took the fact that Quintus Fabius "changed his good customs to the worst" to show "how easily men are corrupted and make themselves assume a contrary nature" (D.I.42).[16] Accordingly, Machiavelli's contrast between nature and habit can also be described as one between first nature and second nature.

Obviously, Machiavelli's distinction of human characteristics into necessary properties and contingent attributes agrees with his ontological assumption that the world is structured by both necessity and contingency. Indeed, this necessity arises in part from the very constancy of human nature; conversely, it is a matter of good fortune when founders arise that endow human beings with law-abiding habits.

First Nature

Soul and Spirit

Most thinkers of the Renaissance considered the intellective soul to be man's immortal essence.[17] Machiavelli mentions it only thrice, and each time ranks it below the good of the city, as when he exclaims "I love my fatherland more than my soul" (L.321.1250).[18] Further, he instructs none other than the Holy Father that "the greatest good to be done and the most pleasing to God is that which one does for one's fatherland"–rather than the soul, as Christian doctrine would have mandated (DF.30). To put the good of the fatherland above the salvation of the soul is indeed necessary for political men in Machiavelli's world; for, as we shall see in chapter 4, rulers must commit wicked deeds in order to make their city prosper, putting their personal salvation at a grave risk. But, as we saw in chapter 2, Machiavelli probably did not even believe in the soul, for his astrological naturalism denies teleological and transcendental world views, such as the Aristotelian and Christian ones, and thus eliminates the realm to which the soul was thought to belong. Add to this that Machiavelli blamed the political decay of Europe in good part on the Christian preoccupation with the salvation of the soul–as when he argues that "our religion . . . seems to have rendered the world weak and given it in prey to criminal men" as the "universality of men, so as to go to paradise, think more of enduring their beatings than of avenging them" (D.II.2.2, mt)[19]–and it becomes evident that his neglect of the soul was a deliberate effort to remove the idea from political life.[20]

Having expunged the soul, Machiavelli is prone to redefine the terms that were used to designate its faculties. Thus, he refers to "reason" (*ragione*) mostly in the discursive sense of argument, cause, ground, or motive, but only rarely in the psychological sense of mental capacity or activity.[21] The few times he mentions "free will" (*libero arbitrio*), he speaks merely of the ability to act without external constraint rather than the soul's capacity to transcend our natural instincts, desires, and habits, as traditionally understood; for instance, a prince should choose wise men as counselors and "only to these should he give *libero arbitrio* to speak the truth to him, and of those things only that he asks about and nothing else" (P.XXIII.94).[22] This redefinition of freedom puts Machiavelli at sharp odds with the humanists, who stressed the freedom of the will in order to exalt the dignity of man; and, at the same time, it makes him a forerunner of Hobbes, who defined liberty as the absence of external impediments to bodily motion.[23]

The live-giving or animating function of the soul is taken over by the "spirit" (*animo*), which is especially needed for actions that take place under adverse conditions. For instance, a prince "needs to have an spirit disposed to change as the winds of fortune and variations of things command him" (P.XVIII.70), "everyone would have admired [Giovampagolo Baglioni's] spirit" if he had been daring enough to kill and despoil the pope and his cardinals when they had entered his city unarmed (D.I.27.2), and the Samnites knew they had to "induce obstinacy in the spirits of their soldiers" to face the battle-harded Romans (D.I.15).[24] Conversely, a "conspiracy is exposed by one party in which the spirit fails" (D.III.6.6). In the absence of the soul, it is the spirit that does the willing and intending, as can be seen from Machiavelli's counsel that those who wish to assassinate a prince should gain his confidence in order to find "every occasion for satisfying [their] spirit" (D.III.2), for it holds in general that "one should not show one's spirit but try to seek to obtain one's desire in any mode" (D.I.44.2).[25]

Going back to the Stoic notion of *pneuma*, spirit was considered by medieval and Renaissance thinkers a rarified substance that mediates the various functions of living organisms; for instance, the experience of anger was thought to consist of the rushing of "vital" spirit toward the extremities, while the faculty of imagination was believed to process impressions in the "animal" spirit that flows through the ventricles of the brain.[26] Machiavelli seems to have accepted this view, for he speaks of the "cooling" of hot spirits,[27] asserts that "false imaginations" come about when you "hear a word, said for another end, that perturbs your spirit and makes you believe it was said about your case" (D.III.6.16),[28] and applies the medical practice of purging a spirit that is contaminated by ill humors to the body politic: "because [Cesare Borgia] knew that past rigors had generated some hatred for Remirro, to purge the spirits of that people and to gain them entirely to himself," he had Remirro cut in half and displayed in the piazza (P.VII.30).

In sum, Machiavelli's first assumptions about human nature are congruent with his ideas about the world at large: just as he rejected the teleological and transcendental in favor of efficient and immanent causes (which are partly psychological and partly occult), so he replaced the soul or *anima* with a medical concept of the spirit or *animo* as the motivating principle of man.[29]

Mind

While the spirit animates us to act, the "mind" (*mente*) tells us how to proceed. Thus, a "prudent orderer of a republic, who has the spirit to wish to help not himself but the common good" should make sure that "any such ordering depend on his mind" alone (D.I.9.2). Regarding the mind's faculties, Machiavelli rather faithfully follows premodern medicine by speaking of imagination (*imaginazione, fantasia*), ingenuity (*ingegno*), and memory (*memoria*), which were collectively known as "inner senses" or mind. Contrary to the soul, the mind had always been considered to lack free will and thus to perform a merely instrumental function–which Machiavelli is only too happy to confirm: "our mind, ever intent on what is natural to it, grants no defense against habit or nature" (AS.I.956).

According to the medical account, the faculty of imagination is housed in the forward ventricle of the brain, where it transforms the fleeting sense impressions streaming in from the sensory organs into more abstract and durable images, which are then carried by the animal spirit into the central ventricle, where the faculty of ingenuity (*ingenium*) or cogitation (*cogitatio*) is located; this faculty then performs the tasks of instrumental reason by correlating newly received images from with old ones, which previously had been deposited in the rear ventricle where the faculty of memory sits; in addition, the faculty of ingenuity or cogitation controls the physical movements of man through animal spirit that flows through spinal cord and nerves to the muscles. Machiavelli most likely referred to this account when he asserted that "each man conducts himself according to his ingenuity and imagination" (L.116.1083), for he used the word "brain" (*cervello*) as a synonym for mind, which suggests that the mental faculties are housed in the ventricles of the brain; for instance, having told us that an orderer of a republic should make "any such ordering depend on his *mind* alone" (D.I.9.2), he later restates that point by saying that ordering a republic is "material for a man who is rare in *brain* and authority" (D.I.55.5, ea).[30]

In particular, the faculty of ingenuity refers to the ability to procure under changing circumstances the means that satisfy one's desires.[31] Thus, private individuals who become princes need "great ingenuity" to know how to act in their new position (P.VII.26); Italians excel in duels and skirmishes on account of their "force, dexterity, and ingenuity" (P.XXVI.104). But Machiavelli also needed "ingenuity" to write the *Discourses* (D.Ded, mt),[32] and Cosimo Rucellai demonstrated the "dexterity of his ingenuity" by composing love poems (AG.I.302), perhaps because writing about political and sexual affairs takes the same faculty as practicing them successfully. The faculty of imagination is mentioned by Machiavelli mostly in terms of its failure to function properly, that is, its tendency to generate images and concepts that do not correspond to reality, which premodern medicine attributed to bad humors. Contrasting the effectual truth of things to their "imagination," he famously heaps scorn on those who "have imagined republics and principalities that have never been seen or known to exist in truth" (P.XV.61); he assesses the difficulties in executing a conspiracy to be such that "every false imagination is able to make [men] turn about" (D.II.32.1);[33] and he claims that men's inability to change results from the fact that they have "turned their imagination for many days to one mode and to one order" (D.III.6.12, mt).

Although Machiavelli does not speak of the faculty of memory in psychological terms, it is nonetheless of great significance with regard to the salutary effect of men's love of glory; for working for the common good in order to gain lasting glory presupposes that others will remember one's deeds. Thus, Stefano Porcari sought to become a founder because he "desired, according to the custom of men who relish glory, to do or at least to try something worthy of memory" (FH.VI.29).[34] The faculty of memory is equally important for the maintenance of political order. A "memorable execution" is needed to secure a new regime against the partisans of the old one (D.III.3), despite the fact that new regimes enjoy "some reverence in the beginning" as long as "the memory of the [previous] prince and the injuries received from him [is] still fresh" (D.I.2.3).[35] In the long run, individuals become accustomed to a princely house if the "memories and causes of innovations are extinguished" (P.II.7), unless they had been living under a republic so that the "memory of their ancient liberty does not and cannot let them rest" (P.V.21).[36] And to forestall corruption in an ongoing republic, wrongdoers must periodically be executed in front of the citizens so that "punishment is brought back to their memory and fear is renewed in their spirits" (D.III.1.3).

Innate differences in these mental faculties of ingenuity, imagination, and memory divide humanity into three major types; for, according to Machiavelli, "there are three kinds of brains: one that understands by itself, another that discerns what others understand, the third that understands neither by itself nor through others; the first is most excellent, the second excellent, and the third useless" (P.XXII.92). The "most excellent" brain that "understands by itself" is clearly needed by men like Moses, Cyrus, Romulus, and Theseus; for Machiavelli calls them the "most excellent" princes, who, since they are "innovators" and introducers of "new orders and modes" (P.VI.23-24), must be able to step beyond the horizon of their time and thus need highly imaginative and independent minds. In second place, the merely "excellent" brain that "discerns what others understand" seems good enough for the ordinary run of princes, like Lorenzo de' Medici to whom the *Prince* is dedicated; for Machiavelli's additional description of this intellect as "one [who] has the judgment to recognize the good or evil that someone does or says, although he does not have the inventiveness by himself" (P.XXII.92) corresponds to his general advice that princes like Lorenzo should "always enter upon the paths beaten by great men, and imitate those who have been most excellent" (P.VI.22). Lacking ingenuity, such men could, perhaps, imitate the work of founders when similar circumstances prevail–as Machiavelli exhorts Lorenzo to do with regard to an Italy that has suffered the kind of degradation which provided Moses, Cyrus, and Theseus with the opportunity,[37] but since these second-rate minds tend to be "deceived by a false good and a false glory," they usually become tyrants who pursue their personal advantage only (D.I.10.1). Nonetheless, as "there is more foresight and more astuteness in the great" (P.IX.40)–who ought to be classed with princes since they usually aspire to become princes–these men are quite capable of manipulate the multitude by various kinds of fraud, such as pretending to be virtuous, manipulating elections, and promoting religious beliefs that sanction their rule.[38] The third and "useless" kind of brain, which "understands neither by itself nor through others," thus comes to light as a characteristic attribute of the common people, especially since we also read that "a multitude without a head is useless" (D.I.44.T).[39] But it should also be noted that useless brains may well belong to princes, who are thus prone to lose their states and meld back into the crowd (for even being a hereditary prince takes "ordinary industry" (P.II.6), that is, diligence combined with skill); likewise, individuals of extraordinary ability may well be born to humble parents, for Fortune sees to it that many of "those who have worked in this world the greatest things . . . have been low and obscure in their beginning and birth" (CC.615). On the whole, the three kinds of brains can thus be associated with founders, princes or great, and multitude or people, but ultimately only in the sense that particular brains tend to ascend or descend to the respective class.

At any rate, the imagination of the many is generally limited to the immediate consequences of actions, so that, "when gain is seen in the things that are put before the people, even though there is loss concealed underneath, and when it appears spirited, even when there is the ruin of the republic concealed underneath, it will always be easy to persuade the multitude of it" (D.I.53.2).[40] But the people are also said to recognize the truth when it is brought up in an assembly:

> If [their] opinions are false, there is for them the remedy of assemblies, where some good man gets up who in orating demonstrates to them how they deceived themselves; and though peoples, as Cicero says, are ignorant, they are capable of truth and easily yield when the truth is told them by a man worthy of faith. (D.I.4.1)[41]

However, the many yield to the truth not so much because they grasp it, but more because they revere the speaker or feel moved by his rhetoric; for excited multitudes are checked by their "reverence for some grave man of authority" (D.I.54), and generals should do "all those things by which human passions are extinguished or kindled" when addressing their troops (AG.IV.354). After all, the people's understanding is fundamentally limited to concrete matters, which "proceeds from men's being very much deceived in general things, not so much in particulars"; for instance, "it appeared generally to the Roman plebs that it deserved the consulate," which spelled danger for the Roman republic, but "as it had to pass judgment on its men particularly, it recognized their weakness" and continued to elect nobles to the consulate (D.I.47.1).[42] In addition to assessing the quality of leaders, the people can also recognize religious fraud when it favors particular persons; for when the ancient oracles "began to speak in the mode of the powerful, and as that falsity was exposed among peoples, men became incredulous and apt to disturb every good order" (D.I.12.1).[43] On the whole, the many can check the power of rulers, but they cannot govern because they fail to grasp remote consequences and the general rules of political theory.[44]

Finally, Machiavelli's emphasis on the various failures of the faculty of imagination has led some commentators to argue that he assumed the world to consist of nothing but appearances.[45] But this is mistaken; for, although Machiavelli surely considered well-manipulated illusions an important means to success, he nonetheless maintained the distinction between how thing appear and what they are, for instance, when he claims that "everyone sees how you appear, few touch what you are" (P.XVIII.71), and that "the generality of men . . . are moved more by things that appear than by things that are" (D.I.25.1). Thus, at least the better minds can "take the world as it really is" (A.983), as founders grasp the true good and ordinary princes are sufficiently knowing of natural things to deceive the many. Actually, even the many can form relatively accurate images of the qualities of particular leaders, and, indeed, see through the use of religious fraud for private gain. In short, Machiavelli takes reality to be independent of its representation by human beings, and assumes that these representations are true in a number of instances.

Desires

Regarding our emotive faculties, Machiavelli mentions both feelings and desires. Feelings like anger, despair, envy, fear, hatred, hope, indignation, love, and pride can attach themselves to various objects, making them of limited use in the construction of a political theory. For instance, in the first and second books of the *Discourses* alone, we read that the good Roman emperors were defended by the love of the Senate, that the Romans loved their fatherland, that republics have a love for acquiring empire and keeping themselves free, that soldiers fight well if they love their ruler, that ancient peoples loved freedom, that cities augment their inhabitants by way of love if they allow free immigration, and that the Senate used a consul's love of glory to hold him in check.[46] Desires, in contrast, aim at specific gratifications and thus provide human action with determinate ends; this, in turn, supplies a theorist like Machiavelli with a major ground for postulating the constancy of human nature: "men . . . have and always had the same passions" (D.III.43.1).[47]

The most basic desire of human beings concerns self-preservation, as "no one is found who wishes to go to a certain death" (D.III.6.2). Nonetheless, highly spirited individuals are able to give up their lives in order to satisfy their desire for glory, like Decius Mus the Younger, who "sacrificed himself to the Roman legions in imitation of his father, so as to acquire with death the glory he had been unable to attain with victory" (D.III.45).[48] In so doing, they seek to exchange a bodily but temporarily limited existence for everlasting life in the minds of posterity, bearing witness to the "desire [men] have to perpetuate the name of their ancestor as well as their own" (FH.Pr). Whereas princely types strive for glory, the many are usually content with mere honor, which prudent rulers should use to their advantage by abstaining from gratuitously offending to their subjects: "Whenever one does not take away either property or honor from the generality of men, they live content" (P.XIX.72); in particular, "of honors taken away from men, that concerning women is most important; after this, contempt of one's person" (D.III.6.2).[49]

These desires for glory and honor endow human beings with a kind of sociality since they are a form of recognition that exists in the opinions of others. Indeed, since people are likely to admire those who benefit them, glory and honor can be used to make self-seeking individuals act for the common good. In Machiavelli's words, to provide citizens with "public ways" of gaining reputation advances the common utility, "because to pass their tests it is necessary for them to attempt to exalt the republic," for instance, by "winning a battle, acquiring a town, carrying out a mission with care and prudence, advising the republic wisely and prosperously" (FH.VII.1).[50] However, this does not mean that these citizens work for the common good as an end in itself, but that they consider it a means to the self-regarding pleasure of being admired by others. Moreover, fame can also be gained by doing "despicable things" (FH.Pr); for instance, had Giovampagolo Baglioni murdered the pope, he would not only have shown his spirit, but "done a thing whose greatness would have surpassed all infamy, every peril, that could have proceeded from it" and "left an eternal memory of himself" (D.I.27.2). On balance, then, the desire for glory and honor endows human beings with an unsocial sociality: They need others to admire them and to acknowledge their status, but treat them as means to their own satisfaction.

In addition to preservation, glory, and honor, human beings seek power or domination, freedom, and wealth. "Greed for dominating" is especially characteristic of noblemen like Jacopo Coppola, who conspired against the king because "having come to so much greatness . . . it did not appear to him that he lacked anything except a kingdom" (D.III.6.3); in the many, by contrast, one usually sees "only desire not to be dominated; and, in consequence, a greater will to live free" (D.I.5.2).[51] However, neither the many nor the princes desire freedom as an end in itself, but merely as a condition for enjoying other goods: "a small part of [men] desires to be free so as to command, but all the others, who are infinite desire liberty so as to live secure" (D.I.16.5). Thus, the love of freedom among the ancients was really a love of dominion and riches, based on the experience that republics prosper in greater measure than tyrannies.[52] And the desire for wealth is coequal with those for preservation and glory, for love of property is said to be "not less than that of life" (AG.IV.353), and Rome's distributional struggle over the Agrarian law shows "honors and belongings . . . as the thing esteemed most by men" (D.I.37.1).[53]

Another desire that figures prominently in Machiavelli's thought is carnal love: His comedies *Mandragola* and *Clizia* consist of ruthless schemes to gain sexual access to women; in *L'Asino,* Machiavelli spices his account of the human condition with a sexual encounter with Circe; and when composing a charter for a "pleasure company," he ordains that "never shall women of the said company wear hoop skirts or anything underneath that may be an impediment."[54] Given the coarseness of these fantasies, it has been charged with good reason that the predatory aspects of Machiavelli's political thought are subliminally related to his problematic understanding of sexuality and manhood.[55] On the conscious level, however, Machiavelli advises rulers to keep sexuality out of politics; for "women have been causes of much ruin and have done great damage to those who govern a city, and have caused many divisions in them" (D.III.26.2).[56]

Humors

As we saw in chapter 2, "humors" are temperamental dispositions that individuals receive from the heavens when they are born. More precisely, "humor" (lit. moisture) was the name that premodern medicine gave to the four bodily fluids of blood, choler, phlegm, and black bile, whose quality and proper mixture determine both the health of an organism and its temperament–making a person more or less sanguine, choleric, phlegmatic, and melancholic. Humors were also believed to affect the inner senses and thus to account for mental differences among men; for instance, a preponderance of black bile results in superior imagination because its coldness reduces the speed at which the animal spirit brings on new sense impressions and because its dryness makes already formed images last longer. And since the humors receive their inherent qualities of hot, cold, dry, and moist from the four elements of earth, water, air, and fire, they also transmit climatic and astral influences to organisms; accordingly, the dry cold of northern lands makes their inhabitants strong, fierce, and long-legged, whereas those born under the dry and hot planet Mars tend to be active, fierce, and short-tempered.

That Machiavelli believed in the efficacy of these humors follows not only from his belief in astrology, but can be seen particularly from his claim to have reconstructed the "speeches and private reasonings" of characters in his *Florentine Histories* according to the "proper humor of the person speaking" (FH.Ded). More generally, humors join the desires as the principal reason for the constancy of human nature: "in all peoples there are the same desires and the same humors, and there always have been. So it is an easy thing for whoever examines past things diligently to foresee future things" (D.I.39.1). In particular, the humoral mix that individuals receive at birth determines their fixed and characteristic "mode of proceeding." Depending on whether their humor is predominantly sanguinic, choleric, phlegmatic, or melancholic, men "proceed variously: one with caution, the other with impetuosity; one by violence, the other with art; one with patience, the other with its contrary" (P.XXV.99). But since a cautious individual is likely to proceed with art and patience and since an impetuous person will tend to be violent and impatient, Machiavelli effectively reduces the humoral modes to a mere two: "some men proceed in their works with impetuosity, some with hesitation and caution" (D.III.9.1).[57]

Following medieval thought, Machiavelli also applied the concept of humors to political bodies.[58] He characterized individuals with brains of the second kind as the humor of "the great" and those with third-rate organs as the humor of "the people," with the result that "in every city these two diverse humors are found, which arises from this: that the people desire neither to be commanded nor oppressed by the great, and the great desire to command and oppress the people" (P.IX.39). And he took the humoral theory of health to justify the mixed regime: Just as the well-being of a body depends on the proper balance of its fluids, the stability of a city rests on the proportionate satisfaction of its constituent groups; for one cannot "believe that republic to be enduring where those humors are not satisfied, which if not satisfied, ruin republics" (DF.24).[59] Moreover, Machiavelli accounted for natural disasters as purges of the ill propensities that accumulate in the human race (D.II.5.2), described the factional hatreds that arise in cities as "malignant humors" (FH.IV.26),[60] and called for law-governed outlets by which these humors can be vented safely.[61]

Ambition

Thus far, our inquiry into the necessary properties of human beings has produced a rather static picture: deeply embedded desires for preservation, glory, power, riches, and lust, that differ to some extent for nobles and commoners; personal humors received at birth that issue in fixed modes of proceeding; faculties of ingenuity and imagination that serve the passions and differentiate humanity into founders, princes, and multitude. Yet, as we shall see presently, this nature is really dynamic in that the mind stimulates the desires to grow without limit, thereby producing the ceaseless ambition so characteristic of Machiavelli's individuals. While this ambition has been given its due in the literature,[62] the psychological process that engenders it has been overlooked, even though it represents the very core of Machiavelli's anthropology, and one of the most important insights he offers.

The mind expands the desires in two ways. First, the faculty of imagination recombines memories of past gratification to create novel images of delight,[63] while ingenuity finds means for attaining them. In Machiavelli's articles for a pleasure company, "pleasant things" are thus made to "grow more pleasant" by a clever mind:

> Whereas at times some schemes have been thought but have had no result, because of lack of diligence by those who have thought them, it has seemed good to those who have some brain and, in the affairs of men and women, some experience, to organize–that is, so to regulate–such a company that each one would be able to imagine, and after imagining to do, those things that to men and women . . . in any way can give delight.[64]

Likewise, Callimaco, the *virtuoso* lover of Machiavelli's *Mandragola*, develops such a sexual craving for Lucrezia after merely having heard of her beauty and manners, that he travels from France to Italy and undertakes a complicated fraud to possess her.[65] And the initially defensive victories of the Swiss engrossed their desires for glory and power to the point where they thought that the "*virtù* of their militia . . . was similar to that of the Romans, and what the reason was that they could not do one day like the Romans," that is, acquire a great empire (L.211.1149).

Second, imagination allows human beings to foresee the very real possibility that future needs might not be met; prompted by the resulting anxiety, ingenuity then suggests that in order to mitigate such a disaster they should acquire as many means of satisfaction as soon as possible. In Machiavelli's words: "the fear of losing generates in [those who possess] the same wishes that are in those who desire to acquire; for it does not appear to men that they possess securely what a man has unless he acquires something else new" (D.I.5.4). More generally, imagination makes us aware of our precarious position in a contingent universe; in allegorical terms, "we see Anxiety prostrate on the floor" of Fortune's palace (F.977).[66]

Using an idea current in the Renaissance, Machiavelli captured the general result of this mental expansion of the desires in the concept of "ambition" (*ambizione*).[67] Accordingly, ambition can be directed toward any end desired by men: glory, as it was when "ambition of the consuls" was to finish the war early "so as to have a triumph" (D.II.6.2); domination, as when certain "persuasions inflamed the ambitious spirit of the duke to a greater desire to rule" (FH.II.34); and wealth, insofar as "ambition results in two kinds of action: one party robs and the other weeps for its wealth ravaged and scattered" (A.986).[68] Important, this ambition is inherently without limit because imagination can always expand the desires further, once a certain level of satisfaction has been attained; thus, "men ascend from one ambition to another" (D.I.46.T), for they "are never satisfied and, having gotten one thing, do not content themselves with that but desire something else" (FH.IV.14).[69]

Arising from the mind and the desires, this ceaseless ambition clearly belongs to the characteristics that human beings have by nature. In other words, "the nature of men is ambitious and suspicious and does not know how to set a limit to any fortune it may have" (D.I.29.1); ambition is a "natural instinct" that "no man has power to drive . . . out of himself" (A.985-86). Accordingly, the fact that new ambitions are acquired characteristics does not make them into contingent attributes like skills or habits, because it is natural for human beings to expand their desires. Hence, it is most precisely here that Machiavelli inverts Aristotle's seminal idea of potentiality and act as applied to man: Rather than actualizing a natural potential for virtue by taming the desires with the help of freely choosing reason,[70] Machiavelli's individuals develop a natural capacity for "ambitious license" (D.I.47.3) through the activity of a mind that stimulates the desires in serving them. In short, man's potential is for vice rather than virtue.

It is this kind of potential that differentiates men from beasts, in that the human powers of imagination and ingenuity expand the limited needs of animals into insatiable cravings. During Machiavelli's imaginary visit with Circe, the ancient witch who transformed people into animals, a muddy porker puts this difference as follows:

> And with regard to temperance, you will plainly see that in this game we have surpassed your side. On Venus we spend but short and little time, but you without measure follow her in every time and place. Our species does not care for other food than the product of heaven without art; you wish that which Nature cannot make. You are not content with one food only, as we are, but, better to fulfil your greedy desires, you journey for such things to the kingdoms of the East. (AS.VIII.974-75)[71]

Thus, the distinctly human faculties of "hands and speech" have "cancelled the good of nature" by causing the incessant growth of ambition (AS.VIII.975). And, given the resultant discontent and anxiety characteristic of humans, the porker concludes that he is happier now than when he was a man: "in this mud I live more happily; here without worry I bathe and roll myself" (AS.VIII.976).

Further, the fact that human brains come in three kinds implies that men differ in their ambition; for the stronger the faculties of imagination and ingenuity, the more they tend to expand the desires. Thus, founders strive for perpetual glory because their first-rate brains enable them to envisage such glory and to invent the orders that will bring it about; the second-rate minds of ordinary princes direct their ambition to the delights of ruling tyrannically, but fail to comprehend the good of founders; and the third-rate imagination and ingenuity of the multitude limit their ambition to being secure in order to enjoy their women and possessions.

But this three-tiered account of human ambition is not entirely accurate; for, upon closer reading, we find that the multitude tends to embrace the ambitions of the great after it has gained security:

> It was not enough for the Roman plebs to secure itself against the nobles by the creation of the tribunes, to which desire it was constrained by necessity; for having obtained that, it began at once to engage in combat through ambition, and to wish to share honors and belongings with the nobility as the thing most esteemed by men. (D.I.37.1)

In Florence, "the pride and ambition of the great was . . . taken from them by our men of the people, who now, by the wont of ambitious men, seek to obtain the first rank in the republic" (FH.III.5).[72] Moreover, if the great are eliminated by the people, its leading men– the "greater plebs" or "popular nobles"–soon begin to lord it over the others and eventually form another set of great.[73] Likewise, it is possible for the great to acquire the ambition of founders, as shown by Stefano Porcari, a man "noble by blood and learning, but much more so by the excellence of his spirit," who sought to "take his fatherland from the hands of prelates and restore it to its ancient way of life, hoping by this, should he succeed, to be called the new founder and second father of that city" (FH.VI.29).

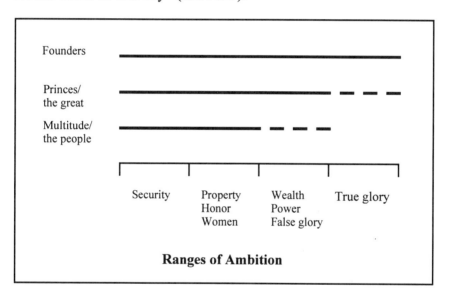

Ranges of Ambition

Hence, differences in ambition depend not only on innate distinctions in mental power, but also on the current level of satisfaction: While they are oppressed, the many imagine to gain security, property, and honor; once they have attained these goods, they begin to imagine the additional delights enjoyed by the great, such as wealth, power, and ordinary glory; the great, in turn, who take these goods for granted, begin to dream of the perpetual glory bestowed on founders. However, there is a limit in this growth of ambition insofar as the many's inability to grasp general things prevents them from understanding the ambition of the founder, who has to benefit the generality of men for the sake of perpetual glory. Overall, the innate quality of their minds situates individuals in one of three ranges of ambition, while circumstances determine the extent to which their ambition expands within their range.

The Vulgar Sameness of Men

Finally, the fact that these quantitatively different ranges of ambition overlap in large measure suggests that human beings have qualitatively the same ends: Whether founder, prince, or commoner, all men want to survive, be recognized by others, dominate them, possess material goods, and enjoy women. In other words, men are natural worshippers of Fortune and Venus, the Roman goddesses who offered long life, prosperity, power, glory, and carnal delight.

Hence, the classical writers went wrong when they portrayed the distinction between the few and the many as an ethical matter, concerning the ends that men pursue; for

> all men particularly, and especially princes, can be accused of that defect of which the [ancient] writers accuse the multitude. . . . The variation in their proceeding arises not from a diverse nature–because it is in one mode in all, and if there is advantage of good, it is in the people–but from having more or less respect for the laws within which both live. (D.I.58.2-3)[74]

Or as a Florentine plebeian put it, the difference between nobility and baseness is merely a matter of appearance:

> Do not let their antiquity of blood, with which they will reproach us, dismay you; for all men, having had the same beginning, are equally ancient and have been made by nature in one mode. Strip all of us naked, you will see that we are alike; dress us in their clothes and them in ours, and without doubt we shall appear noble and they ignoble, for only poverty and riches make us unequal. (FH.III.13)

In other words, the few are just as base as the many in desiring the goods of Fortune and Venus–which gives rise to the fact that "in the world there is no one but the vulgar" (P.XVII.71). At root, this reduction of man to the vulgar level occurs because Machiavelli's denial of the intellective soul deprives people of the capacity to ascend to the rational contemplation of the Good or the beatific vision of God. In short, all men seek material and bodily goods because the goods of the soul are an illusion that belongs with the "imagined republics and principalities that have never been seen or known to exist in truth" (P.XV.61). In reality, the few differ from the many only in the extent to which they have expanded the selfsame desires and the amount of cleverness by which they pursue the resulting ambitions.

Hence, it is no coincidence that Machiavelli's image of man so closely resembles Aristotle's description of the many (*hoi polloi*), who "always ask for more, and go on doing so without limit. For the nature of desire is without limit, and it is with a view to satisfying this that the many live;" in particular, "wealth, goods, power, reputation, and all such things [men] seek to excess without limit."[75] In other words, Machiavelli rejected the classical definition of nature as the fully developed form reached only by a few in favor of its modern definition as the primitive beginning shared by all. Thus, Leo Strauss had a point when he accused Machiavelli of "accepting the ends of the *demos* as beyond appeal," and thereby inaugurating the soulless concerns of modernity.[76]

Second Nature

Habits that form a second nature constitute the most important accidental characteristic in Machiavelli's anthropology. Such habits can either reinforce our naturally rapacious properties, or they can mitigate them by making subjects loyal to their princes and citizens observant of the laws. But good habits that oppose rapacious nature are theoretically more significant than bad ones, since they make possible government in accordance with laws rather than princely will; thus, "laws have need of good customs so as to be observed" (D.I.18.1). To some extent, Machiavelli followed tradition in emphasizing the importance of good habits for a well-ordered political life; for, as Aristotle pointed out, "law has no strength with respect to obedience apart from habit."[77] However, there is an all-important difference: Whereas classical thinkers held that good habits actualize first nature, which they considered a potential for virtue, Machiavelli assumed that good habits *oppose* first nature because it consists of a capacity for ambition and vice.[78]

Human beings form habits when the instrumental reasoning that guides their behavior becomes unconscious on account of frequently repeated performance. To form "bad customs" (D.I.12.2),[79] they only need to imagine the gratification that will arise from a certain behavior in order to repeat it. But to form good habits that oppose their natural inclinations and deprive them of immediate satisfaction, they must be constrained by fear of punishment. In Machiavelli's words, "to inure to good a city" presupposes an "extreme force" (D.I.17.3) and "good customs have need of laws to maintain themselves" (D.I.18.1).

More precisely, individuals initially carry out behaviors that will turn into good habits because their ingenuity suggests that only their performance will allow them to escape punishment at the hands of an autocrat. As this calculation is done over and over, it becomes more and more unconscious; when it has been completely internalized, a habit has formed that engenders performance even after autocratic constraint has been lifted. In other words, individuals for whom it has become second nature to recognize hereditary princes as lords and defend republican institutions no longer consciously calculate the costs and benefits that are currently associated with such actions, but simply repeat what they have done before.[80]

Human beings form their first habits under the constraint of their parents. Asking "whence it arises that one family in one city keeps the same customs for a time," Machiavelli thus writes that when "a boy of tender years begins to hear good or bad said of a thing . . . it must of necessity make an impression on him, which afterwards regulates the mode of proceeding in all the times of his life" (D.III.46.1). He describes as "customs" the lifestyles of "young men," who, "more unrestrained than usual, were spending beyond bounds on dress, banquets, and other similar abandonments" (FH.VII.29). As these statements show, Machiavelli did not make the usual distinction between "customs" as the normative patterns of a society and "habits" as the rote behaviors of individuals,[81] perhaps because he thought that the former must reduce to the latter among people who naturally tend to ambitious license. A more directly political habit has formed when "the minds of men . . . have been accustomed to look only to one man,"[82] that is, the prince, so that obedience to his line becomes their second nature; for instance, it was "natural for Florentine citizens to honor [the Medicean] house, enjoy those favors that proceed from it, and love those things that are loved by it," since "they have followed this habit for sixty years" (DF.25). Such habituation takes more than one generation because the injuries that brought the princely house to power need first to be forgotten, so that the children learn to do from habit what their parents did from fear. Similarly, becoming "accustomed to living by [one's] own laws and in liberty" (P.V.20) takes at least two founders in succession:

> There cannot be one man of such long life as to have enough time to inure to good a city that has been inured to bad for long time. If one individual of very long life or two virtuous ones continued in

succession do not arrange it, . . . it is ruined, unless indeed he makes it reborn with many dangers and much blood. (D.I.17.3)

Thus, the rabble that initially formed the Roman people became a body of law-abiding citizens because it chanced upon three able founders in succession: Romulus, Numa, and Tullus Hostilius.[83] Proper habituation also undergirds military discipline, as good captains "train [their armies] for several months in mock battles and to accustom them to obedience and order" (D.III.38.2).[84] Even religious belief is a kind of habit, since it rests primarily on the performance of "ceremonies, sacrifices and rites" (D.I.12.1).[85] How effective such rituals can be in shaping human beings can be seen from the "custom of the ancient faith" (FH.I.6), that is, pagan religion: "Neither pomp nor magnificence of ceremony was lacking there, but the action of the sacrifice, full of blood and ferocity, was added, with a multitude of animals being killed there. This sight, being terrible, rendered men similar to itself" (D.II.2.2).

At the same time, since good habits remain opposed by first nature, they will eventually succumb to a renewed surge of ambition. Machiavelli's term for this dissolution is "corruption": "because in the process of time that goodness is corrupted, unless something intervenes to lead it back to the mark, it of necessity kills that body" (D.III.1.2).[86] More precisely, good habits are corrupted when opportunities for gratification tempt the desires with such intensity that the mind recalculates the means of satisfying them, and in so doing discovers that rapacious modes are again more rational than cooperative ones, now that autocratic punishment need no longer be feared. In particular, citizens cease to obey the laws unthinkingly when they realize–often by the example of one who got away with crime–that taking a free ride on the law-abidingness of others will gratify their ambition more than emulating it. In Rome, this happened to the ten men (*decem vires*) who had been given absolute authority to reform the laws, but then developed tyrannical aspirations:

> One also notes in the matter of the Decemvirate how easily men are corrupted and make themselves assume a contrary nature, however good and well brought up, considering how much the youths that Appius had chosen around him began to be friendly to the tyranny for the little utility that came to them from it, and how Quintus Fabius, one in the number of the second Ten–though a very good man–blinded by a little ambition and persuaded by the malignity of Appius, changed his good customs to the worst, and became like him. (D.I.42.1)

While corrupting individuals in this fashion is easy, subverting the good customs of an entire civic body is laborious: "a man can indeed begin to corrupt a people of a city with his modes and his wicked means, but for him it is impossible that the life of one individual be enough to corrupt it so that he himself can draw the fruit from it;" instead, "little by little and from generation to generation [the matter] may be led to disorder" (D.III.8.2).

In conclusion, it is this psychological account of how good habits attenuate first nature that resolves the tension between the rapacious and cooperative sides of Machiavelli's image of man–which has vexed his commentators for so long. For it explains from a unified set of assumptions how a number of naturally licentious individuals can be made into loyal subjects and law-abiding citizens by the constraint of an individual of superior *virtù*, whose ambition encompasses perpetual glory. And it explains on the basis of the same assumptions how people lose their good habits by recalculating their behavior in response to tempting opportunities to gratify their first nature. What seemed a contradiction has thus been shown to be a duality with a mechanism that explains in consistent terms how its two aspects are transformed into each other.

Individualism

That Machiavelli assumed human beings to be individuals may seem obvious, for he showed in the *Prince* how to "become princes from private individual" (P.VII.25), and who could be more self-determined than founders like Moses, Cyrus, Theseus, and Romulus, who single-handedly introduced wholly new orders? Moreover, he conspicuously replaces Polybius's claim that early men formed herds like animals with the statement that they "lived dispersed for a time like beasts" (D.I.2.3),[87] describes factional violence as "offense by private individuals to private individuals" (D.I.7.2), and, in the third book of the *Discourses,* seeks "to demonstrate to anyone how much the actions of particular men made Rome great" (D.III.1.6). But Machiavelli also used terms which assume human beings to exist by nature in groups or communities. Thus, when he justifies the mixed regime on the grounds that it satisfies the "humors" of both the great and the people (DF.24), or claims that "principality is caused either by the people or by the great" (P.IX.39), he draws on the medieval belief that such groups are the constituent elements of the body politic.[88] Indeed, when he refers to the humors in terms of *universale,*

università, and *universalità*–for instance, when he tells the prince that
the "*università* of which you judge you have need to maintain yourself
. . . are the people or the soldiers or the great" (P.XIX.77)–he seems
to draw on the medieval concept of *universitas,* that is, a corporation
with the legal status of a person.[89] Similarly, when Machiavelli uses
the Aristotelian concepts of form and matter in order to express the
idea that a founder gives order to a shapeless multitude, he gives us a
reason to assume that he also shared Aristotle's belief that the city
comes before the individuals since the whole is prior to its parts.[90]

This tension between holism and individualism in Machiavelli's
thought can be resolved in favor of the latter by virtue of his acute
awareness of various problems of collective action, that is, situations
in which human beings fail to cooperate in the provision of a good
that would benefit them all; for such problems presuppose self-seeking
individuals endowed with narrow instrumental reason.[91] Machiavelli
generally captures this idea by claiming that "it rarely happens that
individual passions are not harmful to universal advantage" (FH.V.31),
and arguing that "where the prize has to be unequal, men are loathe to
spend equally."[92] He employs it particularly when showing how the
universale of the people dissolves into self-regarding individuals
because they distrust each other and fear the prince:

> The multitude is often bold in speaking against the decisions of their
> prince; then, when they look the penalty in the face, not trusting one
> another, they run to obey. . . . There is nothing, on one side, more
> formidable than an unshackled multitude without a head, and on the
> other side, there is nothing weaker; for even though it has arms in
> hand, it is easy to put it down provided that you have a redoubt that
> enables you to escape the first thrust. For when the spirits of men are
> cooled a little and each sees he has to return to his home, they begin to
> doubt themselves and to think of their safety either by taking flight or
> by coming to accord. (D.I.57.1)

In other words, a leaderless multitude suffers inherently from what is
nowadays called the "prisoner's dilemma," namely, that individuals
fail to cooperate because they fear the consequences of being cheated
by the others more than they desire the advantages of cooperation.
More precisely, the people are capable of forming a destructive mob
as long as the heat of their spirits prevents their minds from realizing
that the individual cost of continued cooperation, such as being killed,
outweighs the individual benefit, such as gaining a share in republican
liberty or the spoils of looting; but once their instrumental reason
functions again, they desist from fear of negative consequences and

lack of trust in each other, and, consequently, fly apart. Indeed, Machiavelli quotes in this very context a Latin passage from Livy, which describes this dissolution of the mob in terms of a transition from what the people are *universis* to what they are *singuli:*

> Titus Livius says these words: 'From being ferocious when together (*universis*) they became obedient when isolated (*singuli*) by each one's fear.' And truly, the nature of the multitude in this part cannot be shown better than demonstrated in this text. (D.I.57.1)

While the prisoner's dilemma thus makes it easier for rulers to control a crowd, the "coordination problem" makes it harder to establish political order in the first place. Thus, the founder of a city "should contrive to have authority alone" because "many are not capable of ordering a thing because they do not know its good, because of the diverse opinions among them" (D.I.9.2). Finally, in an instance of the "free-rider problem," Machiavelli claims that states fail to form alliances because each party wants to let the others do the fighting, hoping to gain the benefit of security without bearing the burden of war: "as soon as a prince and a people come into so much reputation that every neighboring prince and people is afraid for itself to assault it, and fears it, it always happens that none of them will ever assault it if not necessitated to do so"; for, as in the case with the states that faced the Romans, "each of them believed that the other would overcome it."[93]

In sum, Machiavelli used the holistic language of humors and universality merely as a kind of convenient shorthand to describe individuals whose self-interests happen to coincide.[94] In so doing, he participated in the Renaissance and humanist movement whereby "man," in Jacob Burckhardt's words, "became a spiritual individual, and recognized himself as such."[95] However, since Machiavelli did not follow the humanists into a deeper reflection on what it means to have an individual personality–as they had done since Petrarca's discovery of the self on Mont Ventoux[96]–his individualism remained limited to the methodological proposition that the individual is the unit of identity and action. Nonetheless, he thereby took the equally momentous step of conceiving political order as a construct that must be imposed on individuals against their nature, which departs from the classical belief that men live naturally in communities and prepares the modern idea that they naturally exist without government.[97]

Coping with Necessity and Contingency

How will individuals as described above deal with a world that is structured by necessity and contingency? In other words, how does action succeed in light of Machiavelli's ontological and psychological premises?

Human beings encounter necessity above all in the constant nature of their fellows, for, as we know, "the work of men, who have and always had the same passions . . . must of necessity result in the same effect" (D.III.43.1). Accordingly, agents should take advantage of the fact that human beings can be relied upon to seek to preserve themselves and to gain glory, power, wealth, and sexual pleasure. For instance, a general should block the escape routes of his own troops and leave open those of the enemy, in order to "impose every necessity to engage in combat on his soldiers and take it away from those of enemies" (D.III.12.T); for "necessities may be many, [but] strongest is that which forces you either to win or to die" (AG.IV.354). On the reward side, a prince attract followers by satisfying their thirst for honors and riches, as Cesare Borgia did when, in order to weaken his rivals, he "gained to himself all their adherents . . . by giving them large allowances" and honoring them "with commands and with government posts" (P.VII.28). In other words, the clever agent succeeds because he knows what human beings will naturally do in certain situations and then proceeds to manipulate them to his advantage.

Human beings enounter contingency above all in changes of the circumstances that surround their actions, which Machiavelli conceptualizes both as "accidents," unexpected events caused by Fortune, and alterations in the "quality of the times," whereby the heavens (or Fortune in the popular strand of Renaissance astrology) dispose an entire region to peace, war, order, chaos, etc. To succeed in the face of accidents, individuals need to know above all when to seize an opportunity and when to desist from action. Thus, Machiavelli writes about something because he has "opportunity for it anew through a new accident" (D.II.15.2), and bestows praise on Filippo Visconti for "being a very able man and knowing how to take up new policies among new accidents" (D.II.18.4); in contrast, hereditary prince that keep to the ancestral order can "temporize in the face of accidents" (P.II.6, mt).[98] Insofar as accidents are occultly caused, divination can tell the agent when to act; for "before great accidents occur in a city or province, signs come that forecast them, or men that predict them" (D.I.56.T).

Concerning the changing quality of the times, he is "prosperous who adapts his mode of proceeding to the qualities of the times; and similarly, he is unprosperous whose procedure is in disaccord with the times" (P.XXV.99).[99] Again, astrology helps with this adaptation as "he who were so wise that he knew the times and the order of things and accommodated himself to them, would always have good fortune" (L.116.1083).[100] However, the fixity of one's characteristic mode of proceeding, which in turn rests on innate humors and ingrained habits, makes it impossible for individuals to be always in accord with the times: A man "cannot deviate from what nature inclines him to or also because, when one has always flourished by walking on one path, he cannot be persuaded to depart from it"; for instance, "the cautious man, when it is time to come to impetuosity, does not know how to do it, hence comes to ruin" (P.XXV.100).[101] Hence, individual agents must "bide the time"[102] until its quality matches their given mode of proceeding, for instance, by taking "a middle ground until time and the variations of things force him to declare himself, or that he is so firm in his seat that he can join and engage in enterprises according to his spirit."[103] Republics, on the other hand, can overcome this limitation by changing their leaders in such a way that their individual modes of proceeding remain in accord with the times; thus, a republic with its "diverse citizens and diverse humors" has "greater life and has good fortune longer than a principality" because it "can accommodate itself better than a prince can to the diversity of times" (D.III.9.1-2). For instance, the Romans won the Second Punic War because they were first led by Fabius whose cautious mode "was best in times proper for sustaining war," and later by Scipio whose daring mode was superior "in times apt for winning," whereas the Carthaginians relied on Hannibal throughout (D.III.9.1).

Paradoxically, this need to deal with accidents and to match the quality of the times gives rise to secondary kind of necessity, which arises from the very contingency of human affairs. For a prince who is "disposed to change as the winds of fortune and variations of things command him" is also "forced by necessity" to enter into evil (P.XVIII.70); and, instead of blaming Athens for its practice of ostracism, one should "accuse only necessity because of the diversity of accidents" that arose there (D.I.28).[104]

The ability to cope with contingency as necessary also defines Machiavelli's concept of *virtù*;[105] for the central fact about his supreme exemplars of *virtù*–founders like Moses, Cyrus, Romulus, Theseus–is that "opportunities . . . made these men successful, and their excellent *virtù* enabled the opportunity to be recognized"

(P.VI.23). Adopting a humanist commonplace, Machiavelli thus describes the human condition as a struggle between the *virtù* of man and the contingency of Fortune, representing the latter as a violent river: Fortune "shows her power where *virtù* has not been put in order to resist her and therefore turns her impetus where she knows that dams and dikes have not been made to contain her" (P.XXV.98-99); and "true *virtù* does not fear every least accident" (D.III.33.1).[106]

Although *virtù* is also needed by a lover,[107] its greatest calling is in politics; for the "most *virtuoso* works the histories show us" have been performed by "kings, captains, citizens, legislators, and others who have labored for their fatherland," in terms of "ordering republics, maintaining states, governing kingdoms, ordering the military and administering war, judging subjects, increasing empire" (D.I.Pr.2). Since *virtù* implies the ability to recognize opportunities, it is regularly associated with prudence, for instance, when a founder needs to "be so prudent and *virtuoso* that he does not leave the authority he took as an inheritance to another" (D.I.9.2). Since Fortune is herself violent, *virtuoso* men must use force to tame her: "Fortune is a woman; and it is necessary, if one wants to hold her down, to beat her and strike her down" (P.XXV.101). As a result of these two requirements, "forces mixed with prudence . . . are the nerves of all dominions."[108] Of course, there is also need for fraud, as those princes have "done great things who have taken little account of faith and have known how to get around men's brains with their astuteness" (P.XVIII.69). And *virtuoso* men need spirits strong enough to steady them in reversals of fortune, in the manner of true Romans who "'are not weakened in their spirits if they are vanquished, nor are they used to becoming insolent if they are victorious'" (D.III.31.3, mt).

In short, it is clear that Machiavelli's notion of *virtù* does not refer to virtue as in traditional Italian, but, above all, to the ability to succeed in political and military life. Part of this semantic shift had already been effected by other Renaissance writers, who had sought to return the word to its Latin root *virtus,* the glory-winning excellence of a man who performs his duties as patriarch, citizen, and soldier,[109] but only Machiavelli claimed that this could not be done without committing evil deeds (as we shall see in chapter 4).

Given the strongly mental aspect of *virtù,* Machiavelli's three types of man–founder, princes/great, multitude/people–are bound to possess it in different degrees. Superior imagination and ingenuity obviously endows founders with the greatest *virtù.* Ordinary princes come second, as they can only "imitate those who have been most excellent, so that if [their] own *virtù* does not reach that far, it is at least in the odor of it" (P.VI.22). The multitude is by nature without *virtù* since it cannot undertake constructive political action without a leader; at most, anger can heat their spirits to the point where they form a destructive mob, but once their spirits have cooled down they are rent apart by pusillanimity and selfishness. However, the many can acquire the secondary *virtù* of a good citizen by being habituated to republican institutions, so that they will be "brought to life by the *virtù* of a citizen who rushes spiritedly to execute them" (D.III.1.3). Likewise, the *virtù* of soldiers is largely acquired, since "in every country drill makes for good soldiers; because, where nature is lacking, it is made up by industry, which in this case counts more than nature" (AG.I.309).[110] In contrast, habituation to a princely line does not seem to give the subjects any kind of *virtù* in Machiavelli's writings, even though it makes them good at following orders. At any rate, since the acquired *virtù* of citizens and soldiers is caused by the natural *virtù* of the founders and princes that constrains them, the former *virtù* is derivative of the latter.[111]

Notes

1. See Lauri Huovinen, *Das Bild vom Menschen im politischen Denken Niccolò Machiavellis.* Annales Academiae Scientiarum Fennicae, ser. B, tom. 74.2 (Helsinki: Finnische Akademie der Wissenschaften, 1951), 102; Federico Chabod, *Machiavelli and the Renaissance,* trans. David Moore (New York: Harper & Row, 1958), 99; Giuseppe Prezzolini, *Machiavelli,* trans. Gioconda Savini (New York: Farrar, Straus & Giroux, 1967), 52.

2. Although this distinction has been noted by some commentators, they either failed to grasp it accurately or to develop it theoretically; see Leo Strauss, *Thoughts on Machiavelli* (Chicago: University of Chicago Press, 1958), 246; Prezzolini, *Machiavelli,* 51-54; Gian Piero Baricelli, "Rereading 'The Prince': Philosophical Themes in Machiavelli," *Italian Quarterly* 13, no. 52 (spring–summer 1970): 43-62, at 58-59; Herfried Münkler, *Machiavelli: Die Begründung des politischen Denkens der Neuzeit aus der Krise der Republik Florenz* (Frankfurt: Europäische Verlagsanstalt, 1982), 255-56, 269; J. G. A. Pocock, *The Machiavellian Moment: Florentine Political Thought and the Atlantic Republican Tradition* (Princeton: Princeton University Press, 1975), 184.

3. "Second Mission to Sienna," in W.III.457-81, at 475.

4. See Aristotle, *Aristotle's Metaphysics,* trans. Hippocrates G. Apostle (Grinell, Iowa: Peripatetic Press, 1966), D.30.25-30, E.2.9, K.8.26, 34.

5. Cf. FH.IV.1; P.VI.23; D.I.19.1, 4.

6. Francesco Guicciardini, *Maxims and Reflections of a Renaissance*

Statesman [1512-30], trans. Mario Domandi (New York: Harper Torchbooks, 1965), 89, 43, mt.

7. Francesco Alunno, *La Fabrica del Mondo* (Vinegia, 1548), 209, mt; Giacomo Pergamino, *Il Memoriale della Lingua Italiana* (Venice: Gio. Battista Ciotti, 1617), 7, 350, mt.

8. See Aristotle, *Metaphysics,* D.4, 8, 30; E.2, 3; K. 8; Thomas Aquinas, *Aquinas On Being and Essence,* trans. Joseph Bobik (Notre Dame, Ind.: University of Notre Dame Press, 1965), I.5-11, VII.99-113.

9. Cf. D.I.21; FH.II.1; AG.VI.372; AG.VII.377, 385; "Second Mission to Francesco Guicciardini," in W.IV.339-373, at 354.

10. *Discorso o dialogo intorno all nostra lingua* [Discourse or dialogue internal to our language], in TO.923-930, at 928, mt.

11. See P.VII.26; D.I.12.1, 19.3, 33.2, 37.1, 40.7, 56; D.II.Pr.3, 3, 5.2; D.III.27.3, 30.1; FH.II.1, III.13, III.16, V.1, V. 34, VII.33; AG.IV.662; AG.VII.389; M.IV.1; L.116.1083; L .239.1191; *Discorso o dialogo intorno all nostra lingua,* in TO.923-930, at 924.

12. See P.XIV.59; D.I.1.4; D.II.17.5, 32.1; D.III.6.19, 37.1, 39.2; AG.II.321.

13. Cf. P.III.14; P.X.44; D.I.Pr.1, 33.2; D.III.12.1, 21.3, 29; FH.IV.10, VII.23; L.211.1149; "Mission to the Court of Rome," in W.III.283-388, at 313, 320, 334.

14. Cf. P.IX.40; P.XVII.68; P.XVIII, 69-70; P.XXIII.95; D.I.24.2, 29.2, 58.1-3; D.III.8.2, 9.1, 22.1, 22.3, 29, 36.1; FH.II.25, II.34, III.1, IV.27, VI.18; AG.VI.372; F.976; A.985; *Parole da dirle sopra la provisione del danaio, facto un poco di proemio et di scusa* [Words to be spoken about the provision of money, having given a little preface and excuse], in TO.11-13, at 12; *De natura Gallorum* [On the nature of the Gauls], in TO.53-54, at T; *Nature di huomini fiorentini et in che luoghi si possino inserire le laude loro* [Natures of Florentine men and in which places their praise can be inserted], in TO.917-18, at T; "Advice to Rafaello Girolami When He Went As Ambassador to the Emperor," in CW.I.116-19, at 116; L.116.1083.

15. Cf. P.VI.24; P.XXV.99; D.I.40.2.

16. Cf. P.II.7; D.II.6.2; DF.25; L.216.1160. The notion of a second nature goes back to Cicero's dictum that "custom makes something like a second nature (*consuetudo quasi alteram . . naturam effici*)," as well as Galen's stronger claim that "custom is second nature (*consuetudo est altera natura*)." See Cicero, *De Finibus Bonorum et Malorum,* trans. H. Rackham, Loeb Classical Library 40 (Cambridge, Mass.: Harvard University Press, 1914), V.25.74; Galen, *De tuenda valetudine,* 1, quoted in Gerhard Funke, *Gewohnheit,* Archiv für Begriffsgeschichte, vol. 3, ed. Erich Rothacker (Bonn: H. Bouvier,1961), 84, cf. 14, 96-99.

17. See Eckhart Kessler, "The Intellective Soul," in *The Cambridge History of Renaissance Philosophy,* ed. Charles B. Schmitt (Cambridge: Cambridge University Press, 1988), 485-534.

18. Cf. FH.III.8; AG.I.302; "Mission to the Emperor of Germany," in W.IV.83-154, at 111.

19. Cf. D.I.Pr.2; AG.II.332-33.

20. See Strauss, *Thoughts on Machiavelli,* 31, 200; Mansfield, Harvey C. Jr., "Machiavelli's Political Science," *American Political Science Review* 75, no. 2 (June 1981): 293-305, esp. 303-05.

21. Sampling the *Discourses,* we find only one psychological use of "reason" at D.I.6.4, but a host of discursive ones, namely at D.I.4.1, 5.2, 6.4, 11.3, 12.2, 23.4, 24.1, 31.2, 34.1-2, 38.2, 40.5, 46, 49.3, 53.2, 55.4, 55.6, 58.1; D.II.Pr.2, 1.1, 2.1, 12.1, 12.3, 16.1, 17.1, 17.5, 18.1-2, 22.2, 23.3, 24.1, 27.1, 32.1; D.III.5, 8.1, 10.2, 16.1, 21.2, 33.1-2. See also Martin Fleisher, "A Passion for Politics: The Vital Core of the World of Machiavelli," in *Machiavelli and the Nature of Political Thought,* ed. Martin Fleisher (New York: Atheneum, 1972), 114-47, at 133.

22. Cf. P.XXV.98; P.XXVI.103.

23. Quentin Skinner, *The Foundations of Modern Political Thought,* vol. 1, *The Renaissance* (Cambridge: Cambridge University Press, 1978), 97-98; Simon Kemp, *Medieval Psychology* (New York: Greenwood Press, 1990), 82. Among humanist authors, see especially Giovanni Pico della Mirandola, *Oration on the Dignity of Man* [1486], trans. Elizabeth Livermoore Forbes, in *The Renaissance Philosophy of Man,* ed. Ernst Cassirer, Paul Oskar Kristeller, and John Herman Randall, Jr. (Chicago: University of Chicago Press, 1948), 223-54, at §§ 3-7; Thomas Hobbes, *Leviathan: With Selected Variants from the Latin Edition of 1688* [1651], ed. Edwin Curley (Indianapolis: Hackett, 1994), XIV.2.

24. On spirit in conspiracies, see also P.XIX.73; D.III.6.2, 6.8, 6.12-16, 6.20. On spirit in combat, see also P.X.44; P.XIII.56; D.I.31.1; 43.1; D.II.12.3-4, 16.1, 32.1; D.III.12.1, 14.1, 31.2, 31.4, 33.1, 36.2, 37.3, 38.1; "Mission to the Duke of Valentinois," in W.III.141-280, at 179. Further, note that Machiavelli substitutes *spirito* for *animo* in a few places; for instance, whereas he writes in the *Prince* that Fortune provided founders with occasions without which their "*virtù* of *animo* would have been eliminated" (P.VI.23), he states in the *Discourses* that Fortune "elects a man of so much *spirito* and so much *virtù* that he recognizes the opportunities that [she] proffers him" (D.II.29.2); cf. D.III.31.4; L.211.1149.

25. Cf. P.VII.28; P.X.44; D.I.27.1, 29.3, 38.3, 59; D.III.2, 6.4, 6.20, 28, 48.2; L.211.1149.

26. This and other references to medieval and Renaissance psychology are based on Kemp, *Medieval Psychology*; E. Ruth Harvey, *The Inward Wits: Psychological Theory in the Middle Ages and the Renaissance* (London: Warburg Institute, 1975); Katherine Park, "The Organic Soul," in *The Cambridge History of Renaissance Philosophy,* ed. Charles B. Schmitt (Cambridge: Cambridge University Press, 1988), 464-84; Walter Pagel, "Medieval and Renaissance Contributions to Knowledge of the Brain and Its Functions," in *The History and Philosophy of Knowledge of the Brain and Its Functions: An Anglo-American Symposium, London, July 15th-17th, 1957* (Amsterdam: B.M. Israël, 1973), 95-114; Parel, *Machiavellian Cosmos,* 87-92.

27. D.I.57; AG.I.309; "Mission to the Duke of Valentinois," in W.III.141-

280, at 179.

28. Cf. D.I.57.1; D.II.19.2, 31.1.

29. Cf. Mansfield, "Machiavelli's Political Science," 304.

30. Cf. P.XVIII.69; P.XXII.92.

31. Cf. Fleisher, "A Passion for Politics," 133-43; Anthony J. Parel, *The Machiavellian Cosmos* (New Haven: Yale University Press, 1992), 89-90.

32. Cf. D.I.Pr.1.

33. Cf. D.I.40.7, 42; D.II.20.1, 27.1, 32.1; D.III.6.3; 6.16; *I Decennali* [Decennial chronicles], in TO.939-54, at 954.

34. Cf. D.I.1.4, 10.2, 27.2, 29.3; D.II.Pr.1, 4.1-2; D.III.6.14, 8.1-2.

35. Cf. D.I.32.

36. Cf. P.IV.19.

37. See P.VI.23 together with P.XXVI.102.

38. See P.XVIII.70-71; D.I.12.1, 48; D.III.49.4.

39. Cf. D.III.14.2.

40. Cf. D.III.12.3.

41. Cf. D.I.58.3-4.

42. Cf. D.I.58.3; D.III.34.4.

43. Cf. FH.I.25.

44. Cf. Strauss, *Thoughts on Machiavelli*, 129.

45. See Fleisher, "A Passion for Politics," 135; K.R. Minogue, "Theatricality and Politics: Machiavelli's Concept of Fantasia," in *The Morality of Politics,* ed. Bhikhu Parekh and R. N. Berki (London: Allen & Unwin, 1972), 148-63, esp. 152; Sheldon S. Wolin, "Machiavelli: Politics and the Economy of Violence," in *Politics and Vision: Continuity and Innovation in Western Political Thought* (Boston: Little Brown, 1960), 195-238, at 211-13.

46. See D.I.10.4, 11.1, 29.3, 43; D.II.2.1, 3, 33.

47. Cf. C.Pr; D.I.Pr.2, 11.5.

48. Cf. "Mission to Mantua on Business with the Emperor of Germany," in W.IV.195-219, at 207.

49. Cf. D.I.16.3; FH.III.13, III.25; "Mission to the Countess Catherine Sforza," in W.III.6-26, at 19. Note, however, that Machiavelli makes no consistent terminological distinction between glory and honor as two kinds of recognition.

50. Cf. D.I.16.3; D.III.8.1, 22.4, 28, 34.1-4. Cf. Strauss, *Thoughts on Machiavelli*, 280-82.

51. On the passion for domination, see also D.I.1.4; D.III.4; A.986; "Mission to the Court of Rome," in W.III.283-388, at 346, 359.

52. See D.II.2.1, 2.3-4; cf. D.I.16.3.

53. Cf. P.XXV.99.

54. *Capitoli per una compagnia di piacere* [Articles for a pleasure company], in TO.930-932, at 932, mt.

55. See Hannah F. Pitkin, *Fortune Is a Woman: Gender and Politics in the Thought of Niccolò Machiavelli* (Berkeley, Calif.: University of California Press, 1984); Mark Hulliung, *Citizen Machiavelli* (Princeton: Princeton University Press, 1983), ch. IV.

56. Cf. P.XVII.67; P.XIX.72.
57. Cf. P.XXV.101.
58. Parel, *The Machiavellian Cosmos,* 101-04.
59. Cf. D.I.2.5-7.
60. Cf. D.I.37.2; FH.II.10, 12,17, 21; FH.III. 21; FH.IV.7, 28; FH.VII.12; FH.VIII.27.
61. See D.I.7, 8.
62. See Huovinen, *Bild vom Menschen,* 51-82; Fleisher, "Passion for Politics," 119-33; Russell Price, *"Ambizione* in Machiavelli's Thought," *History of Political Thought* 3, no. 3 (November 1982): 383-445.
63. Cf. Minogue, "Theatricality and Politics," 155.
64. *Capitoli per una compagnia di piacere,* in TO.930-932, at 930-31, mt.
65. M.I.1.
66. Cf. Pitkin, *Fortune Is a Woman,* 320-24.
67. In a widely read essay, Gianfrancesco Pico della Mirandola thus argued that "depraved imagination is the mother and nurse of ambition"; see Gianfrancesco Pico della Mirandola, *On the Imagination* [1501], trans. Harry Caplan (New Haven: Yale University Press, 1930), VII.45.
68. Cf. D.I.5.4, 37.1; D.II.8.1; D.III.8.1, 20; FH.III.5; AG.I.306; AG.VII.389; L.211.1149; CC.620. Accordingly, Russell Price is quite mistaken when he limits Machiavelli's notion of ambition to "office, power or domination"; see Price, *"Ambizione* in Machiavelli's Thought," 389.
69. Cf. D.I.29.1, 35, 37.1, 46.1; FH.II.32, IV.2, V.21, VII.23; A.984; AS.975.
70. See Aristotle, *Nicomachean Ethics,* trans. Terence Irwin (Indianapolis: Hackett, 1985),1097b25, 1098a15.
71. Cf. [Exortazione alla penitenza] [Exhortation to penitence], in TO.932-34, 933, mt.
72. Cf. Parel, *The Machiavellian Cosmos,* 106, 125-26.
73. See FH.Pr; FH.III.5, 8, 12, 18, 21, 22.
74. This respect, as we shall see below, is a matter of habituation.
75. Aristotle, *The Politics,* trans. Carnes Lord (Chicago: University of Chicago Press, 1984), 1267b, 1323a.
76. Strauss, *Thoughts on Machiavelli,* 296.
77. Aristotle, *Nicomachean Ethics,* 1103b; Aristotle, *Politics,* 1269a. Cf. Thomas Aquinas, *Summa Theologiae,* trans. Fathers of the English Dominican Province (New York: Benziger Brothers, 1947), II-II, Q. 92, A.1; Strauss, *Thoughts on Machiavelli,* 254-55. For an exhaustive treatment of the concept of habituation in the history of ideas, see Funke, *Gewohnheit.*
78. It is above all his failure to recognize this difference that allows J. G. A. Pocock to place Machiavelli in the Aristotelian tradition; for Pocock's central claim that Machiavelli's republic is a structure of civic virtue depends on the assumption that he considered men to be good by their first nature and bad only by their customary, second nature. See J. G. A. Pocock, "Custom & Grace, Form & Matter: An Approach to Machiavelli's Concept of Innovation," in *Machiavelli and the Nature of Political Thought,* ed. Martin Fleisher (New

York: Atheneum, 1972), 153-74, at 171-74; J. G. A. Pocock, *The Machiavellian Moment: Florentine Political Thought and the Atlantic Republican Tradition* (Princeton: Princeton University Press, 1975), 136, 183-85. For another critique of Pocock, see Vickie B. Sullivan, "Machiavelli's Momentary 'Machiavellian Moment': A Reconsideration of Pocock's Treatment of the *Discourses,*" *Political Theory* 20, no. 2 (May): 309-18.

79. Cf. D.I.17.3; AS.V.967; "Mission to the Court of France," in W.III.90-140, at 76; "Mission to Various Parts of the Florentine Dominion," in W.IV.3-9, at 4.

80. Cf. Funke, *Gewohnheit,* 27-28.

81. See Funke, *Gewohnheit,* 14, 96-97.

82. "Second Mission to the Court of Rome," in W.IV.10-75, at 40.

83. See D.I.19.1.

84. Cf. D.III.14.2.

85. Cf. AS.V.967.

86. Cf. D.III.8.2.

87. Polybius, *The Rise of the Roman Empire,* trans. Ian Scott-Kilvert (London: Penguin Classics, 1979), VI.5; cf. Harvey C. Mansfield, Jr., *Machiavelli's New Modes and Orders: A Study of the* Discourses on Livy (Ithaca: Cornell University Press, 1979), 35-40.

88. Parel, *Machiavellian Cosmos,* 101-02.

89. Cf. D.I.2.6, 7.1, 16.4, 17.3, 25, 32, 39.2, 40.6, 50, 52.2; D.II.2.2, 22.1, 28.1; D.III.3, 6.2, 7, 29, 34.1; FH.III.1, 20; FH.IV.1. On the medieval corporation, see Gaines Post, *Studies in Medieval Legal Thought: Public Law and the State, 1100-1322* (Princeton: Princeton University Press, 1964), chs. 1-3; K. Pennington, "Law, Legislative Authority and Theories of Government, 1150-1300," in *The Cambridge History of Medieval Political Thought c. 350-c. 1450,* ed. J. H. Burns (Cambridge: Cambridge University Press, 1988), 424-53, esp. 444-53.

90. See P.VI.23; P.XXVI.102; D.I.1.5, 6.1, 11.3, 16.2, 17.3, 18.4, 35.1, 45.1, 55.4; D.II.5.2, 23.2; D.III.8.1-2; AG.VII.388; DF.26. Cf. Aristotle, *Politics,* 1252a-1253a.

91. See Olsen, *Logic of Collective Action,* 2; Hardin, *Collective Action,* 2.

92. *Ritratto delle cose della Magna* [Portrait of the Affairs of Germany], in TO.68-71, at 71, mt.

93. Cf. D.III.11.1-2; L.233.1183.

94. William Bluhm even calls Machiavelli a follower of the nominal tradition of William of Occam, who reduced universals to mere names *(nomina);* see William T. Bluhm, *Theories of the Political System: Classics of Political Thought and Modern Political Analysis,* 3rd ed. (Englewood Cliffs: Prentice-Hall, 1978), 22-23.

95. Jacob Burckhardt, *The Civilization of the Renaissance in Italy* [1860], trans. by S. G. C. Middlemore (New York: Modern Library, 1954), 100. On Machiavelli and Renaissance individualism, see also Eduard Wilhelm Mayer, *Machiavellis Geschichtsauffassung und sein Begriff virtù: Studien zu seiner Historik* (Munich: R. Oldenbourg, 1912), ch. 1.

96. Francesco Petrarca, *The Ascent of Mont Ventoux* [1336], trans. Hans Nachod, in *The Renaissance Philosophy of Man*, ed. Ernst Cassirer, Paul Oskar Kristeller, and John Herman Randall, Jr. (Chicago: University of Chicago Press, 1948), 36-46, esp. 44-46.

97. Contrast Aristotle, *Politics*, 1252a-1253a, with Hobbes, Leviathan, ch. XIII.

98. Cf. D.I.3.T, 18.1-2, 33.T, 33.2; D.III.11.1;

99. Cf. D.III.9.1.

100. Cf. P.XXV.100; "Mission to the Court of Rome," in W.III.283-388, at 298.

101. Cf. D.III.8.2; F.978; L.116.1083.

102. "Mission to the Court of Rome," in W.III.283-388, at 301.

103. "Mission to the Court of Rome," in W.III.283-388, at 318, mt.

104. Cf. D.II.23.T.

105. For essays on Machiavelli's concept of *virtù*, see J. H. Whitfield, "The Anatomy of Virtue," in *Machiavelli* (New York: Russell & Russell, 1947), 92-105; Felix Gilbert, "On Machiavelli's Idea of *virtù*," *Renaissance News* 4 (1951): 53-56; Neal Wood, "Machiavelli's Concept of *virtù* Reconsidered," *Political Studies* 15, no. 2 (June 1967): 159-72; John Plamenatz, "In Search of Machiavellian *virtù*," in *The Political Calculus*, ed. Anthony Parel (Toronto: University of Toronto Press, 1972), 157-78; Russell Price, "The Senses of *Virtù* in Machiavelli," *European Studies Review* 3, no. 4 (October 1973): 315-453; Harvey C. Mansfield, "Machiavelli's Virtue," in *Machiavelli's Virtue* (Chicago: University of Chicago Press, 1996), 6-52.

106. Cf. P.I.6; P.VI-VII.21-33; P.XXV.98-101; D.II.1; F.976. On the traditional opposition of *virtus* and *fortuna*, see Pocock, *Machiavellian Moment*, 36-41, 86-88, 92, 95-97; Skinner, *Foundations of Modern Political Thought*, 95-98, 119-20, 186-88.

107. See AS.IV.964-65; M.Pr.

108. *Parole da dirle sopra la provisione del danaio, facto un poco di proemio et di scusa* [Words to be spoken on the provision of money, having given a little preface and excuse], in TO.11-13, at 11, mt; cf. D.I.19.4. According to Eduard Mayer, Machiavelli later combined force and prudence to form the concept of *virtù;* see Mayer, *Machiavellis Geschichtsauffassung*, 89, cf. 20.

109. On the Renaissance usage of *virtù*, see Price, "Senses of *Virtù*," 319-22, 335-36, 344. On Roman *virtus*, see Karl Büchner, "Altrömische und Horazische virtus," in *Römische Wertbegriffe*, ed. Hans Oppermann, Wege der Forschung, vol. 34 (Darmstadt: Wissenschaftliche Buchgesellschaft, 1967), 376-401; Ludwig Curtius, "Virtus und Constantia," in *Römische Wertbegriffe*, ed. Hans Oppermann, Wege der Forschung, vol. 34 (Darmstadt: Wissenschaftliche Buchgesellschaft, 1967), 370-75; D. C. Earl, *The Moral and Political Tradition of Rome* (Ithaca: Cornell University Press, 1967), 21.

110. For other mentions of soldierly *virtù*, see D.II.1.1, 18.3, 24.2; D.III.15.1; FH.VI.24.

111. Cf. Friedrich Meinecke, *Machiavellism: The Doctrine of Raison d' Etat*

and Its Place in Modern History [1924], trans. Douglas Scott (Boulder: Westview, 1984), 32; Skinner, *Machiavelli,* 59; Wolin, "Machiavelli," 231.

Chapter 4

Political Good and Necessary Evil

As we saw in chapter 1, Machiavelli's writings contain a tension between offering instructions in the techniques of power and professing a concern with the common good. To resolve it, we need to think of Machiavelli's thought as operating on two planes: a normative level, where the ends of political action are defined as security, greatness, empire, riches, and liberty, and a technical level, where the means to these ends are analyzed in a purely efficient manner; importantly, these levels are integrated by constructing political order in such a way that princes and the great are constrained to promote the common good in the course of using the techniques of power to satisfy their own ambition.[1] In short, the technical aspect of Machiavelli's thought is instrumental to his normative concern.

The Ends of Political Order

Despite his self-regarding anthropology, Machiavelli clearly believed in the existence of a common or public good. A true founder "has the intent to wish to help not himself but the common good" and works "not for his own succession but for the common fatherland" (D.I.9.1). Republics are superior to principalities because "it is not the particular good but the common good that makes cities

85

great" and "this common good is not observed if not in republics" (D.II.2.1).[2] And Machiavelli wrote the *Discourses* because of his "natural desire . . . to work, without any respect, for those things I believe will bring common benefit to everyone" (D.I.Pr.1).

Machiavelli determines the content of this good in two ways: imitation of the ancients and imitation of nature. Regarding the former, he elevates glory or greatness to the highest good because the "Gentiles, esteeming [the honor of the world] very much and having placed the highest good in it" did not "beatify men if they were not full of worldly glory, as were captains of armies and princes of republics" (D.II.2.2).[3] In the *Discourses,* he limits his analysis to those ancient cities that attained greatness on account of their free origin,[4] and devotes the entire third book to the demonstration of "how much the actions of particular men made Rome great" (D.III.1.6). He assumes that wealth should be public on the grounds that "it was enough to those [Roman] citizens to get honor from war, and everything useful they left to the public" (D.III.25). And he follows the ancient peoples in their "affection for the free [i.e., republican] way of life" on the grounds that "cities have never expanded either in dominion or riches if they have not been in freedom" (D.II.2.1).

That Machiavelli considered imitation of nature a normative warrant can be seen most directly from one of his familiar letters, where he excuses his changing the topic with the claim that "this mode of proceeding, if to someone it may appear disgraceful, to me it appears laudable, because we are imitating nature, which is variable; and he who imitates her cannot be reproved" (L.239.1191). Further, if "all our actions imitate nature" (D.II.3.1) and "states [are] . . . like all other things in nature" (P.VII.26), then the effectual truth about the good has to remain within natural bounds, rather than aiming at lofty ideals. In other words, Machiavelli's naturalistic approach to ethics is already implied by his astrological naturalism, which assumes the world to be governed by immanent causes and thus denies any transcendent level of existence from which human affairs could be assessed. Further, since all men share the vulgar desires for recognition, power, wealth, and sexual pleasure (albeit to different degrees), to derive what is good from what is natural leads to a multitudinous notion of the good. In Machiavelli's words, since "in the world there is no one but the vulgar" (P.XVII.71), "good is what does good to many, and with which many are satisfied" (M.III.4).

However, such a naturalistic ethic must do more than simply affirm whatever desires and practices human beings may have and follow; for, otherwise, it would be reduced to a mere anthropology without any normative content of its own. In Machiavelli's case, such a reduction would lead to "ambitious license" (D.I.47.3), which–although fully natural–is undesirable, since it makes men fight their fellows and thus limits the total satisfaction of their desires. Instead, as we shall see in chapter 5, there needs to be "ordered government" (D.I.47.3) that forces individuals to refrain from attacking each other so that they can maximize their overall satisfaction by jointly despoiling foreigners. Hence, Machiavelli's naturalistic ethic is normative insofar as it requires individuals to defer immediate and lawless gratification of their desires for the sake of an ultimately more rewarding share in the common good. In other words, they ought to overcome the collective-action problem that befalls those who cannot see beyond their most immediate self-interest, as when "the common utility that is drawn from a free way of life is not recognized by anyone while it is possessed: this is being able to enjoy one's things freely, without any suspicion, not fearing for the honor of wives and that of children, not to be afraid for oneself" (D.I.16.3). Hence, Machiavelli's "ought" remains limited to the most effectual satisfaction of human ambition, and thus stays firmly on the ground of man-as-he-happens-to-be.

But what are the particular ends that Machiavelli subsumes under the common good, and how does he distinguish them from their underlying desires? Given Machiavelli's adoption of worldly honor as the highest good, a political order obviously should strive for glory or greatness. And since such greatness depends primarily on the size and stability of a city's dominion, greatness and empire are nearly coterminous ends–as in Machiavelli's claim that imitation of the Romans is "the true way to make a republic great and acquire empire" (D.II.19.1). However, while the greatness of the city is unproblematic as a common good, individuals must pursue glory in "public ways":

Citizens in cities acquire reputation in two modes: either by public ways or by private modes. One acquires it publicly by winning a battle, acquiring a town, carrying out a mission with care and prudence, advising the republic wisely and prosperously. One acquires it in private modes by benefiting this or that other citizen, defending him from the magistrates, helping him with money, getting him unmerited honors, and ingratiating oneself with the plebs with games and public gifts. From this latter mode of proceeding, sects and partisans arise, and the reputation thus earned offends as much as reputation helps when it is not mixed with sects, because that reputation is founded on the common good, not on a private good. (FH.VII.1)[5]

Likewise, wealth belongs to the political good insofar as it is in public hands; for "well-ordered republics have to keep the public rich and their citizens poor," as private riches corrupt good customs (D.I.37.1).[6] And since Machiavelli denies wealth not only its use for private consumption, but also for military might–"money is not the sinew of war" (D.II.10.T), the point of filling the treasury must be to serve the greatness of the city. In contrast, sexual gratification should remain private, for excesses that take on a public dimension "have been causes of much ruin and have done great damage to those who govern a city, and have caused many divisions in them" (D.III.26.2). For instance, the rape of Lucretia by one of the Tarquin princes triggered their expulsion from Rome, and the obscene rites of the Bacchanals undermined the lawful order of the Roman republic.[7]

In addition to greatness, empire, and treasure, the political good obviously includes security, both with regard to protecting the city from outside danger and upholding law and order within. Thus, a prince should not "allow disorders to continue, from which come killings or robberies; for these customarily harm a whole community" (P.XVII.65-66). In contrast to individuals who sacrifice their lives to gain glory, the city must be preserved even at the expense of its reputation, for "the fatherland is well defended in whatever mode one defends it, whether with ignominy or with glory"; thus, the Romans, when having to choose between losing their army gloriously and saving it shamefully, decided on the latter because they reasoned that "if the army saved itself, Rome would have time to cancel the ignominy," and in due course gain even greater glory, whereas "if it did not save itself, even though it died gloriously, Rome and its freedom were lost" altogether (D.III.41). Hence, greatness is the highest good in the sense of making a city most exalted, but security is the primary good in the sense of being a necessary condition for all other ones.

In similar fashion, liberty is esteemed as a prerequisite for greatness, empire, and wealth, since "it is seen through experience that cities have never expanded either in dominion or riches if they have not been in freedom"; for instance, "it is a marvelous thing to consider how much greatness Athens arrived at in the space of of a hundred years after it was freed from the tyranny of Pisistratus" and "how much greatness Rome arrived at after it was freed from the [Tarquin] kings" (D.II.2.1).[8] More precisely, "that city can be called free" where "laws are ordered by which [the] humors of the nobles and the men of the people are quieted or restrained so that they cannot do evil" (FH.IV.1), and where they "observe their laws in a mode that no one from outside or inside dares to seize them" (D.I.55.2).[9] In other words, a city is at liberty when it is ruled by its own laws rather than the wills of tyrants, foreign or domestic. This emphasis on laws means further that liberty is different from license, which implies the lawless pursuit of ambition by individuals; thus, corrupt citizens can be said to have "preferred their own license to the liberty of all" (D.I.40.4, mt).

Justice, finally, which was the central political good of the classical tradition, plays only a minor role in Machiavelli's thought. Since human beings lack a soul, they have no natural capacity for a virtue such as justice, but must derive it from the laws that order their cities. In their original condition, men thus had no "knowledge of things honest and good, differing from the pernicious and bad," and it was only after a strongman had become their "head" that they were "making laws and ordering punishments for whoever acted against them: hence came the knowledge of justice" (D.I.2.3).[10] In other words, Machiavelli has a positivist understanding of justice as a mere means to the good of political order.[11] This can be seen most clearly from his *protestatio de iustitia,* a formal oration on justice delivered in Florence at the installation of a new government, where he claims that once Justice had deserted mankind, "she never again returned to earth to dwell universally among men, but particularly in this or that city; and while she was there she made the city great and powerful."[12] A similar expediency makes Machiavelli counsel princes to cultivate virtues other than justice, such as mercy, piety, and humanity: "by appearing to have them, *they are useful,* as it is to appear merciful, faithful, humane, honest, and religious, and to be so"; but when it becomes more useful to practice the corresponding vices, then a prince must know how to act "against faith, against charity, against humanity, against religion," in short, "how to enter into evil" (P.XVIII.70, ea); for "something appears to be virtue, which if pursued would be one's ruin, and something else appears to be vice, which if pursued results in one's security and well-being" (P.XV.62).

In sum, Machiavelli understood the good of political order to consist of greatness, empire, and treasure as its ultimate ends and security and liberty as its proximate ends. These ends largely correspond to what the Romans called *bona fortunae,* the goods of Fortune, which Machiavelli himself lists as "power, honor, riches, and health" (F.978).[13] They arise in naturalistic fashion from the corresponding desires of individuals for recognition, preservation, power, and wealth, but cannot be reduced to them since individuals ought to subordinate their private and immediate gratification to the public satisfaction in the long run. In particular, citizens must limit their pursuit of recognition to public ways, accept personal austerity for the sake of public wealth, prevent their sexual affairs from disrupting public order, and allow their freedom to be regulated by laws. Hence, it is these constraints on individual ambition that give normative content to Machiavelli's naturalistic ethic.

Good Effects Excuse Evil Deeds

To satisfy their own ambition, *virtuoso* individuals must create and maintain political order with the help of Machiavelli's technical maxims, and thus provide for the political good. Above all, founders establish institutional orders that benefit generations of men because they thereby gain "perpetual honor" (D.I.10.1). For instance, Moses, Cyrus, Romulus, and Theseus became "powerful, secure, honored, and prosperous" while "their fatherlands were ennobled by [their *virtù*] and became very prosperous" as well (P.VI.23, 25); and the addressee of the *Prince* should realize that "there is matter [in Italy] to give opportunity to someone prudent and *virtuoso* to introduce a form that would bring honor to him and good to the community of men there" (P.XXVI.102).[14] In republics, as we saw above, ambitious men should pursue personal glory in public ways, which tends to advance the common good because the people are more likely to celebrate those who benefit them, by "winning a battle, acquiring a town, carrying out a mission with care and prudence, advising the republic wisely and prosperously" (FH.VIII.1).

Indeed, Machiavelli seems to think that those who are capable of seizing the reins for the common good have an obligation to do so; for he deplores the fact that many princes,

> deceived by a false good and a false glory, either voluntarily or ignorantly, let themselves go into the ranks of those who deserve more blame than praise; and though, to their perpetual honor, they are able to make a republic or a kingdom, they turn to tyranny. (D.I.10.1)

Caesar, for instance, wasted the last opportunity to reform the corrupt Roman republic, and instead became "the first tyrant in Rome, such that never again was that city free" (D.I.37.2). Piero Soderini, on the other hand, failed to defend the Florentine republic by refusing to use extralegal means at all:

> Such respect [for proceeding lawfully] was wise and good; nonetheless he should never allow an evil to run loose out of respect for a good,

when that good could easily be crushed by that evil. Since his works and his intention had to be judged by the end, he should have believed that if fortune and life had stayed with him, everyone could certify that what he had done was for the safety of the fatherland and not for his own ambition. (D.III.3.1)[15]

In other words, the capacity to generate the political good imposes on *virtuoso* men what Max Weber called an "ethic of responsibility."[16] Of course, given the natural selfishness of human beings, Machiavelli does not expect princes to sacrifice their personal ambition altogether, but merely wants them to understand that far greater glory and security can be attained by working for the common good than by subverting it. Again, it is this idea that integrates the technical and normative levels of Machiavelli's thought.

Machiavelli makes no secret of the fact that the techniques which he wants founders, princes, and the leading men of republics to use often violate the traditional rules of morality. When speaking of well-used cruelties he qualifies his counsel with the clause "if it is permissible to speak well of evil" (P.IV.37); he famously advises princes "to be able not to be good" (P.XV.61) and to "know how to enter into evil, when forced by necessity" (P.XVIII.70); and he states categorically that someone who leaves the private life to become a king can no longer take the "way of the good" but "must enter into this evil one if he wishes to maintain himself" (D.I.26).[17]

To render such evil permissible, Machiavelli resorts to a consequentialist approach to ethics, which assesses the moral status of an action by its effects or consequences–rather than by the character of the action itself. He develops this idea most precisely in assessing the violent deeds committed by Romulus, the founder of Rome. To begin with, Machiavelli asserts that the actions of Romulus were clearly evil when considered by themselves, that is, separately from his intention and the eventual outcome:

Many will perhaps judge it a bad example that a founder of a civil way of life, as was Romulus, should first have killed his brother, then consented to the death of Titus Tatius the Sabine, chosen by him as partner in the kingdom. . . . That opinion would be true if one did not consider what end had induced him to commit such a homicide. (D.I.9.1)

Next, Machiavelli ascertains that it holds as a general rule that the deeds in question are necessary to obtain the good consequences:

> This should be taken as a general rule: that it never or rarely happens
> that any republic or kingdom is ordered well from the beginning or
> reformed altogether anew outside its old orders, unless it is ordered by
> one individual. Indeed it is necessary that one alone give the mode and
> that any such ordering depend on his mind. (D.I.9.2)

Finally, he takes the good consequences to "excuse" the evil quality
of the deeds, thus making their commission permissible and, indeed,
obligatory:

> Nor will a wise understanding ever reprove anyone for any extraordinary
> action that he uses to order a kingdom or constitute a republic. It is
> very suitable that when the deed accuses him, the effect excuses him,
> and when the effect is good, as was that of Romulus, it will always
> excuse the deed; for he who is violent to spoil, not he who is violent to
> mend, should be reproved. (D.I.9.2)

This consequentialist approach to ethics is already implicit in
Machiavelli's commitment to the "effectual truth of the thing"; for if
the truth of a thing lies in its effects or consequences, then the ethical
part of this truth will reside there as well. Moreover, consequentialism
is the natural ethic for a world where all men are vulgar; for "to look
into the mirror of the many" is to "judge things by the end and not by
the means" (L.116.1082).[18]

Since Machiavelli assumed human beings to be individuals, his
consequentialism can also be understood as the sacrifice of a few to
the many. Thus, Cleomenes killed the ephors of Sparta and anyone
else capable of opposition, "since it appeared to him that because of
the ambition of men he could not do something useful to many
against the will of the few" (D.I.9.4); likewise, a prince should follow
the example of Cesare Borgia–"whose cruelty restored the Romagna,
united it, and reduced it to peace and faith"–when subduing a lawless
multitude, because the killings and robberies that result from anarchy
"customarily harm an entire universality, but the executions that
come from the prince harm one particular person" (P.XVII.65-66,
mt).[19] In other words, Machiavelli comes close to formulating a
utilitarian doctrine, whereby an act is considered right if its negative
utility for some is outweighed by its positive utility for others. At the
same time, he falls short of utilitarianism by maintaining that such
deeds are wicked; for a true utilitarian would judge acts that injure a
few to the greater advantage of many to be good deeds, as he has no
other principle than net utility to decide what is right.[20]

That Machiavelli stopped short of taking consequentialism to this extreme is further suggested by his claim that the good effects "excuse" the wicked deed, rather than justify it;[21] for an excuse is typically an admission of fault, whereas justification implies denial of fault and assertion of innocence.[22] In other words, had Machiavelli embraced the adage that the end *justifies* the means–as often but erroneously thought–he would have argued that the good of the effect cancels the evil of the deed and thus makes it just. Then, Romulus and others like him would be innocent of crime and we ought to embrace them as truly good men; but, insofar as their deeds can only be excused on account of their being necessary for the political good, they remain guilty and we may celebrate their *virtù*, but not their virtue. That Machiavelli really understood the difference between excuse and justification is further suggested by his claim that a prince or people, who deny their general his due reward, make "an error that has no excuse but rather brings with it an eternal infamy" when they are motivated by avarice, but deserve "some excuse" when they are driven by fear of his power (D.I.29.1); also, Cesare Borgia said that "he should be sorry to be obliged to injure others, but . . . felt that he would be excused by God and by men, . . . as being forced to it by necessity."[23]

The Scope of Necessity

Machiavelli's writings caused a scandal in Christendom. According to Cardinal Pole (1539), who visited Florence only a few years after Machiavelli's death, the latter had introduced a "new art of ruling" (*nova ars regnandi*) in the *Prince,* which must have been "written by the finger of Satan."[24] In 1559, the Church thus placed Machiavelli's writings on the papal Index of Prohibited Books, where they remained until 1890.[25] Indeed, Innocent Gentillet's *Anti-Machiavel* (1576) spawned an entire genre of "anti-Machiavellian" works that sought to refute the Florentine's maxims for good, including a tract titled *Machiavellism Decapitated.*[26] In the twentieth century, finally, Leo Strauss described Machiavelli as a "teacher of evil" who "challenge[d] not only the religious teaching but the whole philosophical tradition as well."[27] But what was it precisely that made Machiavelli's thought such a challenge to the Western tradition?

Machiavelli's preference for the immanent goods of Fortune surely places him in conflict with a transcendental religion, such as Christianity, which depreciates the pleasures of this life and exalts the salvation of the soul in the next one. At the center of this conflict over the ends of man lies glory, adored by the Romans as well as Machiavelli as the foremost reward for manly deeds in the service of the state, but condemned by Augustine as praise of self instead of God.[28] In this sense, Machiavelli's admiration for the ancients who placed the highest good in "the honor of the world" and his concomitant scorn for Christians who put it in "humility, abjectness, and contempt of things human" (D.II.2.2) represent a revaluation, or, more precisely, an effort to undo the revaluation that occurred when Christianity took glory from man and gave it to God. But this revision had already been underway when Machiavelli burst onto the scene, largely due to the work of humanists who revived the ancient esteem of glory as the proper reward of *virtus,*[29] and thus could not have been the reason for identifying Machiavelli with the devil (who, in turn, became known as "Old Nick," in reference to Machiavelli's first name).

Thus, Machiavelli's innovation lies not so much with his determination of ends, but rather with the kinds of means he advocated in pursuing them. In other words, Machiavelli's far-reaching consequentialism challenged the absolutist core of the Western tradition, which holds that abusing human beings for the satisfaction of others is always wrong.[30] However, this challenge is not a simple one, for classical thinkers had been well aware of "cases of dire necessity" (*casus dirae necessitatis*)–when agents feel forced to act even though they know that action in pursuit of one good will inevitably diminish another–and, under certain circumstances, had allowed seemingly consequentialist resolutions to such moral problems.

This can be most clearly seen from the writings of Cicero, whose penetrating analysis of acts of necessity remained the standard well into early modernity. Accordingly, the "reason of the republic" (*ratio reipublicae*) commands magistrates and citizens to do what is expedient (*utile*) or necessary (*necessarius*), instead of what accords with the *formal* rules of morality (*honestum*)–such as keeping promises, respecting property, observing the laws, and abstaining from violence, intimidation, deceit, and slander–if the *substantive* welfare of the republic and its members (*salus rei publicae*), which in turn consists of their security, liberty, majesty, honor, and property, cannot be preserved by other means.[31] In particular, the magistrates may proceed by extralegal means, such as putting men to death without trial, against known threats to the republic, but only with the explicit consent of the Senate, except when times were so pressing that even this limitation could be suspended; indeed, should the authorities fail to protect the republic, individual citizens are permitted to take matters into their own hands: Thus, to Cicero's mind, Tiberius Gracchus, the Roman tribune who was assassinated in 133 B.C. by an aristocratic faction for his policy of allocating public lands to impoverished plebeians, was actually "put to death by an uprising of the republic itself" on account of "his most seditious tribuneship"; indeed, since both Tiberius and his younger brother Gaius, who strove for land reform as well and was slain twelve years later, "were not approved by the good while they lived," they are "numbered among those whose murder was justifiable."[32]

On the other hand, to break formal rules for the sake of goods that do not belong to the substance of republican life, such as territorial aggrandizement or wealth, or to commit acts which are so heinous (*magnae turpitudinae*) that even the substantive welfare of the republic could not justify them, constitutes "false public utility" (*publicae utilitatis species*), and is never permitted:

> There are some acts either so repulsive or so wicked, that a wise man would not commit them, even to save his country. Poseidonius has made a large collection of them; but some of them are so shocking, so indecent, that it seems immoral even to mention them. The wise man, therefore, will not think of doing any such thing for the sake of his country; no more will the country consent to have it done for her.[33]

Although Cicero shies away from enumerating these heinous acts here, we may surmise that they consist of deeds that undermine the very substance of society, such as killing complete innocents, abjuring the gods, tyrannizing over one's fellows, promoting incest, etc.[34] For the assumption that such deeds tend to destroy society as such implies that they can never be truly expedient for the public weal:

> The problem is the more easily disposed of because the occasion cannot arise when it could be to the state's interest to have the wise man do any of these things.[35]

Accordingly, Romulus was actuated by a "specious appearance of expediency" (*species utilitatis*) when he killed his brother in order to reign alone, and "threw away piety as well as humanity so that he could attain what seemed expedient but was not"[36]–in glaring contrast to Machiavelli's celebration of Romulus's fratricide as a paradigmatic case of necessity. In short, as Cicero repeats tirelessly, "nothing is really expedient (*vero utile*) that is not at the same time morally right (*honestum*)."[37]

Conversely, to assume that what is morally wrong can be useful to the political good is to lapse into a contradiction,[38] for morality is fundamental to political order:

> not even those who live by wickedness and crime can get on without some small element of justice. For if a robber takes anything by force or by fraud from another member of the gang, he loses his standing even in a band of robbers; and if the one called "Pirate Captain" should not divide the plunder equally, he would be either deserted or murdered by his comrades.[39]

In other words, expedient wickedness carries the seeds of its own destruction as "injustice is fatal to social life and fellowship between man and man."[40]

Actual Roman law reflected Cicero's doctrine. In the early days of the republic, the magistrates were entitled to appoint a dictator in emergencies, who could put to death any citizen without due process.[41] In 146 B.C., the Senate attained the right to issue emergency decrees (*senatus consulta ultima*) and therewith to declare anyone an enemy of the republic (*hostis publicus*) that ought to be killed on sight. Should the authorities fail to proceed against threats to the republic, any citizen could use force to act in their place. During the times of the Empire, the *princeps* could act outside the law on grounds of his *imperium*, the fullness of power granted to him by the Roman people. At the same time, all of these emergency provisions were conceived to be of a "necessarily ephemeral nature,"[42] that is, exceptions to the domestic rule of law where crime had to be delt with by due process in court. In Justinian's *Corpus juris civilis* (535 A.D.), finally, the Roman conception of cases of necessity was distilled into a number of succinct legal maxims, such as *necessitas legem non habet* (necessity knows no law), *quod principi placuit legis habet vigorem* (what pleases the prince has the force of law), and *princeps legibus solutus* (the prince is not bound by the laws).[43]

Drawing on these Latin sources, a number of medieval thinkers—such as John of Salisbury (ca. 1115/20-80), Henry of Ghent (ca. 1279), Jean Petit (d. 1411), and Jean Gerson (1363-1429)—then developed the concept of "reason of state" (*ratio status*), which they understood as the reasoning that guides the ruler in upholding the public welfare (*utilitas publica*); accordingly, they argued that war was just as long as defense against an aggressor made it necessary, that a just war permitted the king to levy extraordinary taxes and to confiscate property, that danger to the realm justified the use of torture in cases of treason, that laws should be disregarded if they conflicted with peace, and that the pope could authorize breaches of canonic law for the welfare of the Christian faith and its Church.[44] Again, this medieval consequentialism "was often sincerely believed to be in conformity with that reason which comes from God, participates in the law of nature, and approves the moral entity of the State," with the result that "extraordinary measures . . . were not in reality contrary to law and justice"; in particular, an "act needed to defend the State in a *casus necessitatis* was neither illegal nor immoral," but only to the extent that it "was indeed a *casus* and therefore could be adduced only *casualiter,* not *normaliter*"–that is, accidentally, not normally.[45]

This classical belief in the coherence of the moral world received its final elaboration by Thomas Aquinas, who argued that moral perplexity–situations where an agent must do one wrong in order to avoid another–can arise only *secundum quid,* that is, consequent to a prior wrongdoing by the agent; for it is a natural consequence of mortal sin that it entangles the sinner in circumstances where he cannot but commit others.[46] For instance, a murderer may find himself in a situation where he must either resist the authorities in order to escape punishment or abandon his wife and children to penury by allowing himself to be arrested; or, an adulterer may face the choice between lying to his wife or hurting her feelings by admitting his sin. In short, the classical tradition–whose moral core consists of Jewish, Stoic, and Christian ideas[47]–maintains throughout that cases of necessity are mere accidents in a world where it is natural and ordinary for morally right actions to have good consequences.

This reassuring assumption Machiavelli tore to shreds when he claimed in the *Prince* that there is a *"natural and ordinary* necessity which requires that one must always offend those over whom he becomes a new prince, both with men-at-arms and with infinite other injuries" (P.III.8, ea). This holds above all for the founder, who must use force to impose a new order on men who naturally want to retain their old way of life; thus, when the Israelites had reverted to worshipping the golden calf, an idol of fertility and sexuality, "Moses was forced to kill infinite men who, moved by nothing other than envy, were opposed to his plans" (D.III.30.1). But even well-ordered republics must injure men in order to prosper, since the majority has to override the interests of the minority in order to procure the common good:

> It is not the particular good but the common good that makes cities great. And without doubt the common good is not observed if not in republics, since all that is for that purpose is executed, although it may

turn out to harm this or that private individual, those for whom the aforesaid does good are so many that they can go ahead with it against the disposition of the few crushed by it. (D.II.2.1)

Further, to prevent the law-abiding customs of the citizens from being corrupted, they must be frequently exposed to punishments that are "excessive" and thus go beyond what is truly just (D.III.1.3). Once corruption has nonetheless spread through the civic body, the rulers must "go to the extraordinary, such as violence and arms" (D.I.18.1) in order to make the city "reborn with many dangers and much blood" (D.I.17.3). Indeed, all moral constraints are off when the safety of the fatherland is at stake:

> The fatherland is well defended in whatever modes one defends, whether with ignominy or with glory . . . for where one deliberates entirely on the safety of his fatherland, there ought not to enter any consideration either of just or unjust, merciful or cruel, praiseworthy or ignominous; indeed every other concern put aside, one ought to follow altogether what saves its life and maintains its liberty. (D.III.41.1)[48]

Should those who are sacrificed protest against the injustice done to them, Machiavelli stands ready to tell them that "you have to recognize every good of yours from [the fatherland]; so if it deprives itself of a part of its citizens, you would be obligated to thank it for those whom it lets be, rather than to defame it for those whom it eliminated."[49] Foreign affairs, finally, are such that a violent struggle for empire is unavoidable, making the political good rest on the unjust means of preventive war and domination of others; thus the Romans "knew that war may not be avoided but is deferred to the advantage of others. So they decided to make war with Philip and Antiochus in Greece in order not to have to do so in Italy" (P.III.12). In short, injustice is essential to the good of political order.

And this was an idea that nobody had dared to espouse in the West since Plato and his successors had been able to suppress the archaic view that "justice is doing good to friends and harm to enemies" and sophistic claim that "the just is nothing other than the advantage of the stronger"[50]–both of which had made political order coterminous with the injury of either foreigners or fellows. Machiavelli shocked Christendom by claiming that cases of necessity occur not only accidentally, that is, when prior transgressions have upset the natural order, but regularly, making expedient wickedness a fundamental aspect of political life. The import of this claim was enormous: No longer ought we to believe that human beings are capable–at least in principle and under the right circumstances–of living together without doing wrong to each other. The ethical community of classical thought, designed to cultivate all the virtues in harmony, belongs not only to the "imagined republics and principalities that have never been seen or known to exist in truth" (P.XV.61), but is a veritable impossibility.

The Incoherence of Reality

As we saw above, Machiavelli describe acts of political necessity as "evil" and merely "excuses" them, rather than justifying them on grounds of their good consequences, as a thoroughgoing utilitarian would. In other words, he clings in some measure to the absolutist idea that certain acts are inherently wrong.

But what may account for this scruple? There are no premises in Machiavelli's thought from which such a moral judgment could be derived: Ontologically, his belief in astrological naturalism and concomitant rejection of Christianity exclude revelation and divine law as transcendent sources of absolute norms; epistemologically, his commitment to the effectual truth prevents him from evaluating actions in intrinsic terms; in psychological terms, his denial of free will prevents mind as well as spirit from going beyond what ingenuity and imagination suggest in order to satisfy and engross the desires. In other words, Machiavelli's thought is deeply inconsistent in this regard: Whereas his premises entail a purely consequentialist ethic, his propositions maintain an absolutist notion of right and wrong.

To be sure, Machiavelli took diabolical delight in proclaiming his disdain for traditional morality, perhaps no more so than when professing disappointment that Giovampagolo Baglioni had failed to seize the opportunity to murder and despoil the pope and his cardinals, for such a deed that would have been "honorably wicked," that is, a "malice [that] has greatness in itself or is generous in some part" (D.I.27.1).[51] Likewise, he is by no means reluctant or anguished when advising princes to enter into evil; rather, the words burst out of him like a raging torrent:

> It is much safer to be feared than loved, if one has to lack one of the two. For one can say this generally of men: that they are ungrateful, fickle, pretenders and dissemblers, evaders of danger, eager for gain. While you do them good, they are yours, offering you their blood, property, lives, and children, as I said above, when the need for them is far away; but when it is close to you, they revolt. And that prince who

has founded himself entirely on their words, stripped of other preparation is ruined; for friendships that are acquired at a price and not with greatness and nobility of spirit are bought, but they are not owned and when the time comes they cannot be spent. And men have less hesitation to offend one who makes himself loved than one who makes himself feared; for love is held by a chain of obligation, which, because men are wicked, is broken at every opportunity for their own utility, but fear is held by a dread of punishment that never forsakes you. (P.XVII.66-67)

But where such rage is present, there is often an underlying and largely suppressed yearning for goodness that has been bitterly disappointed.[52] This genealogy of Machiavelli's morals is particularly suggested by his claims that make necessary evil a function of the others' wickedness; in addition to the above passage, we thus read that "if all men were good, this teaching would not be good; but because they are wicked and do not observe faith with you, you also do not have to observe it with them" (P.XVIII.69), and that a "man who wants to make a profession of good in all regards must come to ruin among so many who are not good" (P.XV.61).

Indeed, Machiavelli's awareness of the moral ideal–to which he thought men compare so poorly–was probably shaped by the very Christianity which he attacked so vehemently in other places; for he once belonged to a Company of Piety,[53] and, perhaps in this function, wrote a traditional oration on penitence and charity, whose forcefulness suggests something more than mere rhetoric:

Man is created for the good and honor of God, who gave him speech that he might praise him, gave him sight, turned not to the ground as with the other animals but turned to the sky, in order that he might always see it, gave him hands in order that he might build temples, offer sacrifices in his honor, gave him reason and intellect in order that he might consider and know the greatness of God. See then, with how much ingratitude man rises against such a great benefactor! And how much he merits punishment when he perverts the use of these things and turns them toward evil! And that tongue made to honor God blasphemes him; the mouth, by which he has to be nourished, he makes into a sewer and a way of satisfying the appetite and the belly with delicate and superfluous foods; those considerations about God he converts into considerations about the world; that appetite to preserve the human species becomes lust and a thousand other kinds of lasciviousness. And so, by these base deeds, man transforms himself from a rational animal into a brute animal.[54]

Thus, Machiavelli's anthropological pessimism has been associated with Augustine's doctrine of original sin, when man fell away from God and turned his gifts to wicked use.[55] But Machiavelli's pessimism goes much deeper than Augustine's; for the latter construed human wickedness as the contingent defect of a being created to be good and destined in time to be redeemed by the grace of its maker.[56] There is no such hope in Machiavelli. Since our first nature is a soulless potential for vicious license, any habituation to a civil way of life can only be temporary and is readily reversed by a fresh surge of ambition. This fact is exacerbated by the absence of a moral order in the world that could provide a pattern for human society in the form of natural or divine law: the occult order of the heavens consists merely of the mindless churning of a celestial mill, devoid of *telos* and thus bringing peace in one age and war in the next, without any permanent advance toward the good; and Fortune delights in afflicting the good and elevating the wicked.

On balance, Machiavelli undoubtedly issued a fundamental challenge to the classical tradition when he claimed that unjust violence represents an ordinary necessity for political order and excused it on consequentialist grounds, but he also–and probably unwittingly–drew on that same tradition when he described such violence as "evil." According to Eduard Wilhelm Mayer, the "leap into the transcendental is impossible for Machiavelli. He only believes in the world he sees. But he sees it in the deep shadow that was really a contrast to that world of light which for him was past and bygone."[57]

This clinging to the light of absolutist morality creates not only an inconsistency in Machiavelli's thought, but suggests nothing less than an incoherence in human reality itself: Since the creation and maintenance of political order necessitates deeds that men who "make a profession of good in all regards" (P.XV.61) would never do, one can either be a effective ruler or a truly good man–but not both. Machiavelli describes this incoherence primarily as a tension between public and private life: "a republic and a people [act] very differently from a private person";[58] and war is a "profession by which men cannot live decently all the time, which cannot be done as a profession except by a republic or a kingdom" (AG.I.305). Most important, when discussing the maxim that new princes should make everything new in their states–in imitation of Philip of Macedon who "transferred men from province to province as herdsmen transfer their herds"–Machiavelli states that

these modes are very cruel, and enemies to every way of life, not only
Christian but human; and any man whatever should flee them and wish
to live in private than as a king with so much ruin to men.
Nonetheless, he who does not wish to take this first way of the good
must enter into this evil one if he wishes to maintain himself. But men
take certain middle ways that are very harmful, for they do not know
how to be either altogether wicked or altogether good. (D.I.26)

The human condition is such that men face a stark choice: they can
either uphold absolutist morality by remaining in private life, or they
must enter into consequentialist evil if they want to succeed in
political life.[59] Politics requires men who can make tough choices and
are not afraid of getting their hands dirty, who are prepared to sell
their souls to the devil in order to procure the goods of Fortune for
their city, even if it means abandoning their hopes for personal
salvation–as Machiavelli seems to have been eager to when he cried
"I love my fatherland more than my soul" (L.321.1010).[60]

But even the private sphere ultimately cannot escape the need for
unjust force and fraud, as Machiavelli's comedies readily suggest.[61] In
Mandragola, the young and fiery Callimaco lusts for Lucrezia, a
young woman married to an old man. Disguising himself as a doctor,
Callimaco persuades the couple that their barrenness would end if
Lucrezia betook of a potion called "mandrake" (which lends the play
its name). However, since it is quite possible that the man who first
lies with Lucrezia will die from the medicine's side-effects, an
unwitting youth must be found who takes her husband's place during
the first night. This youth, of course, will be no other than Callimaco
in disguise. To persuade the pious Lucrezia to participate in this
scheme, which involves not only adultery but risks an innocent life,
the corrupt Brother Timoteo resorts to a consequentialist argument
that compares her to Lot's daughters, who committed incest with
their father as the necessary means for propagating the human race.
Once the fraud has succeeded, Callimaco drops his mask and professes
his passion for Lucrezia, who shows her true colors by readily taking
him as her secret lover on grounds of his superior virility.

In Machiavelli's comedy *Clizia,* the aged Nicomacho plans to
have surreptitious intercourse with his step-daughter by marrying her
to a servant who would let Nicomacho take his place in the conjugal
bed under the cover of darkness. However, this scheme is undone by
the counter-fraud of his clever wife Sofronia, who gets another
servant to disguise himself as Clizia, to resist Nicomacho's advances
in the bridal chamber with force, and, finally, abandon his disguise to
make a laughingstock of the old man. Thoroughly shamed, Nicomaco

submits to Sofronia's rule.

The principal inference from these vulgar farces seems to be this: by withdrawing into private life, human beings may be able to shun the wholesale slaughter and dislocation that rulers have to impose on their subjects in order to generate the political good, but they cannot avoid deception, adultery, indeed, negligent homicide in order to realize the sexual good.[62] Absolutist morality thus clashes with consequentialist wickedness in private life as well.

Hence, there is no single overarching truth with regard to how we should live; for what is politically and sexually expedient is morally wrong–insofar as a city's prosperity rests on injury to innocents and carnal success on manipulation and violence, and what is morally right is politically and sexually ineffective–insofar as saintly leaders fail to protect their communities and scrupulous men fail to seduce the most alluring women. Thus, Socrates was wrong when he equated the Good and the True and claimed in particular that the "just come to light as wiser and better and more able to accomplish something" than the unjust; conversely, the sophist Thrasymachus was right when he avered that "injustice, when it comes into being on a sufficient scale, is mightier, freer, and more masterful than justice."[63] In other words, success in attaining the goods of Fortune and Venus is incompatible with doing what is right.

This incompatibility can also be understood as the historical conflict between, on the one hand, the ethic of the pre-Socratic Greeks and pagan Romans, and, on the other, that of the Hebrew, Socratic, and Christian traditions; for the former was consequentialist insofar as it readily sacrificed individuals to the safety and greatness of the city, whereas the latter discovered that certain actions are essentially wrong and therefore always prohibited. In other words, Machiavelli uncovered a clash between two ultimate sets of ends: the worship of glory, mastery, wealth, and sexuality as opposed to the cultivation of the goods of the soul. In the words of Isaiah Berlin,

> Machiavelli's cardinal achievement is . . . his uncovering of an insoluble dilemma, the planting of a permanent question mark in the path of posterity. It stems from his *de facto* recognition that ends equally ultimate, equally sacred, may contradict each other, that entire systems of value may come into collision without possibility of rational arbitration, and that not merely in exceptional circumstances, as a result of abnormality or accident or error . . . but (this was surely new) as part of the normal human situation.[64]

More concretely, "there exist at least two sets of virtues–let us call them the Christian and the pagan–which are not merely in practice, but in principle, incompatible."[65]

Moreover, insofar as we accept that something in both of these ethics is true, we must abandon the "idea of the world and of human society as a single intelligible structure," that is, the "unifying monistic pattern . . . at the very hearth of traditional rationalism, religious and atheistic, metaphysical and scientific, transcendental and naturalistic, that has been characteristic of Western civilization."[66] In other words, if we thoroughly examine ourselves, we will arrive at the unsettling conclusion that there are at least two mutually exclusive ways of life that appeal to us intrinsically, and that we possess no nonarbitrary criterion by which to judge their comparative merit. For instance, we cannot help but feel admiration for the artistic and intellectual achievements of the Greeks and the great empire of the Romans, but, after centuries of Socratic and Christian teaching, have also come to sense intuitively that every human being deserves respect. Yet, slavery may have been the necessary means for the flowering of Greek civilization, and brutal wars of conquest surely were a prequisite for the greatness of the Roman Empire–which seems to render at least some kinds of great achievement incompatible with respect for persons. But how are we to decide between these goods, none of which we can give up entirely?

In other words, the world is not a *cosmos* where everything is ultimately subsumed under a supreme final cause, such as the Platonic Idea of the Good or the will of God, but a *chaos* where actions in pursuit of one set of ends are detrimental to the attainment of another. Thus, Machiavelli reaches back to the world of Homeric epos and Greek tragedy, where human beings are caught up in the pursuit of antagonistic principles that tend to their destruction. Accordingly, there is a kinship between *virtù* which enables Machiavelli's princes to cope with the vicissitudes of Fortune, and *arete* which makes heroes like Achilles overcome their fear of death and savor cataclysmic conflict.[67] Indeed, Machiavelli seems to suggest as much when he makes Achilles the model for princes who need to know "how to use the beast and the man," that is, fight not only with laws but also with force and fraud (P.XVIII.69).[68] However, this comparison is wanting at least in this respect: Whereas Homeric and tragic heroes contemn the vulgar concern with comfortable existence and destroy themselves and their dependents in a reckless quest for honor and mastery, Machiavelli wants his princes to use violence economically in order to secure themselves and to provide for the common good, which, in turn, puts the preservation of the city before its reputation. In other words, if Nietzsche is to be believed, the pre-Socratic Greeks and Romans had the "pessimism of strength" to affirm the *agon* (strife) as an occasion to discharge their will to power,[69] whereas Machiavelli deplored it as an evil because he had already been enfeebled by Christian morals.

Notes

1. Cf. G. H. R. Parkinson, "Ethics and Politics in Machiavelli," *Philosophical Quarterly* 5, no. 18 (January 1955): 37-44; David E. Ingersoll, "The Constant Prince: Private Interests and Public Goals in Machiavelli," *Western Political Quarterly* 21, no. 4 (December 1968): 588-96.

2. Cf. DF.25; FH.III.1.

3. On ancient and especially Roman ideas of glory, see Ulrich Knoche, "Der römische Ruhmesgedanke" [1937], in *Römische Wertbegriffe,* ed. Hans Oppermann, Wege der Forschung, vol. 34 (Darmstadt: Wissenschaftliche Buchgesellschaft, 1967), 420-45; Maria Rosa Lida de Malkiel, *L'idée de la gloire dans la tradition occidentale: Antiquité, moyen-age occidental, Castille* [1952], trans. Sylvia Roubaud (Paris: C. Klincksieck, 1968), 17-86; Günther B. Philipp, "Zur Problematik des römischen Ruhmesgedankens," *Gymnasium: Zeitschrift für Kultur der Antike und humanistische Bildung* 62, no. 1 (1955): 51-82; D. C. Earl, *The Moral and Political Tradition of Rome* (Ithaca: Cornell University Press, 1967), passim. On glory and its synonyms in Machiavelli, see Russell Price, "The Theme of *gloria* in Machiavelli," *Renaissance Quarterly* 30, no. 4 (winter 1977): 588-631.

4. See D.I.1.3 together with D.I.2.1.

5. Cf. D.III.28.1.

6. Cf. D.II.6.1-2, 19.1; D.III.16.2, 25.1.

7. See D.III.2, 5, 26.2, 49.1. Cf. Livy, *The Early History of Rome: Books I-V of* The History of Rome From Its Foundation, trans. Aubrey de Sélincourt (London: Penguin Books, 1960), I.57-60; Livy, *Rome and the Mediterranean: Books XXXI-XLV of* The History of Rome From Its Foundation, trans. Henry Bettenson (London: Penguin Books, 1976), XXXIX.8-22.

8. On Machiavelli's notion of liberty, see also Marcia L. Colish, "The Idea of Liberty in Machiavelli," *Journal of the History of Ideas* 32, no. 3 (July-September 1971): 323-50. Quentin Skinner, "The Republican Ideal of Political Liberty," in *Machiavelli and Republicanism,* ed. Gisela Bock, Quentin Skinner, and Maurizio Viroli (Cambridge: Cambridge University Press, 1990), 293-309.

9. Cf. D.I.2.1, 18.3.

10. Cf. Polybius, *The Rise of the Roman Empire,* trans. Ian Scott-Kilvert (London: Penguin Classics, 1979), VI.5.

11. See Anthony J. Parel, "Machiavelli on Justice," *Machiavelli Studies* I (1987): 65-81.

12. *Allocuzione fatto ad un magistrato* [Address given to a magistrate], in

TO.36-37, at 36, mt.

13. Cf. P.VI.25; D.I.10.1. On the goods of Fortune in antiquity, see Quentin Skinner, *Machiavelli* (New York: Hill and Wang, 1981), 25; Thomas Flanagan, "The Concept of *Fortuna* in Machiavelli," in *The Political Calculus,* ed. Anthony Parel (Toronto: University of Toronto Press, 1972), 127-56, at 143.

14. Cf D.III.5.1.

15. Cf. D.I.37.3; D.III.6.4; FH.VI.30.

16. Max Weber, *Politics As a Vocation* [1921], in *From Max Weber: Essays in Sociology,* trans. H. H. Gerth and C. Wright Mills (NewYork: Oxford University Press, 1946), 77-128, esp. 115-21.

17. Cf. P.VIII.38; D.I.18.4; 44.2.

18. Cf. P.XVIII.71; FH.III.13; "Mission to the Court of Rome," in W.III.284-388, at 291.

19. Cf. P.XVI.63.

20. Cf. Parkinson, "Ethics and Politics in Machiavelli."

21. See Michael Walzer, "Political Action: The Problem of Dirty Hands," *Philosophy and Public Affairs* 2, no. 2 (winter 1973): 160-80, at 170, 175-76; cf. Carl. J. Friedrich, *Constitutional Reason of State* (Providence, R.I.: Brown University Press, 1957), 23-24, note 15.

22. See J. L. Austin, "A Plea for Excuses," in *Philosophical Papers,* ed. J. O. Urmson and G. J. Warnock (Oxford: Oxford University Press, 1961), 123-52.

23. "Mission to the Duke of Valentinois," in W.III.141-280, at 269; cf. D.I.10.3, 6. Note also that Machiavelli refers to the murders which Cleomenes committed to renew the laws of Sparta as "just and praiseworthy," before reiterating that "for the death of Remus and Titus Tatius, Romulus deserves excuse and not blame" (D.I.9.4-5).

24. Reginald Cardinal Pole, *Apologia Reginaldi Poli ad Carolum V. Caesarem* [1539], in *Epistolarum Reginaldi Poli S. R. E. Cardinalis et aliorum ad ipsum collectio,* ed. Angelo M. Quirini, vol. I (Brescia, 1744-57; reprinted Farnborough, England: Gregg Press, 1967), 66-172, at 151, 137. On Cardinal Pole and Machiavelli, see also Peter S. Donaldson, *Machiavelli and Mystery of State* (Cambridge: Cambridge University Press, 1988), ch. 1.

25. Leslie J. Walker, "Introduction by the Translator," in *The Discourses of Niccolò Machiavelli,* trans. Leslie J. Walker (New Haven: Yale University Press, 1950), vol. I, 1-164, at 3, 7.

26. See Innocent Gentillet, *Anti-Machiavel* [1576], ed. C. Edward Rathé (Geneva: Librairie Droz, 1968), whose original title was *Discours sur les moyens de bien gouverner et maintenir en bonne paix un royaume ou autre principauté–contre Nicolas Machiavel;* Claudio Clemente, *El machiavellismo degollado* (1637), quoted in Richard C. Clark, "Machiavelli: Bibliographical Spectrum," *Review of National Literatures* 1, no. 1 (spring 1970): 93-135, at 99. For general surveys of Machiavelli's reception across the centuries, see also Eric W. Cochrane, "Machiavelli: 1940-1960," *Journal of Modern History* 33, no. 2 (June 1961): 113-36; Giuseppe Prezzolini, *Machiavelli,* trans. Gioconda Savini (New York: Farrar, Straus & Giroux, 1967), chs. 6-7; Felix Gilbert,

"Machiavellism," in *Dictionary of the History of Ideas,* ed. Philip P. Wiener (New York: Scribner's Sons, 1973), 116-26.

27. Leo Strauss, *Thoughts on Machiavelli* (Chicago: University of Chicago Press, 1958), 9, 232.

28. See Augustine, *The City of God,* in *Political Writings,* trans. Michael W. Tkacz and Douglas Kries (Indianapolis: Hackett, 1994), 3-201, at V.15-19; XIV.13, 28; XIX.13, 19; XXII.30.

29. See Lida de Malkiel, *L'idée de la gloire,* 107-150; Quentin Skinner, *The Foundations of Modern Political Thought,* vol. 1, *The Renaissance* (Cambridge: Cambridge University Press, 1978), 80, 91-101, 118-22; Quentin Skinner, "Machiavelli's *Discorsi* and the Pre-humanist Origins of Republican Ideas," in *Machiavelli and Republicanism,* ed. Gisela Bock, Quentin Skinner, and Maurizio Viroli (Cambridge: Cambridge University Press, 1990), 121-41, at 123-34.

30. Alan Donagan, *The Theory of Morality* (Chicago: University of Chicago Press, 1977), 36, 81-90, 151, 152, 154-55, 173. For modernity, this principle has been framed by Kant as the second formulation of the categorical imperative: *"Act in such a way that you always treat humanity, whether in your own person or in the person of any other, never simply as a means, but always at the same time as an end"*; see Immanuel Kant, *Groundwork of the Metaphysics of Morals* [1785], trans. H. J. Patton (New York: Harper Torchbooks, 1964), 96.

31. See Cicero, *On Duties,* trans. Walter Miller, Loeb Classical Library 30 (Cambridge, Mass.: Harvard University Press, 1913), I.vii.20, 23, 41, I.x.31-32, I.xxx.108-109, II.xiv.51, II.xxi.73-73, II.xxiv.85, III.vi.30-31, III.xxiii.90, III.xxiv.93, III.xxv.95, III.xxix.107; Cicero, *De Inventione,* trans. H. M. Hubbell, Loeb Classical Library 386 (Cambridge, Mass.: Harvard University Press, 1949), I.xxxviii.68-69, II.xxv.75, II.lvi-lviii.168-75; Cicero, *De Legibus,* trans. C. W. Keyes, Loeb Classical Library 213 (Cambridge, Mass.: Harvard University Press, 1928), III.iii.8, III.xviii.42; Cicero, *De Oratore,* trans. E. W. Sutton and H. Rackham, Loeb Classical Library 348-349 (Cambridge, Mass.: Harvard University Press, 1942), I.xlv.201, I.xlviii.211, II.lxxxii.334-35; Cicero, *De Partitione Oratoria,* trans. H. Rackham, Loeb Classical Library 349 (Cambridge, Mass.: Harvard University Press, 1942), xxiv.83-88, xxx.104-106; Cicero, *De Re Publica,* trans. C. W. Keyes, Loeb Classical Library 213 (Cambridge, Mass.: Harvard University Press, 1928), III.xxii.34-35.

32. Cicero, *Brutus,* trans. G. L. Hendrickson, Loeb Classical Library 342 (Cambridge, Mass.: Harvard University Press, 1971), xxvii.103; Cicero, *On Duties,* II.xii.43, mt. Cf. Cicero, *On Duties,* III.iv.19; Cicero, *De Partitione Oratoria,* xxx.104-106; Cicero, *De Re Publica,* II.xxv.46.

33. Cicero, *On Duties,* I.xlv.159. Note that Machiavelli directly–and in all likelihood wittingly–negates this passage, when he writes that "where one deliberates entirely on the safety of his fatherland, there ought not to enter any consideration of either just or unjust, merciful or cruel, praiseworthy or ignominious" (D.III.41).

34. Cicero, *On Duties,* I.xxiv.82, I.xlv.159, III.v.21-22, III.vi.28, III.x-

xv.40-64, III.xxi.83, III.xxii.86-88, III.xxv.95; Cicero, *De Amicitia,* trans. W. A. Falconer, Loeb Classical Library 154 (Cambridge, Mass.: Harvard University Press, 1923), xvii.61.

35. Cicero, *On Duties,* I.xlv.159.

36. Cicero, *On Duties,* III.x.40-41, mt.

37. Cicero, *On Duties,* III.vii.34; cf. II.iii.9, II.xii.42, III.iii.11, III.iv.19-20, III.vii-viii.33-36, III.x.40, III.xii.49, III.xv.64, II.xviii-xxi.74-85, III.xxviii.101, III.xxx.110.

38. Cicero, *On Duties,* III.iii.11, III.viii.34-35, III.xviii.75.

39. Cicero, *On Duties,* II.xi.40.

40. Cicero, *On Duties,* III.v.21.

41. See Theodor Mommsen, *Römisches Staatsrecht* [1888], 4th ed. (Tübingen: Wissenschaftliche Buchgemeinschaft, 1952), I.687-97; III.1240-51.

42. Mommsen, *Römisches Staatsrecht,* I.697.

43. Paul Krüger and Theodor Mommsen, eds., *Corpus iuris civilis,* vol. 1, 17th ed. (Hildesheim: Weidmann, 1963), *Digestes* 1.4.1, 1.4.2, 1.3.31; *Institutiones* 1.2.6. Cf. P. G. Stein, "Roman Law," in *The Cambridge History of Medieval Political Thought c. 350-c.1450,* ed. J. H. Burns (Cambridge: Cambridge University Press, 1988), 37-47; Gaines Post, *Studies in Medieval Legal Thought: Public Law and the State, 1100-1322* (Princeton: Princeton University Press, 1964), 258-60.

44. See Post, *Medieval Legal Thought,* ch. 5; Friedrich Meinecke, *Machiavellism: The Doctrine of Raison d' Etat and Its Place in Modern History* [1924], trans. Douglas Scott (Boulder: Westview Press, 1984), 27-29.

45. Post, *Medieval Legal Thought,* 251, 306. Cf. Kurt Kluxen, *Politik und menschliche Existenz bei Machiavelli: Dargestellt am Begriff der Necessità* (Stuttgart: W. Kohlhammer, 1967), 29-29; Berlin, "Originality of Machiavelli," 189, 200.

46. See Aquinas, *Summa Theologiae,* Pt. I-II, Q. 19, A. 6; Pt. II-II, Q. 62, A. 2; Pt. III, Q. 64, A. 6. Cf. Donagan, *Theory of Morality,* 144-45.

47. Donagan, *Theory of Morality,* 2-7.

48. Cf. FH.V.8.

49 *Discorso o dialogo intorno all nostra lingua* [Discourse or dialogue internal to our language], in TO.923-30, at 924, mt.

50. *Plato's Republic,* 2nd ed., trans. Allan Bloom (New York: Basic Books, 1968), 332d, 338c.

51. Cf. "Second Mission to the Court of Rome," in W.IV.10-75, at 35-36.

52. Cf. Sebastian De Grazia, *Machiavelli in Hell* (New York: Random House, 1994), ch. 4.

53. Oreste Tommasini, *La vita e gli scritti di Machiavelli nello loro relazione col machiavellismo,* vol. 2 (Rome: E. Loescher, 1911), 386.

54. [*Exortatione alla penitenzia*] [Exhortation to penitence], in TO.932-34, at 933, mt; cf. GA.VIII.974-75; A.984. Cf. Donald Weinstein, "Machiavelli and Savonarola," in *Studies on Machiavelli,* ed. Myron P. Gilmore (Florence: Sansoni, 1972), 253-64, esp. 260-62; De Grazia, *Machiavelli in Hell,* 73-75.

55. See Giuseppe Prezzolini, "The Christian Roots of Machiavelli's Moral

Pessimism," *Review of National Literatures* 1, no. 1 (spring 1970): 26-37; Silvia Ruffo-Fiore, "Machiavelli and Reinhold Niebuhr: Politics and Christian Pragmatism," *Machiavelli Studies* I (1987): 127-36.

56. See Augustine, *City of God,* IV.33, XI.17, XII.1, XII.28, XIII.14, XIV.6, XIV.11.

57. Eduard Wilhelm Mayer, *Machiavellis Geschichtsauffassung und sein Begriff virtù: Studien zu seiner Historik* (Munich: R. Oldenbourg, 1912), 9, mt. Cf. Heinrich von Treitschke, *Politics* [1897], trans. Blanche Dugdale and Torben de Bille (New York: Macmillan, 1916), I.84.

58. "Mission to the Emperor of Germany," in W.IV.83-154, at 96. Note that the report in which this statement appears was signed by Francesco Vettori, but reportedly written by Machiavelli.

59. Cf. Ernesto Landi, "The Political Philosophy of Machiavelli." *History Today* 14, no. 7 (July 1964): 550-55, at 554.

60. Cf. FH.III.8; AG.I.302; "Mission to the Emperor of Germany," in W.IV.83-154, at 111. According to Pasquale Villari, Machiavelli gleaned this notion from the Florentine chronicles of Gino di Neri Capponi, who wrote of choosing "for the Ten of the Balìa practical men who love the commune better than their own welfare and their own souls," since it was impossible to maintain the government in accordance with Christian precepts. See Pasquale Villari, *The Life and Times of Niccolò Machiavelli,* new ed., trans. Linda Villari (London: T. Fisher Unwin, 1892), II.87, 433.

61. Cf. Mark Hulliung, *Citizen Machiavelli* (Princeton: Princeton University Press, 1983), 103-04.

62. Thus, sexual activity is reckoned by Machiavelli not only as one of our principal desires, but also elevated to a good–in agreement with his naturalistic approach to ethics. Indeed, he suggests as much when he introduces *Mandragola* with the same reference to ancient greatness as the *Discourses:* "from ancient *virtù* the present age *in everything* is degenerate" (M.Pr, ea); "no sign of that ancient *virtù* remains with us" (D.I.Pr.2). In other words, a man of *virtù* should worship Fortune in public and Venus in private.

63. *Plato's Republic,* 352b, 344c.

64. Berlin, "Originality of Machiavelli," 201.

65. Berlin, "Originality of Machiavelli," 195.

66. Berlin, "Originality of Machiavelli," 194.

67. See John H. Geerken, "Homer's Image of the Hero in Machiavelli: A Comparison of *arete* and *virtù,*" *Italian Quarterly* 14 (1970): 45-90. Cf. Michael Palmer, "Machiavellian *virtù* and Thucydidean *arete:* Traditional Virtue and Political Wisdom in Thucydides," *Review of Politics* 51, no. 3 (summer 1989): 365-85.

68. Cf. P.XIV.60.

69. According to Nietzsche, "pessimism of strength" is "an intellectual predilection for the hard gruesome, evil, problematic aspect of existence, prompted by well-being, by overflowing health, by the *fullness* of existence," a "sharp-eyed courage that tempts and attempts, that *craves* the frightful as the enemy, the worthy enemy, against whom one can test one's strength." See

Friedrich Nietzsche, *The Birth of Tragedy and The Case of Wagner* [1872], trans. Walter Kaufmann (New York: Random House, 1967), 17-18; cf. 20-21.

Chapter 5

Principalities and Republics

The Natural Condition of License

Machiavelli's assumption that human beings are individuals implies that they can exist in a prepolitical condition, where organized collectivities, such as principalities and republics, are absent. Machiavelli first of all describes this condition in historical terms. Drawing on Polybius's account of the origin of political society, he asserts that "since the inhabitants were sparse in the beginning of the world, they lived dispersed for a time in likeness to beasts" (D.I.2.3)– even though Polybius states that they were "herding together like animals."[1] In other words, whereas the Greek historian maintained the classical assumption that human beings are by nature social animals, Machiavelli emphasizes their individual nature.[2] He also gives an astrological gloss to Polybius's claim that natural disasters have repeatedly destroyed the human race, eliminating all knowledge of arts and social institutions and throwing men back into their original condition:[3]

> The memories of times are eliminated by diverse causes, of which part come from men, part from heaven. Those that come from men are the variations of sects and languages. . . . And because these sects vary two or three times in five or in six thousand years, the memory of the things done prior to that time is lost. . . . As to the causes that come

from heaven, they are those that eliminate the human race and reduce the inhabitants of part of the world to a few. This comes about either through plagues or through famine or through an inundation of waters. The most important is the last, both because it is more universal and because those who are saved are all mountain men and coarse, who, since they do not have knowledge of antiquity, cannot leave it to posterity. (D.II.5.1-2)[4]

Second, Machiavelli conceives this prepolitical condition as a state of "license" or anarchy, to which men revert when neither a prince nor good customs prevent them from acting on their first nature. In Florence, this happened "after 1494, when the princes of the city had been expelled . . . and no ordered government was there, but rather a certain ambitious license, and public things were going from bad to worse" (D.I.47.3). Machiavelli ascribes such license to the common people rather than the nobility, because the primary ambition of the people is to be free from all constraint in order to enjoy their possessions, whereas the great seek to rule and thereby tend to impose order: "the ministers of license . . . are the men of the people" while "the ministers of servitude . . . are the nobles" (FH.IV.1).[5] Overall, human beings live in one of three conditions: "principality or liberty or license" (P.IX.39); for they live either without government, that is, in license, or under government, of which there are only two stable forms, namely principality and republic (i.e., liberty).[6] In short, Machiavelli's notion of license refers to the natural condition of individuals in the absence of central authority–akin to Hobbes's concept of the state of nature.[7]

As with Hobbes, the principal result of this condition is a state of war among individuals. According to a Florentine plebeian, "men devour one another and . . . those who can do less are always worst off. Therefore one should use force whenever the occasion for it is given" (FH.III.13). Or as King Ferdinand the Catholic put it, "men often act like certain lesser birds of prey, in whom there is such a desire to catch their prey, to which nature urges them, that they do not sense another larger bird that is above them so as to kill them" (D.I.40.7).

On the occult level, this condition of *homo homini lupus* can be explained by the malicious agency of Fortune, who, "to deprive us of peace and to set us at war, to take away every quiet and every good, sent two furies to inhabit earth," namely Ambition and Avarice (A.984).[8] On the psychological level, the causes of conflict are two: ambition for greater satisfactions than hitherto attained, and fear of being attacked that prompts a first strike; in Machiavelli's words, "since some men desire to have more and some fear to lose what has been acquired, they come to enmities and to war" (D.I.37.1).[9] More precisely, conflict arises from ambition when two or more individuals strive for goods that cannot be enjoyed jointly, such as the greatest glory, sole dominion, private property, and the exclusive favors of a woman. Thus, the struggle between the nobles and the plebs of Rome intensified when the latter began "to engage in combat through ambition, and to wish to divide honors and belongings with the nobility as the thing most esteemed by men" (D.I.37.1). In other words, ambition leads to strife when one man's gain implies another's loss; in Machiavelli's words, "ambition results in two kinds of action: one party robs and the other weeps" (A.986).

While Machiavelli's explanation of conflict from ambition is straightforward and traditional, his explanation from fear is complex and innovative, foreshadowing Hobbes's notion of "anticipation" by several centuries.[10] Conflict arises from fear when an individual imagines it possible or even likely that another might seek to deprive him of a particular good, and then tries to forestall such an event by seizing the good or attacking the other before the latter can do so in turn. Machiavelli clearly draws on this anticipatory reasoning when he explains how a prince responds to his fear of conspiracies: "conspiracies by their example give him cause to fear; and in fearing, to secure himself; and securing himself, to injure" (FH.VIII.1).[11] The same reasoning gives rise to the ingratitude of princes toward victorious generals:

> It is impossible that the suspicion suddenly arising in the prince after the victory of his captain not be increased by that same one because of some mode or term of his used insolently. So the prince cannot but think of securing himself against him; and to do this, he thinks either of having him put to death or of taking away the reputation that he has gained for himself in his army and in his peoples. (D.I.29.1)

Moreover, the incentive to strike first doubles when we have reason to believe that the others suspect us of aggressive designs and thus have an incentive to strike first in their turn; this happens, for instance, when "necessity constrains you to do to the prince that which you see that the prince would like to do to you, which is so great that it does not give you time except to think about securing yourself" (D.III.6.10).[12] Since such a reason can never be fully excluded, there arises a vicious circle of mutual fear that soon makes anticipatory violence a perceived necessity on all sides. Republics are ruined in this way, as "the desire to defend liberty made each one try to prevail so much that he oppressed the other," for

> the order of these accidents is that when men seek not to fear, they
> begin to make others fear; and the injury that they dispel from
> themselves they put upon another, as if it were necessary to offend or to
> be offended. (D.I.46.1)[13]

Conflict from fear thus arises as the unintended consequence of our
desire to preserve ourselves and the goods we enjoy. This consequence
is ultimately a necessary one, because most of our goods, such as life,
power, possessions, liberty, are already threatened by the mere
presence of others with the capability to deprive us of them,
regardless of their intentions; for we can never know for certain what
they intend to do and must assume the worst to minimize the risk of
losing what is dearest to us.

The Generation of Political Order

Although the condition of license is natural to human beings, it entails
severe problems. Given the absence of central authority, the
possession of goods is very insecure, as "God and nature have put all
the fortunes of men in their midst, where they are exposed more to
rapine than to industry and more to wicked than to good arts"
(FH.III.13). Without a government to protect and organize them,
men also fail to increase the total amount of goods through
cooperation, as "riches are seen to multiply [in republics] in larger
number . . . for each willingly multiplies that thing and seeks to
acquire those goods he believes he can enjoy once acquired"
(D.II.2.3). And glory–the highest good–cannot exist among
individuals that live dispersed because they lack the shared opinion
that bestows recognition.

    To overcome these difficulties, men living in license must form a
political order. Thus, "cities are built . . . when it does not appear, to
inhabitants dispersed in many small parts, that they live securely,
since each part by itself, because of the site and because of the small
number, cannot resist the thrust of whoever assaults it" (D.I.1.1).[14]
There are two fundamental ways of organizing a dispersed multitude
into a political order: by a kind of social contract and by the authority
of a prince; in Machiavelli's words, "to flee these dangers [of the
original condition], moved either by themselves or by someone
among them of greater authority, they are restrained to inhabit

together a place elected by them, more advantageous to live and easier to defend" (D.I.1.1). In an instance of a self-moved founding, those Romans who, in the fifth century, had fled from the Huns to the islands at the tip of the Adriatic Sea "began among themselves, without any particular prince who might order them, live under the laws that appeared to them most apt to maintain them," thus forming the city of Venice (D.I.1.2).[15] However, this leaderless founding succeeded only because the place enjoyed natural defenses: "it turned out happily for them because of the long idleness that the site gave them, since the sea had no exit and the peoples who were afflicting Italy had no ships able to plague them: so any small beginning would have enabled them to come to the greatness they have" (D.I.1.2).

But natural defenses are exceptions; in general, cities need to be founded by princes in order to grow to greatness. This can be seen from the two most glorious ancient cities–Athens and Rome; for Athens "was built . . . by the dispersed inhabitants [of Attica] under the authority of Theseus" (D.I.1.2), and Rome was established by Romulus and Numa, who "imposed" laws that made it "full of as much *virtù* as has ever adorned any other city" (D.I.1.5). Consequently, "this should be taken as a general rule: that it never or rarely happen that any republic or kingdom is ordered well from the beginning . . . unless it is ordered by one individual. Indeed it is necessary that one alone give the mode and that any such ordering depend on his mind" (D.I.9.2). The reason lies with the collective-action problem that befalls a leaderless multitude, as "many are not capable of ordering a thing because they do not know its good, which is because of the diverse opinions among them" (D.I.9.2).

To "have authority alone" (D.I.9.2), a founder needs to eliminate his rivals to power as well as those who dispute his designs. Thus, Romulus, as we know, killed his brother Remus and consented to the death of Titus Tatius with whom he had shared rule, and Moses put to death thousands who had worshipped the golden calf. Likewise, Cleomenes "had all the ephors and anyone else who might be able to stand against him killed" in order to renew the laws of Lycurgus at Sparta (D.I.9.4). Among contemporary princes, Cesare Borgia laid "good foundations for his power" by ridding himself of the Orsini; first he "gained to himself all their adherents . . . by making them his gentlemen and by giving them large allowances," and then "waited for an opportunity to eliminate the Orsini chiefs"–which came when, trusting his professions of friendship, they came as his guests to Sinigaglia, where he had them strangled (P.VII.29).[16]

New Principality

When founders like "Moses, Cyrus, Theseus, Romulus" impose order
on a licentious multitude, they thereby create "principalities that are
altogether new both in prince and in state" (P.VI.21-22). Being
endowed with a first-rate brain that "understands by itself"
(P.XXII.92), these dominators realize that a condition of license–or,
alternatively, enslavement by foreigners–provides an "opportunity to
someone prudent and *virtuoso* to introduce a form that would bring
honor to him and good to the universality" (P.XXVI.102, mt).
Hence, "it was necessary for anyone wanting to see the *virtù* of Moses
that the people of Israel be enslaved in Egypt, and to learn the
greatness of spirit of Cyrus, that the Persians be oppressed by the
Medes, and to learn the excellence of Theseus, that the Athenians be
dispersed" (P.XXVI.102); "such opportunities . . . made these men
successful, and their excellent *virtù* enabled the opportunity to be
recognized; hence their fatherlands were ennobled by it and became
very prosperous" (P.VI.23).

In contrast, men with a second-rate brain–one that "discerns what
others understand" (P.XXII.92)–tend to become new princes by
usurping authority in an already existing order, like the mercenary
captain Francesco Sforza, who "became duke of Milan from private
individual" by turning his arms against his employer (P.VII.26).[17]
Since such men are usually "deceived by a false good and a false
glory," they "turn to tyranny," even "though, to their perpetual
honor, they are able to make a republic or a kingdom" (D.I.10.1). For
instance, the "*virtù* of spirit and body" of Agathocles was such that it
enabled him to rise through the ranks of the Syracusan military, until
he had enough power to kill the leading men of the city and become
its tyrant; however, since he "kept to a life of crime at every rank of
his career," rather than using his power to introduce good orders, he
cannot be "celebrated among the most excellent men" (P.VIII.34-
35), that is, true founders.

Both founders and usurpers rule autocratically; for to "become
prince" of a city is to be "able to dispose it in one's own mode"
(D.I.18.4). In other words, princely will constitutes the ordering
principle of a new principality. In contrast, as we shall see below, the
ordering principle of hereditary, mixed, and ecclesiastical
principalities is custom, and that of civil principalities and republics
consists of laws and institutions. Further, the reasons why people obey
these fonts of authority will be threefold as well: (1) fear of injury at
the hands of prince, magistrates, gods, and foreigners; (2) habituation

to a line of princes, to a set of laws, or to gods and religious rituals; (3) expectation of benefits in exchange for obedience. Thus, to return to the present topic, how do new princes make themselves obeyed?

In new principalities, the fundamental cause of compliance is dread of violent punishment by the prince. Hence, principalities "are acquired either with the arms of others or with one's own" (P.I.6), and "one must always offend those over whom he becomes a new prince, both with men-at-arms and with infinite other injuries" (P.III.8). This holds especially in a condition of license "full of robberies, quarrels, and every other kind of insolence," which requires a "cruel and ready man" to be restored to "peace and unity" (P.VII.29).[18] Further, there is no surer way to impose one's will on others than to threaten them with violence because almost everyone will submit rather than suffer injury or death. True, there are cases where individuals have chosen death for the sake of honor; but, as a general rule, it holds that "there is no proportion between one who is armed and one who is unarmed" (P.XIV.58).[19] Hence, a prince should make himself feared rather than loved in order to be obeyed, as "fear is held by a dread of punishment that never forsakes you" (P.XVII.67). In other words, force is a quasi-objective cause of compliance because the threat of death generates supreme necessity in the spirits of men.

On the other hand, the injuries inflicted by a new prince should not go beyond what is necessary. He should "make himself feared in such a mode that if he does not acquire love, he escapes hatred," and "this he will always do if he abstains from the property of his citizens and his subjects, and from their women" (P.XVII.67). More precisely, those "cruelties . . . can be called well used . . . that are done at a stroke, out of the necessity to secure oneself, and then are not persisted in," whereas "those cruelties are badly used which, though few in the beginning, rather grow with time than are eliminated"; hence, a new prince should "examine all the offenses necessary for him to commit, and do them all at a stroke, so as not to have to renew them every day" (P.VIII.37-38). In Sheldon Wolin's felicitous phrase, Machiavelli thus aims at an "economy of violence."[20]

Next, a new prince can strengthen his position by religious fraud, that is, make the subjects believe that they will be punished by the gods if they disobey his will. Numa, the second king of Rome, thus "pretended to be intimate with a nymph who counseled him on what he had to counsel the people . . . because he wished to put new and unaccustomed orders in the city and doubted that his authority would suffice"; as a result of the religion introduced by Numa, the Romans "feared to break an oath much more than the laws, like those who esteem the power of God more than that of men" (D.I.11.1-2). In psychological terms, Numa generated false images in the minds of the many, exploiting their inability to understand the world at large, for a founder "knows many goods that do not have in themselves evident reasons with which one can persuade others. Thus wise men . . . have recourse to God" (D.I.11.3).

Since religious fraud constrains men through fear of divine punishment it is a form of coercion. However, compared to the quasi-objectivity of force, it suffers the drawback of resting on beliefs that are ultimately subjective. This can be seen most clearly from the failure of prophets like Girolamo Savonarola, who relied on religious oratory to found a new Florentine state, and "was ruined in his new orders as soon as the multitude began not to believe in them" (P.VI.24). Accordingly, religious fraud needs to be backed up by violence, so that "when [peoples] no longer believe, one can make them believe by force," making Moses–who killed those who did not believe him–the "armed prophet" par excellence (P.VI.24). Likewise, Numa was able to establish Roman religion "with the arts of peace" because he was preceded by the warlike Romulus and succeeded by the equally ferocious Tullus Hostilius.[21] But the deeper reason for this dependence of religion on force rests on the fact that religious beliefs are habits: since any religion that commands obedience to the public good runs afoul of the licentious urges of first nature, individuals must be habituated to religious belief by repeatedly perfoming the corresponding rituals under princely constraint.

Once his state has been secured by physical and religious coercion, a new prince should also seek the obedience of his subjects by "benefiting them in such a mode that it would not be reasonable for them to desire to change fortune" (D.II.23.2). The primary benefit which a new prince can offer in exchange for obedience is security, both from the predations of the state of license, domestic as well as foreign, and badly-used cruelties of his own. Thus, a prince "to gain the people to himself . . . should be easy . . . when he takes up its protection" (P.IX.40), for the people "are easily satisfied by making orders and laws in which universal security is included" (D.I.16.5).[22] Concerning the cruelties that are indispensable, a prince should commit them "at a stroke," so that "by not renewing them" he can "secure men and gain them to himself with benefits" (P.VIII.38). Beyond the fundamental good of security, a prince "can gain the people to himself in many modes, for which one cannot give certain rules because the modes vary according to circumstances" (P.IX.40-

41). Nonetheless, we may infer from Machiavelli's other utterances that the people can also be won over by administering justice, promoting the arts, awarding honors and offices, showing favors to individuals, inspiring men with great enterprises, and entertaining them with festivals and spectacles.[23] In so doing, a prince should again be economical, for one that spends too liberally will soon have to "burden the people extraordinarily, to be rigorous with taxes, and to do all those things that can be done to get money," which "will begin to make him hated by his subjects" (P.XVI.63). Finally, a prince "should appear all mercy, all faith, all honesty, all humanity, all religion" (P.XVIII.70), for "being held virtuous gives him obedience" while "affability, humanity, mercy . . . give him love" (D.III.22.5). Note, however, that the people cannot be assumed to love the prince's virtue as an end in itself, for virtue is a good of a soul that men do not possess; instead, they support the prince because they understand his apparent virtue as a sign that he will benefit them with bodily and external goods; for instance, they love a prince who appears merciful because they expect not to be mistreated.

Whereas security is a good that can be enjoyed jointly, honors, offices, and riches are possessed by one to the neglect or even detriment of the others. With regard to such exclusive goods, a prince must therefore decide whom to benefit in exchange for support against the others. The most obvious support group for a prince are his soldiers; for "if those whom you arm are benefited, once can act with more security toward the others. The difference of treatment that they recognize regarding themselves makes them obligated to you" (P.XX.83). In general, however, princes "have to contrive with all industry to avoid the hatred of those universalities [i.e., groups] which are most powerful" (P.XIX.76), Thus, they should favor the people over the great, because they "can never secure [themselves] against a hostile people, as they are too many" (P.IX.39).[24]

Customary Regimes

A "hereditary principality" forms when the heirs of a new prince maintain their state and the memory of the initial cruelties fades away, so that the next generation of subjects takes for granted what the previous one accepted primarily fear; in other words, the subjects become increasingly habituated to being ruled by a particular line of princes. In Machiavelli's words, when "the memories and causes of innovations are extinguished" by the "antiquity and continuity of the dominion," a "hereditary state accustomed to the blood line of their prince" has come into being (P.II.6-7). Indeed, insofar as obedience to a princely house has become second nature to the subjects, the hereditary prince can be considered a "natural prince" (P.II.7). In the kingdom of France, for instance, there is an "ancient multitude of lords, acknowledged in that state by their subjects", who "recognize them as lords and hold them in natural affection" (P.IV.17).

Since the ordering principle in such a hereditary principality is ultimately not the will of the prince, but the customary order that has grown around the rule of his predecessors, it is usually enough for hereditary princes "of ordinary industry" not to "depart from the order of [their] ancestors, and then to temporize in the face of accidents" in order to maintain their state (P.II.6). Being able to rely on habituation as the first cause of compliance, the hereditary prince also "has less cause and less necessity to offend; hence it is fitting that he be more loved. And if extraordinary vices do not make him hated, it is reasonable that he will naturally have the good will of his own" (P.II.7). This good will makes it very difficult for conquerors to secure territories used to living under hereditary princes, as the Romans found out when they had occupied Spain, Gaul, and Greece: There "arose frequent rebellions . . . because of the numerous principalities that [had] existed in those states," and it was only "when their memory was eliminated with the power and long duration of the empire [that] the Romans became secure possessors of them" (P.IV.19). But, the fact that hereditary princes rule by custom also means that they "begin to lose their state at the hour they begin to break the laws and those modes and those customs that are ancient, under which men have lived a long time" (D.III.5).

A "mixed principality" comes into being when a hereditary prince adds a new province to his state. If the old and new parts are alike in "language, customs, and orders," it is relatively easy to gain the allegiance of the new subjects, for when "customs are similar" men "can easily bear with one another" (P.III.9). On the other hand, if the new province is dissimilar, the way to secure it is to move one's own poeple there, either "to go there to live in person . . . as the Turk has done in Greece" or "to send colonies" as the Romans did (P.III.10).

An "ecclesiastical principality," finally, centers on the customary order of a religion and is ruled by a cleric. In Machiavelli's words, "ecclesiastical principalities . . . are sustained by orders that have grown old with religion, which have been so powerful and of such a kind that they keep their princes in the state however they proceed and live" (P.XI.45); for instance, the pope is "sustained and defended by spiritual power and reputation" (FH.VIII.18). In addition to religious habit, ecclesiastical principalities are maintained by the fear that god will punish those who disobey the ruler–which Machiavelli may have had in mind when he wrote that they "subsist by superior causes" and "are exalted and maintained by God" (P.XI.45). However, there are again limits to this religious form of coercion; for, when Pope Boniface excommunicated and proclaimed a crusade against his personal rivals, the "arms which had been used *virtuosamente* for the love of faith, when used for his own ambition against Christians, began not to cut" (FH.I.25).

This weakness of religious coercion implies further that force is needed to establish ecclesiastical principalities; in Machiavelli's words, "they are acquired either by *virtù* or by Fortune" (P.XI.45), that is, either with one's own arms or the arms of others. Thus, the Papal States were founded in 754 by the arms of the Frankish king Pepin, who gave Rome and the Exarchate of Ravenna to Pope Stephen II. Likewise, an already established ecclesiastical prince needs to use force and fraud to add new provinces to his dominion; according to Machiavelli, "Alexander VI . . . showed how far a pope could prevail with money and forces" and "did all the things I discussed above in the actions of Cesare Borgia" (P.XI.46), who pacified the Romagna with cruelties, murdered his guests, and cut a loyal servant in half to please the crowd.

The Civil Way of Life

Laws and Orders

The regimes we have encountered thus far arise rather spontaneously: A new principality is born when the most *virtuoso* man, aiming to secure himself and to satisfy his ambition, wins the struggle for domination that rages among individuals in the natural condition of license; the customary orders of hereditary, mixed, and ecclesiastical principalities arise from the human propensity to become habituated to activities that are often repeated or situations that last for a long time. In contrast, regimes that center on a "civil way of life" (*vivere civile*)–or, synonymously, a "political way of life" (*vivere politico*) or "free way of life" (*vivere libero*)[25]–are constructed by conscious reflection on the rules needed to coordinate the multifarious actions of individuals in an effective manner. This construction began in the original condition, where men were "reduced to making laws and ordering punishments for whoever acted against them" (D.I.2.3), and continued when "some [cities] were given laws by one alone and at a stroke, either in their beginning or after not much time, like those that were given by Lycurgus to the Spartans," whereas "some had them by chance and at many different times, and according to accidents, as had Rome" (D.I.2.1). For instance, to resolve the enmity between the great and the people, the Romans "sent Spurius Postumius with two other citizens to Athens for examples of the laws that Solon gave to that city so that they could found the Roman laws on them," and for a year granted unlimited authority to ten citizens "to create such laws without any hesitation" (D.I.40.2).[26]

More precisely, to act in a civil manner means first of all to pursue one's ambition through laws rather than violence, which can be seen from the Florentine government's request to some rebellious plebeians that "if you ever wish something new, be pleased to ask for it with civility and not with tumults and arms" (FH.III.11).[27] Second, the laws must be designed and applied in such a way that they do not exclude any humor from all participation in political life. The Roman plebs observed this maxim well, whereas the common people of Florence sought to exclude the nobility from all offices and thus destroyed their civil way of life:

> The people of Rome desired to enjoy the highest honors together with the nobles, while the people of Florence fought to be alone in the government without the participation of the nobles. And because the desire of the Roman people was more reasonable, offenses to the nobles came to be more bearable, so that the nobility would yield easily and without resorting to arms. Thus, after some differences, they would come together to create a law whereby the people would be satisfied and the nobles retain their dignities. On the other side, the desire of the Florentine people was injurious and unjust, so that the nobility readied greater forces for its own defense; and that is why it came to the blood and exile of citizens, and the laws that were made afterwards were not for the common utility but were all ordered in favor of the conqueror. (FH.III.1)[28]

Further, a party that eliminates all others will not be able afterwards to reconstitute a civil life by itself, for naturally licentious individuals will turn on each other once the common enemy has been vanquished; thus, "in the city that prefers to maintain itself with sects rather than with laws, as soon as one sect is left there without opposition, it must of necessity divide from within itself" (FH.III.5).[29]

In addition to laws, Machiavelli describes the civil way of life in terms of "orders" (*ordini*). Wider in compass and more stable than laws, these institutions determine where political authority resides and how it is to be exercised, including the making of the laws itself.[30] In the Roman republic, for instance,

> there was the order of the government, or truly of the state, and afterwards the laws, which together with the magistrates checked the citizens. The order of the state was the authority of the people, of the Senate, of the tribunes, of the consuls; the mode of soliciting and creating the magistrates; and the mode of making the laws. These orders varied hardly or not at all in accidents. The laws that checked the citizens varied–such as the law on adulteries, the sumptuary [law], that on ambition and many others–as the citizens little by little became corrupt. (D. I.18.2)

In other words, authority in a civil, free, or political way of life is institutionalized. Obedience is not owed to concrete persons but to holders of public office, who carry out laws that have been ratified by an assembly of citizens, for that "private men find themselves in the councils of public things . . . is contrary to every civil order" (DF.24).[31] Indeed,

> in a republic, one would not wish anything ever to happen that has to be governed with extraordinary modes. For although the extraordinary mode may do good then, nonetheless, the example does ill; for if one sets up a habit of breaking the orders for the sake of good, then later, under that coloring, they are broken for ill. (D.I.49.1)

These orders function almost like a constitution that checks the licentious ambitions of men. For instance, the orders of the Roman republic circumscribed the office of dictator in such a way that giving so much power to an individual proved beneficial rather than harmful to the civil way of life; in contrast, the rule of the Ten (the Decemvirate) led to tyranny precisely because all other orders had been suspended:

> When the dictator was created, the tribunes, consuls, and Senate remained with their authority; nor was the dictator able to take it away from them. If he had been able to deprive one of them of the consulate, one of the Senate, he could not annul the senatorial order and make new laws. So the Senate, the consuls, the tribunes, remaining in their authority, came to be like a guard on him to make him not depart from the right way. But in the creation of the Ten it happened all the

contrary; for they annulled the consuls and the tribunes; they gave them authority to make laws and do any other thing, like the Roman people. (D.I.35)

Indeed, Machiavelli shows an incipient sense of due process when he asserts that "accusations have need of true corroborations" (D.I.8.2), and that the "authority to shed blood against its own citizens . . . was well ordered in Rome because one could appeal to the people ordinarily," that is, through established orders (D.I.49.3).[32]

As with laws, Machiavelli had a thoroughly positivist conception of orders. They are created by founders like Romulus, who "ordered a Senate with which he took counsel and by whose opinion he decided," making the "first orders of [Rome] more conformable to a civil and free way of life than to an absolute and tyrannical one" (D.I.9.2). Further, a city's orders need to be changed in response to newly arising problems–a maxim that the ordinarily savvy Romans failed to observe:

By holding steady the orders of the [Roman] state, which in corruption were no longer good, the laws that were renewed were no longer enough to keep men good; but they would indeed have helped if the orders had been changed together with the innovation in laws. (D.I.18.2)

Although Machiavelli's laws and orders emulate those of the Roman republic, the fact that they merely seek to regulate–rather than eliminate–competition for glory, power, and wealth implies a sharp break with tradition; for classical republicanism–from Aristotle to Cicero and the humanists of fifteenth-century Florence–conceived *res publica* as a moral community of men harmoniously joined by a shared way of life.[33] For such a community to maintain its harmony, there had to be a deeply felt agreement among the citizens with regard to the beliefs, virtues, and customs of their particular way of life– called *homonoia* or "like-mindedness" by the Greeks and *concordia* or "common-heartedness" by the Romans; and the citizens needed to form networks of friendship that consisted not only of exchanges for pleasure and utility, but, more importantly, of the mutual recognition of virtue.[34] To foster such concord and friendship, ancient thinkers thought that republics should limit their size to enable the citizens to know each other's character and deliberate together, restrict foreign contacts to keep out unwholesome ideas and practices, and provide an education (*paideia, disciplina*) to implant specific virtues in the citizens: in particular, men had to develop prudence in order to rule well, justice to give every one his fair share, courage to defend the city, moderation to take no more than their allotted share, and piety to obey the laws from fear of divine punishment.[35] It was in this way that classical republicans sought to bring out the best in man and to perfect his nature as a political animal.[36]

Machiavelli broke with this organic conception of republican order when he argued that it was precisely "the disunion of the plebs and the Roman Senate that made that republic free and powerful," notwithstanding the fact that this disunion implied "the people together crying out against the Senate, the Senate against the people, running tumultuously through the streets, closing shops, the whole plebs leaving Rome"–which had been roundly condemned by ancient writers (D.I.4.T-1). In particular, the "confusions, noises, and dangers of scandals" (D.I.3.2), which arose from the people's resistance against the oppressive tendencies of the nobles, led to the creation of the Tribunes, whose ability to veto any law and intercede with any magistrate became the "guard of Roman freedom" (D.I.4.2). Moreover, "if you wish to make a people numerous and armed so as to be able to make a great empire, you make it of such a quality that you cannot manage it in your mode"; hence, "to tolerate the enmities that arise between the people and the Senate" was "an inconvenience necessary to arrive at Roman greatness" (D.I.6.3-4).

At same time, Machiavelli makes it clear such enmities must stop short of factional violence when he praises the fact that "from the Tarquins to the Gracchi, which was more than three hundred years, the tumults of Rome rarely engendered exil and very rarely blood" (D.I.4.1). To this end, the founder of a civil way of life should first of all eliminate all "gentlemen," that is, feudal lords who "live idly in abundance from the return of their possessions . . . command from a castle and have subjects that obey them . . . for such kinds of men are altogether hostile to every civility" (D.I.55.4, mt); in other words, great inequalities of wealth and rank undermine a *vivere civile* because they enable the few to break its laws and circumvent its orders with impunity. Thus, "if one wanted to create a republic in Milan, where the inequality of the citizens is great, one would have to extinguish all the nobility, and reduce it to an equality with the others; for among them are so many extraordinary [men] that the laws are not enough to repress them" (DF.27). Insofar as men become rich later, cities need to prevent them from using their wealth to acquire reputation in "private ways," that is, to "benefit this or that other private individual–by lending him money, marrying his daughters for him, defending him from the magistrates"; for such favors "make men into "partisans to oneself and give spirit . . . to corrupt the republic and to breach the laws" (D.III.28).[37] Thus, when Spurius Maelius gained a following among the Roman plebs by doling out grain, the "Senate, thinking of the inconvenience that could arise from that liberality of his, so as to crush it before it could pick up more strength, created a dictator over him and had him killed" (D.III.28). A similar problem is posed by citizens who have gained great glory by benefiting their city in extraordinary ways, for such a man "has an audacity and confidence that he can do some work that is no good without fearing punishment," so that in a "short time he will become so insolent that any civility will be dissolved" (D.I.24.1). Thus, ancient cities merit "excuse" for persecuting excessively glorious men despite the fact that they had not committed any crimes–as the Romans did with the great Scipio–for "a city could not call itself free where there was a citizen who was feared by the magistrates" (D.I.29.3). Finally, cities that seek to maintain a civil way of life ought to have procedures by which private individuals can accuse others in "a way ordered by the laws," for when the "malignant humors that arise in men" at any rate "do not have an outlet by which they may be vented ordinarily, they have recourse to extraordinary modes that bring a whole republic to ruin" (D.I.7.1,5). Whereas the Romans observed this maxim and thus made sure that "accusations have need of true corroboration and of circumstances that show the truth," the Florentines allowed private calumnies to fester, so that "on every side hatred surged; whence they went to divisions; from divisions to sects; from sects to ruin" (D.I.8.2-3).[38]

On the whole, whereas classical republicans sought to foster moral unity among unequals by instilling nobles and commoners with complementary virtues, Machiavelli abandons this project as an idle hope that fails to reckon with the permanence of conflict among like individuals who compete by nature for the largely exclusive goods of glory, power, and wealth. Accordingly, those who found a civil way of life must assume that man's true nature tends to vice rather than virtue:

> As all those demonstrate who reason on civil way of life, and as every history is full of examples, it is necessary to whoever disposes a republic and orders laws in it to presuppose that all men are bad, and that they always have to use the malignity of their spirit whenever they have a free opportunity for it. (D.I.3.1)[39]

At best, human ambition can be channeled into nonviolent competition that provides individuals with incentives to benefit the common good in order to gratify their own desires:

> Those who hope that a republic can be united are very much deceived
> in this hope. It is true that some divisions are harmful to republics and
> some are helpful. Those are harmful that are accompanied by sects and
> partisans; those are helpful that are maintained without sects and
> partisans. Thus, since a founder of a republic cannot provide that there
> be no enmities in it, he has to provide at least that there not be sects
> [by allowing citizens to gain reputation only by public ways]. . . . And
> although even among citizens so made one cannot provide by any
> mode that there will not be very great hatreds, nonetheless, having no
> partisans to follow them for their own utility, they cannot harm the
> republic; on the contrary, they must help it, because to pass their tests
> it is necessary for them to attempt to exalt the republic and to watch
> each other particularly so that civil bounds are not transgressed.
> (FH.VII.1)

It is on this ground that Machiavelli can be said to have introduced
the modern idea of interest politics, which similarly disregards the
ideal of a virtuous community and encourages the various interests of
society to use public institutions for the advancement of their
particular aims, as pointed out by Sheldon Wolin.[40]

Finally, since it is possible to "order a political way of life either
by way of republic or of kingdom" (D.I.25), there are two regimes
that rest on a civil way of life: republics and "civil" principalities (or
law-governed kingdoms).

Republics

The Mixed Regime

Drawing on the ancient idea that the ruling element in simple
regimes–kingship, aristocracy, and popular government–tends to
become despotical, Machiavelli defines the republican form of the
civil way of life as a mixed regime, where "one [element] guards the
other since in one and the same city there are the principality, the
aristocrats, and the popular government" (D.I.2.5).[41] Having banned
virtue from politics, he prefers the mixed regime on grounds of
stability alone: "Those who prudently order laws . . . avoiding each of
these [simple] modes by itself, chose one that shared in all, judging it
firmer and more stable"; Lycurgus, for instance, "who in Sparta
ordered his laws so as to give their roles to the kings, the aristocrats,

and the people . . . made a state that lasted more than eight hundred years" (D.I.2.5-6). This stability arises first of all from the fact that those who hold executive power are prevented from using it for licentious ends; for it is "not good that citizens who have the state in hand should not have those who observe them, and who make them abstain from actions that are not good, relieving them of the authority that they use wickedly" (DF.29-30). Second, mixed regimes are more enduring because they satisfy the major "humors" of a city, that is, groups of individuals who share temperament, outlook, and interests, such as "the people" and "the great" (D.I.4.1), or, alternatively, the "powerful, middle, and low" (FH.II.42);[42] for one "cannot believe a republic to be lasting, where those humors are not satisfied, which, if not satisfied, ruin republics" (DF.24).[43] As we saw in chapter 3, premodern medicine believed the health of the human body to depend on the proper balance of its four fluids or "humors"– blood, choler, phlegm, and black bile, which make a person's temper correspondingly sanguine, choleric, phlegmatic, and melancholic. Applied to the body politic, this theory suggests that a city will stay healthy as long as its humors participate in government in the right proportion. It is mainly on these grounds that Machiavelli argues for a participatory kind of politics:

> There is no other way to flee [the evils of factional violence] than to proceed in such a mode that the orders of the city by themselves can stand firm; and they will always stand firm when everyone has a hand there, and when everyone knows what he has to do and in whom he has to confide, and no rank of citizen, either by fear of oneself or by ambition, has to desire innovation. (DF.31)

Accordingly, the various republics of Florence were short-lived because they did not mix their constitutions properly. In the regime from 1393 to 1434, the magistracy "had little reputation and too much authority, being able to dispose without appeal of the life and property of citizens," and, as a result, became not "the defender of the state, but the instrument of ruining it whenever a reputed citizen was able either to command or trick it"; moreover, "the people did not have its part in it" (DF.24). The republic from 1494 to 1512 failed to adopt a "mode that would be durable because the orders did not satisfy all the humors of the citizens, and, on the other hand, were not able to punish them"; in particular, the chief magistrate "did not have around him those who could defend him, if he were good, nor those who could either curb or correct him, if he were bad" (DF.25).

The far more successful mixed regime of Rome had its first beginning in the kingship of Romulus, who "ordered a Senate with which he took counsel and by whose opinion he decided," reserving for himself only the authority of "commanding the armies when war was decided on and that of convoking the Senate" (D.I.9.2). When the city became a republic in 510 B.C., the powers of the king were vested in two consuls, to be elected annually by the entire people from among the nobility.[44] But the truly popular element was introduced in 494 B.C., thanks to the resistance of the Roman plebs against the arrogance of the nobility: When the Senate rejected a motion to relieve the plebeians of their crushing debts, they marched out of the city under arms and set up camp on Mons Sacer, three miles distant from Rome; alarmed by the possibility of their secession and the concomitant loss of military manpower, the Senate accepted the creation of special officials–the Tribunes of the Plebs–who would have authority to protect the plebeians from vetoing any legislation and interceding with the acts of any magistrate.[45] As a result, "the state of that republic came to be more stabilized, since all three kinds of government there had their part"; and "remaining mixed" in this fashion for centuries, Rome "made a perfect republic, to which perfection it came through the disunion of the plebs and the Senate" (D.I.2.7).

In Machiavelli's republic, which is closely modelled after the Roman, the magistrates are elected by the assembly of the people, which judges the quality of the candidates according to their reputation: "the people in its distributing [of offices] goes by what is said of one individual through public word and fame when one does not otherwise know him through his known works, or through the presumption or opinion that one has of him" (D.III.34.2). Since it is with regard to "particular things concerning distributions of ranks and dignities" that "the people does not deceive itself" (D.I.47.4), this generally leads to election of *virtuoso* men–at least as long as the city remains uncorrupt and threatened by foreign enemies.[46] During the early years of the Roman republic, the plebs thus rejected men from its own ranks who stood for offices with consular authority, for "as it had to pass judgment on its men particularly, it recognized their weakness and judged that none of them deserved" the posts (D.I.47.1); but once the Mediterranean world had been subdued, "this security and this weakness of their enemies made the Roman people no longer regard *virtù* but favor in bestowing the consulate, lifting to that rank those who knew better how to entertain men rather than those who knew better how to conquer enemies" (D.I.18.3).

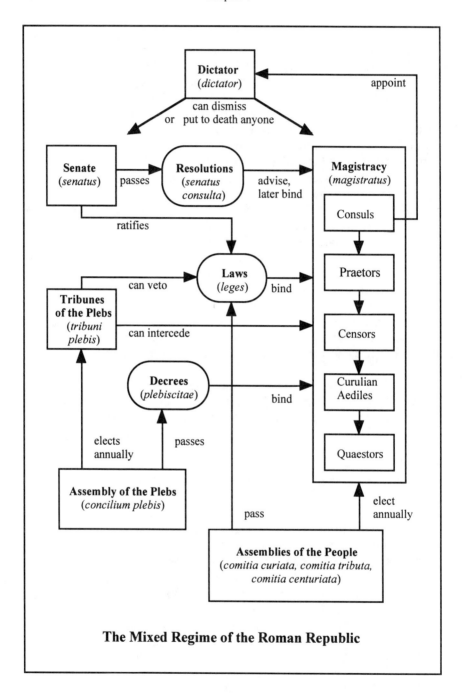

The Mixed Regime of the Roman Republic

While capable of selecting good leaders under particular circumstances, the common people are generally unable to make good laws or to govern effectively; for such matters require a grasp of abstract ideas and the many are "very much deceived in general things" (D.I.47.1). Thus, even the "remedy of assemblies" (D.I.4.1) will be of little avail when affairs of state are at issue, especially when crafty demagogues sway public opinion to their private advantage. Drawing on Thucydides, Machiavelli thus reports that "in the city of Athens, Nicias, a very grave and prudent man, was never able to persuade that people that it might not be good to go to assault Sicily; so when that decision was taken against the wish of the wise, the entire ruin of Athens followed from it" (D.I.53.4).[47]

To prevent the many from governing, the leading men of Rome manipulated the elections of public officials by the people:

> When the Senate feared that tribunes with consular power would be made of plebeian men, it held to one of two modes: either it had [the position] asked for by the most reputed men in Rome; or . . . it corrupted some vile and very ignoble plebeian who, mixed with the plebeians of better quality who ordinarily asked for it, also asked them for it. This last mode made the plebs ashamed to give it; the first made it ashamed to take it. (D.I.48)

In addition to stacking the slate, the Romans engaged in what nowadays would be called "gerrymandering":

> Because of the liberality that the Romans practiced in giving citizenship to foreigners, so many new men were born in Rome that they began to have so much share in the votes that the government began to vary, and it departed from the things and from the men with which it was accustomed to go. When Quintus Fabius, who was censor, perceived this, he put all these new men from whom this disorder derived under four tribes, so that by being shut in such small spaces they could not corrupt all Rome. (D.III.49.4)

Thus, we have arrived at another significant reason for the superiority of the mixed regime: it accords to the people that share of authority which they are competent to exercise, namely to choose among candidates for public office, to adjudicate crimes, to sanction laws proposed to them by the leaders, and, in general, to check the insolent tendencies of the nobles; at the same time, the tasks that are beyond the many, namely to legislate and govern, are placed in the hands of men who have demonstrated their *virtù* by benefiting the republic or, at a minimum, by successfully campaigning for office.

The offices of such a republic will most often be won by individuals from the ranks of the great, who have not only the ambition to command but also possess the wealth, influence, and reputation to stand out in the public eye. In general, this fact is beneficial to republics since "there is more foresight and astuteness in the great," they possess "*virtù* in arms and the generosity of spirit," and are "more prudent and more knowing of natural things" (P.IX.40).[48] Nonetheless, Fortune sees to it that many of "those who have worked in this world the greatest things . . . have been low and obscure in their beginning and birth" (CC.615). Michele di Lando, for instance, had been a humble wool carder before he was made Gonfalonier (chief magistrate) of Florence by the acclamation of a rebellious mob; but "because he was a sagacious and prudent man who owed more to nature than to fortune, he resolved to quiet the city and stop the tumults" (FH.III.16), which were eventually "settled solely by the *virtù* of the Gonfalonier," who "in spirit, prudence, and goodness . . . surpassed any citizen of his time and deserves to be numbered among the few who benefited their fatherland" (FH.III.17). Accordingly, Machiavelli endorses the eligibility of commoners for magistral office not only because men who are asked to fight and die for the republic "cannot be given trouble without a reward," but also because "it would be a very harmful thing for the city not to be able to avail itself" of a youth or, by extension, any man, who has "so much *virtù* that he makes himself known in some notable thing" (D.I.60). Thus, the fact that the Romans "went to find *virtù* in whatever house it inhabited," so that "the way to any rank whatever and to any honor whatever was not prevented for you because of poverty" (D.III.25), greatly contributed to the strength of their republic; for as capable "men of the people could be placed in the administration of the magistracies, the armies, and the posts of empire together with the nobles, they were filled with the same *virtù* as the nobles, and that city, by growing in *virtù,* grew in power" (FH.III.1). Aiming at the effectual truth, Machiavelli thus wants rulers to be selected according to ability, similar to the modern notion of a *carrière ouverte aux talents* (career open to talents). Thus, when speaking of the "first citizens"[49] or "princes of a republic" (D.I.12.1), he does not refer simply to the nobility, but to all men capable and willing to assume leadership on account of their *virtù*–whether as magistrates, senators, tribunes, military officers, or private citizens.

Causes of Compliance

What explains the willingness of these *virtuoso* men to act for *res publica,* the "public affair"? Most readily, republics offer many opportunities for capable individuals to gain personal glory, for instance, by "winning a battle, acquiring a town, carrying out a mission with care and prudence, advising the republic wisely and prosperously" (FH.VII.1). Thus, whereas republics should close the private ways of gaining reputation, as discussed above, they "ought to open to citizens the [public] way to honor and to put up rewards both for counsels and for works" (D.III.28). Again, Rome provides the example: "to reward whoever worked well for the public, it ordered triumphs and all the other honors that it gave to its citizens; and to harm whoever sought under various colors to make himself great by private ways it ordered accusations" (D.III.28).[50] Indeed, this exchange of personal glory for public service is so important that "a republic without reputed citizens cannot stand, nor can it be governed well in any mode" (D.III.28).

While the leaders are motivated by personal glory, the commons obey them above all from fear of punishment: "for fear of being accused citizens do not attempt things against the state; and when attempting them, they are crushed instantly and without respect" (D.I.7.1). In particular, no respect should be paid to previously acquired merit when using force to punish citizens for their current transgressions: "no well-ordered republic ever cancels the demerits with the merits of its citizens; but . . . having rewarded one for having worked well, if that same later works badly, it punishes him without any regard for his good works" (D.I.24.1).

In addition to punishment by the magistrates, there is punishment by the gods to keep the many in line. Thanks to the religion introduced by Numa, the second founder of Rome, "for many centuries there was never so much fear of God as in that republic, which made easier whatever enterprise the Senate or the great men of Rome might plan to make" (D.I.11.1-2). Indeed, religious coercion is a necessity for a republic that arms its people in order to augment its military manpower: "to rein in armed men neither the fear of laws nor of men is enough"; hence, the "ancients added the authority of God" (AG.VI.370). The chief instruments of this authority were oaths and omens. Regarding the former, the Romans "with very great ceremonies . . . had their soldiers swear to observe military discipline, in order that if they acted against it, they would have to fear not merely the laws and men but God" (AG.VI.370). As a result, the plebs,

who had sworn obedience to a consul for the sake of recapturing the
Capitol, continued to obey his successor from mere "fear of religion,"
even though the tribunes explained to them that they were led out to
war to prevent them from voting on a law which would have reduced
the power of the consuls (D.I.13.2). Concerning omens, a plague and
a famine once occurred after the Roman people had elected mostly
plebeians to the tribuneship with consular power, and there were
reports of other heavenly signs, such as fires blazing in the sky, the
earth trembling, cows talking; promptly, the "nobles used the
opportunity . . . to say that the gods were angry because Rome had
used the majesty of its *imperium* [consular power] badly, and that
there was no remedy for placating the gods other than to return the
election of tribunes to its place," with the result that in the next
election "the plebs, terrified by this religion, created as tribunes all
nobles" (D.I.13.1). When omens pointed the wrong way, clever
reinterpretation did the trick: "when reason showed them a thing they
ought to do–notwithstanding that the auspices had been adverse–they
did it in any mode. But they turned it around with means and modes so
aptly that it did not appear that they had done it with disdain for
religion" (D.I.14.1).

Further, the people obey their rulers in exchange for the personal
safety and opportunities that exist under republican government.
Thus, the ancient "peoples" had such an "affection for the free way
of life" (D.II.2.1), because

> larger peoples are seen there, because marriages are freer and more
> desirable to men since each willingly procreates those children he
> believes he can nourish. He does not fear that his patrimony will be
> taken away, and he knows not only that they are born free and not
> slaves, but that they can, through their *virtù,* become princes. Riches
> are seen to multiply there in large number, both those that come from
> agriculture and those that come from the arts. For each willingly
> multiplies that thing and seeks to acquire those goods he believes he
> can enjoy once acquired. (D.II.2.3)[51]

In addition to actually benefiting the people, the leaders can also
assuage them with promises and then delay their fulfillment. Thus,
when the Roman plebs demanded to be eligible for consular office, "it
was fitting at an early hour that the plebs have hope of gaining the
consulate, and it was fed a bit with this hope without having it; then
the hope was not enough and it was fitting that it come to the effect"
(D.I.60).

But neither punishment nor benefits are quite enough to make naturally ambitious individuals observe the laws and work for the common good. Physical punishment cannot reach and deter all individuals; sooner or later, some will get away with illicit behavior, and moreover there are transgressions of such a kind that "one of these things . . . left unpunished is capable of ruining a republic" (D.III.28). Religious punishment overcomes this problem insofar as it makes people believe that the gods see and punish transgressions that escape the attention of the magistrates; but, being subjective in nature, faith can dissipate quickly, as "unarmed prophets" tend to find out (P.VI.24). Benefits are limited in that the nobles have not only a strong ambition to become sole rulers, but can attain even greater glory, power, and wealth by usurping authority than by respecting it. The common people typically fail to understand that cooperation is their most beneficial choice because they fail to grasp such general ideas as enlightened self-interest, that is, the insight that everyone is better off by working together to augment the public good than by proceeding individually. In other words, there are two collective-action problems that limit the effectiveness of benefits as causes of compliance: *virtuoso* individuals are actually better off by taking a "free ride" on the compliance of others; the many lack the far-sighted rationality needed to overcome their "coordination problem."

Machiavelli's general solution to these compliance problems consists of "good customs," that is, the habituation of citizens to the laws and orders of a civil way of life; for "laws have need of good customs so as to be observed" (D.I.18.1), and, conversely, "well-ordered laws do not help" when the "matter . . . is corrupt," that is, has a "bad habit" (D.I.17.3). Indeed, a city that has "good laws and bad customs" will of necessity be destroyed (AS.V.967). Good customs are thus an integral part of any civil way of life, which can be seen from Machiavelli's statement that the Romans acted "beyond every civil mode and *custom,*" when the reform effort of the Gracchi "inflamed so much hatred between the plebs and the Senate that they came to arms and bloodshed" (D.I.37.2).

In particular, the customs needed to undergird a republic consist of being "content with those goods, to live by those foods, to dress with those woolens that the country provides," as opposed to the "usage of a gentleman," who lives "idly in abundance from the returns of [his] possessions without having any care either for cultivation or for other necessary trouble in living" (D.I.55.3-4). Similarly, a republic is in trouble when "both sexes at every age are full of foul customs," for "from this grows the avarice that is seen in our citizens and the appetite, not for true glory, but for the contemptible honors on which hatreds, enmities, differences, and sects depend" (FH.III.5); in other words, a "city . . . full of courtly delicacies and customs" is "contrary to all well-ordered civility" (FH.VII.29). In addition to habits that support civil living, citizens need to be shaped for military discipline. Thus, the Romans "were accustomed to serve in the military on their own," that is, without pay (D.I.51), and "they did not esteem it a dishonorable thing to obey now one whom they had commanded at another time, and to find themselves serving in the army of which they had been princes," a "custom [that] is contrary to the opinions, orders, and modes of citizens in our times" (D.I.36). Finally, both civility and warlikeness are served by the right kind of religious habits, for the fact that "in ancient times peoples were more lovers of freedom that in these [times]" arises from "the difference between our education and the ancient, founded on the difference between our religion and the ancient"; in particular, whereas the ferocious rituals of the pagans made men strong, the mild ceremonies of Christianity have rendered them weak (D.II.2.2).

Such customs help solve collective-action problems in that they make people act from habit, that is, without calculating the associated costs and benefits. For instance, men accustomed to frugal living are far less likely to consider whether the prospect of enjoying the delights available to a tyrant are worth the risk of conspiring against the republic; they simply continue to live their ordinary lives because that is what people of their station have always done. In contrast, gentlemen, who have no such frugal habits but a taste for luxuries, are prone to reckon whether they could gratify their ambitions even more by seizing the state and becoming its tyrant. Likewise, citizens used to serving in the army without pay are far less likely to calculate whether their small personal share in the city's liberty and greatness is worth the grave risk of being killed or maimed; they simply do their duty because that is what men of their sort have always done. Mercenaries, in contrast, readily desert their employer because they have no such habitual motivation and thus figure their personal costs and benefits with precision; as a result, "they have no love nor cause to keep them in the field other than a small stipend, which is not sufficient to make them want to die for you" (P.XII.48-49). In other words, men lapse into ambitious license because their faculties of ingenuity and imagination suggest noncooperative ways to increase the satisfaction of their desires; good customs block these faculties and thus make people fit to be republican citizens.

This emphasis on good customs suggests further that republics do not prosper on account of well-organized institutions alone, but need citizens with the right kind of attributes to sustain them. In Machiavelli's words, "orders have need of being brought to life by the *virtù* of a citizen who rushes spiritedly to execute them against the power of those who transgress them" (D.III.1.3). Thus, the Roman practice of awarding high offices only to self-nominated candidates "was a good order as long as the citizens were good," for only those who "judged themselves worthy asked for them"; but it became pernicious when the citizens became corrupt, so that "not those who had more *virtù* but those who had more power asked for the magistracies" (D.I.18.3). Likewise, that any citizen could propose a law in the popular assembly "was a good order when the citizens were good," but when they "have become bad, such an order becomes the worst, for only the powerful propose laws" (D.I.18.3). Here, Machiavelli's daring proposal to institutionalize the conflict between the great and the people has reached its limit; for he knows that ultimately something other than interest–on which punishments as well as benefits act–must bind individuals to institutions for the latter to function well. Thus, his anticipation of the modern concept of interest politics stops short of the related idea that character is altogether irrelevant in political life.

Return to the Beginnings

But good customs are readily corrupted by a surge of ambitious license, for the latter is rooted in the necessary properties of first nature whereas habits are merely contingent attributes. Thus, the good customs that citizens acquired under the founder tend to decline once they are left to govern themselves. In Machiavelli's words, while "all the beginnings of sects, republics and kingdoms must have some goodness in them," in the "process of time that goodness is corrupted," which "of necessity kills that body" (D.III.1.2).[52] To prevent such corruption of the body politic, "it is necessary to draw it back often toward its beginning" (D.III.1.T), that is, to renew good customs by reenacting the coercive constraint that created them during the founding of the city; for when a certain amount of "time is past, men begin to vary in their customs and to transgress the laws," unless "something arises by which punishment is brought back to their memory and fear is renewed in their spirits" (D.III.1.3). This salutary fear can arise from an "external beating," such as the sack of Rome by the Gauls in 395 BC, which shocked the Romans into restoring the customary piety and law-abidingness that undergirded their civil way of life (D.III.1.2). But such "extrinsic force" is obviously too accidental to serve as a reliable remedy for corruption that spreads continuously, and, moreover, is "so dangerous that it is not in any way to be desired" (D.III.1.6).

To make a return to the beginnings more reliable and less perilous, it needs to be institutionalized in the manner of "the orders that drew the Roman republic back toward its beginning," which consisted of "the tribunes of the plebs, the censors, and all the other laws that went against the ambition and the insolence of men" (D.III.1.3). More precisely, these orders need to be executed by punishing transgressors in such a way that the thought of emulating them fills the others with dread:

> Notable among such executions before the taking of Rome [by the Gauls in 395 B.C.] were the death of the sons of Brutus, the death of the ten citizens, and that of Maelius the grain dealer; after the taking of Rome it was the death of Manlius Capitolinus, the death of the son of Manlius Torquatus, the execution of Papirius Cursor against his master of the cavalrymen Fabius, and the accusation of the Scipios. Because they were excessive and notable, such things made men draw back toward the mark. (D.III.1.3)

What made these punishments "excessive and notable" in the eyes of Machiavelli? The sons of Brutus conspired to overthrow the young Roman republic and were put to death by their own father, Lucius Junius Brutus, who was consul at the time; according to Machiavelli, "it is an example rare in all memories of things to see the father sit on the tribunals and not only condemn his sons to death but be present at their death" (D.III.3).[53] In the case of Maelius the grain dealer, who, as we know, was put to death for feeding the plebs, the excess in his punishment arose from the fact that his work appeared "merciful" and could not "reasonably be condemned" (D.III.28).[54] The punishment of Manlius Capitolinus, who was sentenced to death by the Roman people for agitating the plebs and planning revolution, was notable in that he had once been celebrated as a hero for retaking the Capitoline hill from the enemy, but now "was without any respect for his merits thrown headlong" from the very rock that he had once saved "with so much glory for himself" (D.I.24.2).[55] Manlius Torquatus was commander of the Roman army when his own son disobeyed his order not to engage the enemy; even though the young man had been provoked and achieved victory, Manlius had him decapitated.[56] Likewise, Papirius Cursor, as dictator in charge of the legions, "wished to have Fabius [his cavalry commander] killed for having engaged in combat with the Samnites contrary to his command" (D.I.32.2).[57] The two Scipios, who so gloriously had saved Rome from the Carthaginian menace and made her mistress of the Mediterranean, were tried and fined for the mere fact that their greatness caused the magistrates to fear them.[58]

Among the orders that returned the Roman republic to its beginnings, the censors, charged with keeping the citizen rolls and supervising morals, were of particular importance: for when they "had become arbiters of the customs of Rome, they were a very powerful cause why the Romans delayed more in corrupting themselves" (D.I.49.1). For instance, when Cato the Elder was censor and noticed how the Roman youth were flocking to the subversive teachings of Diogenes and Carneades, two sceptical philosophers who had come as ambassadors from Athens, "he saw to it that no philosopher could be accepted in Rome," for the "strength of well-armed spirits cannot be corrupted by a more honorable leisure than that of letters" (FH.V.1).

In addition to fear, a return to the beginnings can also be generated by the exemplary deed of a *virtuoso* individual, since habits are also formed by emulation. In Machiavelli's words,

> this drawing back of republics toward their beginning arises also from the simple *virtù* of one man, without depending on any law that stimulates you to any execution; nonetheless, they are of such reputation and so much example that good men desire to imitate them and the wicked are ashamed to hold to a life contrary to theirs. In Rome, those who particularly produced these good effects were Horatius Cocles, Scaevola, Fabricius, the two Decii, Regulus Attilius, and some others who with their rare and *virtuoso* examples produced in Rome almost the same effect that laws and orders produced. (D.III.1.3)

Again, what did these men do? Horatius Cocles single-handedly took on the entire Etruscan army to shield the retreat of his comrades, and Mucius Scaevola thrust his hand into fire to show the Etruscan king what kind of men he was dealing with in fighting against Romans.[59] The two Decii sacrificed their lives in battle to inspire their fellow soldiers.[60] Gaius Fabricius refused to betray his fatherland for the gold offered to him by a foreign king.[61] Regulus Attilius, having been taken prisoner by the cruel Carthaginians and released on the condition that he would return from Rome with an offer of peace, showed that a Roman values his word more than his life by returning to Carthage even though the Senate had declined peace, and was promptly tortured to death.[62] That such heroic actions had indeed a salutary effect on the customs of the Romans is attested by Livy, who wrote that "the public recognition of Mucius [Scaevola]'s heroism inspired even the women of Rome to emulate him."[63]

However, Machiavelli's claim that *virtuoso* examples had "almost the same effect" as excessive and notable punishments needs to be qualified: Renewal through example is inherently limited to cases where the good customs of would-be emulators have remained partly intact; for once good customs have dissipated entirely, individuals consist only of their licentious nature and bad customs, and thus have no motivational basis for imitating *virtuoso* deeds. Machiavelli actually suggests as much when he refers to the "two Catos" as exemplars of *virtù* who failed to renew the morals of the late Roman republic because corruption had already spread too far: "they remained so alone, that with their good examples they were not able to do any good work–and especially the last Cato, who, finding the city in good part corrupt, was not able to make the citizens become better with his example" (D.III.1.3).[64]

Further, these returns to the beginnings–excessive and notable punishments as well as examples of *virtù*–must recur at a certain interval for corruption to be held at bay continuously; otherwise, it keeps spreading until "so many delinquents join together that they can be no longer punished without danger" (D.III.1.3). In the first chapter of the third book of the *Discourses,* Machiavelli seems to define this interval as "at least every ten years," seemingly taking his cue from the rulers of Florence, who claimed that "it was necessary to regain [*ripigliare*] the state every five years" (D.III.1.3) and who, "because ten years had already passed since the beginning of their state . . . judged it necessary to take it up again [*ripigliarlo*] by . . . beating down their enemies" (FH.VI.8), but also from the doctors of medicine who "speaking of the bodies of men say 'that daily something is added that at *some* time needs cure'" (D.III.1.2, ea). However, in the last chapter of the third book of the *Discourses,* Machiavelli alters this medical metaphor to say that "in a great city accidents arise *every day* that have need of a physician" (D.III.49.1), in order to suggest surreptitiously that the necessary interval is really one day. In other words, as the chapter's title puts it, "a republic has need of new provisions every day if one wishes to maintain it free" (D.III.49.T).[65] That "provisions" really refers to the punitive aspect of return to the beginnings can be seen from the examples that Machiavelli gives; for they are of the same kind as his examples of excessive and notable punishments in the first chapter: putting to death the Roman wives who had conspired to poison their senatorial husbands, summarily executing thousands suspected of participating in the subversive rites of Bacchus, sentencing to death an entire legion or city, and "decimating" an army for cowardice, that is, executing every tenth man regardless of personal guilt.[66] In other words, we must conclude that exemplary punishments have to occur continuously for good customs to remain intact.

This conclusion casts serious doubt on the effectiveness of good customs as a cause of compliance, for we took their significance to be that well-habituated individuals will observe the laws even in the absence of punishment. To clarify this question, we need to make an analytical distinction between those individuals who administer punishment at any given moment and the many others who dread it. Then, we see that good customs play only a supportive role in the compliance of the multitude, but also that they are indispensable to the motivation of office-holders and private citizens who sustain the civil life by punishing transgressors; for the actual enforcers cannot be motivated by fear of punishment themselves (since this would lead to an infinite regress), nor by fear of divine punishment (since *virtuoso* men see through religious fraud), nor by expectation of benefits (since tyranny is more advantageous to them); hence, it can only be good customs that drive some individuals to defend law and order. In other words, good customs are Machiavelli's answer to the vexing question of *quis custodiet ipsos custodes* (who guards the guardians). To establish layer upon layer of institutional safeguards can take us only so far in making self-regarding and ambitious individuals work for the public good. At least some of them need to have an impulse that suppresses their self-interest in favor of a direct attachment to that good; and this impulse comes from cooperative habits.

But human affairs are inescapably contingent. Thus, it will happen again and again that particular transgressions go unpunished, allowing additional citizens to change their customs from good to bad, until their number is such that the magistrates can no longer hold them in check, whence the republic collapses. In Rome, this terminal phase "arose from the corruption which the Marian parties had put in the people" at the beginning of the first century B.C., so that in 42 B.C., at the battle of Philippi, "the authority and severity of Brutus, together with all the eastern legions, were not enough" to defend republican liberty against the usurper Mark Anthony, who had taken up Caesar's mantle (D.I.17.1).[67] Hence, the theoretical possibility of making a republic last forever by continuously returning its citizens to the beginnings—which Machiavelli hints at in one place[68]—can never be realized; in practice, "it is impossible to order a perpetual republic, because its ruin is caused through a thousand unexpected ways" (D.III.17). Ultimately, even the mixed regime cannot escape the cycle of generation and corruption that plagues simple regimes. Eventually the wickedness of first nature dissolves good customs to the point where the "dams and dikes" (laws and orders) erected by the founder's *virtù* will be pierced by ambitious individuals, and then it is only a matter of time before Fortune's violent rivers "flood the plains, ruin the trees and the buildings, lift earth from this part, drop it in another" (P.XXV.98).

Once corruption has spread to the entire citizen body, it is impossible to renew a republic "by means of [its] orders" (D.III.1.1), that is, returns to beginnings whereby officeholders punish law-breakers in exemplary ways; for "neither laws nor orders can be found that are enough to check a universal corruption" (D.I.18.1). Then, a civil way of life can only be restored by a new prince, for to "inure to good a city that has been inured to bad for a long time" (D.I.17.3), it is "not enough to use ordinary terms, since the ordinary modes are bad; but it is necessary to go to the extraordinary, such as violence and arms, and before everything else become prince of that city, able to dispose it in one's own mode" (D.I.18.4-5). In short, since most men have returned to a condition of ambitious license, another founding is needed. Thus, Machiavelli's maxim that a "prudent orderer of a republic" must be alone in authority holds equally for a city that "is ordered well from the beginning or reformed altogether anew outside its old orders" (D.I.9.2).

At the same time, founders who work with rustic peoples, whose licentiousness arises only from their first nature, face an easier task than founders who have to deal with corrupt city-dwellers, whose foul customs have aggravated their licentious nature. Thus, Romulus, Lycurgus, and Solon "could easily impress any new form whatever" on their matter since the "men with whom they had to labor were crude" (D.I.11.3), and "neither of them had a subject stained with the corruption" that prevailed in Rome when the republic fell (D.I.18.5). Anyone who "wished to make a republic in the present times," would thus "find it easier among mountain men, where there is no civilization, than among those who are used to living in cities, where civilization is corrupt" (D.I.11.3); for no "good sculptor . . . thinks to make a beautiful statue from a badly blocked-out piece of marble, but may well from a raw one" (AG.VIII.388).

Consequentialist Institutions

To make the above distinction between returns to the beginnings and a renewed founding is crucial for upholding the institutional quality of Machiavelli's republic; for otherwise the fact that excessive violence is used in both instances might suggest that Machiavelli wanted us to combine the dailiness of returns to the beginnings with the autocratic nature of founding, and thus to realize that republics are really tyrannies of its leading men–as Leo Strauss seems to have concluded.[69] But, as we have seen, returns to the beginnings are clearly defined by Machiavelli as punishments that "arise from . . . a law" and proceed *"by means of their orders"* (D.III.1.1-2, ea), whereas renewed founding means that a republic is "reformed altogether anew *outside its old orders*" (D.I.9.2). In other words, returns to the beginnings are administered by public officals within established institutions, whereas renewed foundings are done by autocrats that act outside all institutions. Hence, the fact that returns to the beginnings need to take place every day does not negate their institutional character–as long as they are carried out in accordance with established laws and orders.

Similarly, the fact that Machiavelli's officials routinely violate the norms of absolutist morality in order to promote the public good as such does not deny the institutional quality of their actions; for Machiavelli explicitly construes the laws and orders of his republic so that they allow for a consequentialist approach to ethics. This can be most clearly seen from his discussion of the order of "accusations" by which an "outlet is given by which to vent, in some mode against some citizen, those humors that grow up in cities"; for there, he unhesitatingly gives a consequentialist answer to the vexing question of whether innocents should be sacrificed to the mob in order to prevent the latter from going on a rampage that injures many more or even "brings a whole republic to ruin" (D.I.7.1). According to Machiavelli, historical example shows

> how far it may be useful and necessary that republics give an outlet with their laws to vent the anger that the universality conceives against one citizen; for when these ordinary modes are not there, one has recourse to extraordinary ones, and without doubt these produce much worse effects than the former. For if a citizen is crushed ordinarily, there follows little or no disorder in the republic, even though he has been done a wrong. For the execution is done without private forces and without foreign forces, which are the ones that ruin a free way of life; but it is done with public forces and orders, which have their particular limits and do not lead beyond to something that may ruin the republic. (D.I.7.1-2)

Hence, the institutions of Machiavelli's republic are certainly immoral, but nonetheless real; for they regulate the actions of the rulers and turn them toward the public utility–as opposed to the private advantage of the powerful.

On the other hand, the fact that Machiavelli's leaders manipulate the commons by various kinds of fraud–stacking the electoral slate, gerrymandering, making promises and delaying their delivery, using oaths and omens cleverly–*does* diminish the institutional quality of his republic, for this manipulation implies that power is exercised contrary to the laws and orders that ought to regulate it. For instance, when the Roman nobility used omens to make the plebs elect nobles as tribunes, they subverted the mixed regime, which assumes that the tribunes give voice to the interests of the commons. As Machiavelli was quite aware, such abuses of religious fraud undermine republics; for instance, when the oracles of antiquity "began to speak in the mode of the powerful, and as that falsity was exposed among peoples, men became incredulous and apt to disturb every good order" (D.I.12.1). Nonetheless, as this passage suggests as well, Machiavelli ultimately believes in the ability of the commons to assert their interests against the tyrannical tendencies of the nobles to some extent, and thus to maintain the mixed regime by their own effort. Thus, he makes it clear that Rome became a truly mixed regime when "the people rose up against" the insolence of the nobles and forced the "creation of the tribunes of the plebs" (D.I.2.7), and that the "guard of freedom" belongs therefore "in the hands of the plebs" (D.I.5.T-1).

On balance, then, Machiavelli surely denies that republican institutions can observe the norms of absolutist morality if they are to be effective. Moreover, he limits the significance of even these consequentialist institutions by advising leaders to circumvent them by fraud when necessary. But the purpose of this advice is to make republican institutions more effective rather than abolish them, for Machiavelli is quite certain that republics will not attain greatness–the highest good–unless they are generally governed through laws and orders that grant the people a share in authority. This expedient institutionalism can be seen most clearly from his praise of the Roman dictator, an office whose "authority extended to being able to decide by himself regarding remedies for . . . urgent danger, and to do everything without consultation, and to punish everyone without appeal" (D.I.34.2). More precisely,

> in a republic, one would not wish anything ever to happen that has to be governed with extraordinary modes. For although the extraordinary mode may do good then, nonetheless the example does ill; for if one sets up a habit of breaking the orders for the sake of good, then later

under that coloring, they are broken for ill. So a republic will never be perfect unless it has provided for everything with its laws and has established a remedy for every accident and given the mode to govern it. So, concluding, I say that those republics that in urgent dangers do not take refuge either in the dictator or in similar authorities will always come to ruin in grave accidents. (D.I.34.3)

In other words, the dictator belongs to the orders that stem corruption by returning a republic to its beginnings. In contrast, a prince who founds a corrupt city anew operates outside all orders. Hence, it is in this sense that Machiavelli should be believed when he asserts the superiority of a "civil and free way of life" over an "absolute and tyrannical one" (D.I.9.2).[70]

Well-Ordered License

As we saw in chapter 4, Machiavelli defines the purpose of political order as the collective generation of security, greatness, empire, and treasure. Some of these goods can be attained internally, as citizens may enjoy the reputation and power of office and produce a certain amount of wealth through agriculture, crafts, etc. But this internal generation is limited by the institutional nature of the domestic realm: Glory must not be acquired by private ways, magistrates cannot abuse others at will, and prosperity is limited to lawful business. In contrast, the foreign realm, where the natural condition of license has remained intact, offers nearly unlimited opportunities for acquiring greatness by fighting cataclysmic battles and conquering huge territories, and building mighty empires, for savoring power by subduing entire peoples and turning scores of individuals into slaves, and for ammassing wealth by plundering rich cities and levying heavy taxes. Hence, it arises that a republic lives "by laws within, and by arms without" (FH.II.10). Metaphorically put,

> ambition uses against external people that fury which neither the law nor the king consent to inside; wherefore one's own fury almost always ceases; but she is sure to keep disturbing the sheep-folds of others, wherever her violence puts down the banner. (A.985)

Conversely, Machiavelli's citizens need to make war abroad in order to maintain liberty and peace at home. In other words, a well-ordered republic prevents its citizens–whose first nature tends to ambitious license–from venting their rapacity on each other by directing it toward foreigners.

In addition to serving as an outlet for ambition, foreign war also provides the condition that makes it rational for self-regarding individuals to cooperate with their fellows, insofar as the threat from abroad outweighs the risks of cooperation at home. At the most basic level, Machiavelli's republic is thus an alliance of certain individuals (called citizens) against all others (called foreigners), with the purpose of gratifying the former and exploiting the latter. This can be most clearly seen from cities where lack of good customs leaves human ambition without fetters. Florence's fortune, for instance, "is such that when wars outside are ended, those inside begin" (FH.III.11); for "when peace came . . . the city was left without war and without a check. As a result, wicked humors grew without any hesitation" (FH.IV.28).[71]

This need for war and the outward deflection of ambition also makes republics far more aggressive in foreign affairs than principalities, since princes can exploit their own subjects whereas citizens must turn on foreigners. Thus, "of all hard servitudes, that is hardest that submits you to a republic" because the "end of the republic is to enervate and to weaken all other bodies so as to increase its own body"; in contrast, "a prince who makes you submit does not do this, if that prince is not some barbarian" (D.II.2.4). Imperial exploitation of foreigners is therefore the real import of Machiavelli's claim that the ancients had such an "affection for the free way of life" since "it is seen through experience that cities have never expanded either in dominion or riches if they have not been in freedom" (D.II.2.1). And Machiavelli's love of liberty and elevation of the republic to the best regime ultimately reduces to its superior ability to acquire imperial greatness by war; for "the best armies that can be, are those of armed peoples, and they cannot be resisted except by armies similar to themselves" (L.214.1156).

Accordingly, the deeper purpose of republican institutions in Machiavelli's thought is this: to organize the natural efforts of men at satisfying their desires in such a way that they collectively generate a far greater amount of glory, dominion, and wealth than they could have attained by proceeding individually. Instead of cancelling their efforts by fighting each other in a natural condition of license, men are aggregated into a political order that enables them to combine their energies and jointly exploit those who have remained outside. It is above all in this sense that Machiavelli's best regime–and therewith his political thought as a whole–can be characterized as "well-ordered license," that is, a political order that constrains men's licentious impulses so that they can be gratified more effectively on the collective level.[72] In other words, Machiavelli's republic substitutes war made on foreigners by citizens who are accustomed to a civil way of life for unconstrained conflict among individuals who consist merely of their first nature. Accordingly, when Machiavelli extols liberty and defines it as self-government under laws he really speaks of an institutionalized kind of license, which places its exploitative burden on outsiders.

Again, Machiavelli is at loggerheads with classical republicans; for they strove to suppress ambition in order to make men virtuous and provide them with the goods of the soul, whereas he makes ambition supremely successful in order to win the goods of Fortune. In Aristotle's terms, Machiavelli's republic is nothing more than an "alliance" (*symmachia*), that is, a "partnership in location and for the sake of not committing injustice against each other and of transacting business," and definitely not a "community of the good life" (*eu zen koinonia*) that aims to "make the citizens good and just."[73] Likewise, Machiavelli did not understand the "civil way of life" (*vivere civile*) as the mutual dependence of citizens with regard to actions that realize virtue–as the civic humanists did,[74] but as the institutionalization of two kinds of conflict: the struggle between nobility and plebs and their joint war on foreigners.

The Problem of Patriotism

As we have seen, there is strong evidence that Machiavelli did not conceive republics as communities in the classical sense. Nonetheless, there is one aspect of his thought that seems to suggest otherwise: namely, his utterances about "love of fatherland" (*amore della patria*). For he seems to think that those who love their fatherland work for the common good not merely as a means to personal gratification, but also as an end in itself. Thus, Machiavelli claims about himself that "whenever I could honor my fatherland, even to my burden and danger, I have done it willingly,"[75] and we are told that a city "lives politically" when "love of fatherland [is] able to do more in all than any other respect" (D.III.8.1), including, as we know, the salvation of the soul.[76] Indeed, Machiavelli goes as far as to suggest that patriotism is a natural rather than acquired characteristic when he speaks of a "natural affection which every man ought to feel for his fatherland,"[77] and when he asserts that "love of fatherland is caused by nature" in contrast to love of one's general, which depends on his *virtù* and is therefore acquired (AG.IV.354).[78] The deeper reason for this naturalness may rest with his assumption that the endowments human beings receive from nature are mediated by their native land: a man's "being and then all of good that Fortune and nature have conceded him there depend on [the fatherland]; and so much is he greater in them as the fatherland happens to be more noble."[79] Apart from patriotism, this mediation also seems to result in the naturalness of one's native language, which Machiavelli calls the "fatherland's tongue" (*lingua patria*) and ascribes to first nature in contrast to art.[80] Such language further plays a role in Machiavelli's maxim that hereditary princes who acquire new subjects will govern them with ease, if they have customs in common with their old subjects and are "of the same province and same language" (P.III.9). In short, when Machiavelli speaks of the fatherland he seems to believe in a community that consists not only in shared customs, but is rooted by nature in the fact of having been born in the same country.

But Machiavelli's seeming belief in this patriotic community– where it is natural for men to work for the common good–can neither be squared with his otherwise ubiquitous assumption that human beings are naturally licentious individuals, who at best can be habituated to cooperate for selfish gain, nor with his equally prominent proposition that coercion must be used on a regular basis to keep the citizens of republics in line. Hence, we have arrived at another real inconsistency in Machiavelli's thought: Whereas the vast majority of his utterances attains its meaning and coherence from the assumption that men are by nature self-regarding individuals, the few passages cited above take them to be born patriots; in other words, whereas Machiavelli generally gives priority to the part over the whole, here he does the opposite.

To remain consistent, Machiavelli should have described love of fatherland as one of the good customs that citizens acquire under constraint and that enable the leading men to defend the republic's institutions against transgressors. Indeed, there is at least one passage where Machiavelli follows this advice, namely when he ascribes lack of patriotism to corruption, that is, the absence of good customs:

> Men who are used to living in a corrupt city, where the education has not produced any goodness in them . . . and to obtain their wish and to satisfy their perversity of spirit, they would be content to see the ruin of their fatherland. (D.III.30.1)

That Machiavelli committed an intellectual error when ascribing patriotism to nature is further suggested by the fact that what he calls the "fatherland's tongue" is clearly acquired in early childhood and can even be lost through extreme disuse–an error we commit ourselves when referring to "native" language. When combined with the overwhelming weight of Machiavelli's contrary assumptions and propositions, this reasoning ought to permit the conclusion that Machiavelli made a mistake when ascribing patriotism to nature.

Civil Principality

As mentioned above, the institutionalized authority of a civil way of life can be exercised not only by the elected officials of a republic but also by a prince, making his state a law-governed kingdom or "civil principality." Besides pharaonic Egypt, which, according to Machiavelli, was "governed with laws," the most significant instance of such a civil principality is the kingdom of France, which "is moderated more by laws than any other kingdom of which knowledge is had in our times" (D.I.58.2). More precisely, the French "kings are obligated by infinite laws," as "he who ordered that state wished those kings to act in their own mode as to arms and money, but in every other thing they should not be able to to dispose except as the laws order" (D.I.16.5). Interestingly, early Rome thus comes to light as a civil principality as well, for "he who considers well the authority that Romulus reserved for himself will see that none other was reserved except that of commanding the armies when war was decided on and that of convoking the Senate," and thus see that "all the first orders of [Rome] were more conformable to a civil and free way of life than to an absolute and tyrannical one" (D.I.9.2).

Since the greatest challenge to a civil way of life consists of the enmity between the great and the people, the "one who ordered" the kingdom of France constituted the parlements as a "third judge" to check both the "ambition of the powerful and their insolence" and the "hatred of the generality of people against the great" (P.XIX.74-75). Thus, among the "infinite good institutions" of France (P.XIX.74), "parlements are those who maintain [its] laws and orders, especially that of Paris"; in particular, "they are renewed by it whenever it makes an execution against a prince of that kingdom and when it condemns the king in its verdicts" (D.III.1.5). In other words, the authoritative acts of the parlement renew the good customs of the French in another instance of "return to the beginnings"; for "kingdoms also have need of renewing themselves and bringing back their laws toward their beginnings" (D.III.1.5).

In addition to being founded, civil principalities can also arise from republics when their civil way of life is about to collapse, and one humor feels so threatened by the other that it clamors for protection by a strongman; in Machiavelli's words, "a private citizen becomes prince of his fatherland . . . with the support of his fellow citizens (which one could call a civil principality . . .)" when "the great see they cannot resist the people" and "begin to give reputation to one of themselves," in order to "make him prince so that they can satisfy their appetite under his shadow"; alternatively, "the people, when they see cannot resist the great, give reputation to one, and make him prince so as to be defended with his authority" (P.IX.38-39). Machiavelli's model for this kind of civil principality was Florence under Cosimo de' Medici (d. 1464), who "alone in Florence was prince" (FH.VII.5) even though the city retained its republican institutions. "Made with the favor of the people," the "state of Cosimo . . . inclined more toward the principality than toward the republic," insofar as "things [were] done according to the will of one, and decided with the consent of many" (DF.24-25). To maintain this intermediate condition between absolute and republican government, Cosimo took care that in "his conversations, in his servants, in riding on horse, in his whole mode of living, and in his marriage alliances, he was always like any modest citizen," in other words, that he "never overstepped civil modesty" (FH.VII.5). But not all civil princes are as tempered as Cosimo: Driven by ambition, they often "break the bridle [i.e., the laws] that can correct them" (D.I.58.2), with the result that "these principalities customarily run into peril when they are about to ascend from a civil order to an absolute one" (P.IX.41-42).

Machiavelli provided something of a blueprint for a civil principality in his *Discursus Florentinarum Rerum* (ca. 1520), where he advised a Medici pope on how to establish a durable regime in Florence, of which the Medici had regained control in 1512. The proposed regime appears to be a "republic," if considered "without your [i.e., the Pope's] authority," but really is a "monarchy, because you command the arms, command the criminal judges, and have the laws in your bosom" (DF.30).[81] In particular, its republican or, better, civil aspect of consists of three institutions that give a share of authority to the "three qualities of men" in the city. To satisfy the most ambitious individuals, sixty-five citizens of gravity and influence should be appointed for life to fill the highest offices of the Signoria (i.e., the magistracy) on a rotating basis. The middling sort will be represented by a Council of Two Hundred, also appointed for life, whose task is to advise the Signoria. To satisfy the lowest rank, the "universality of citizens" should be allowed to elect a Council of Thousand, which would allot all offices and magistracies, except for the Sixty-Five, and should be given Gonfaloniers who—in the manner of Roman tribunes–can veto the decisions of the Signoria and the Two Hundred, and appeal them to the Thousand. The princely aspect of this regime consists first of all of the fact that the Sixty-five, Two Hundred, the Gonfaloniers, and the Eight of the Balia–a committee with arbitrary power to remodel government–are to be appointed by the Pope. Second, whenever the Council of Thousand allots offices, the pouch containing the names of the candidates should be kept by eight "couplers," who are selected by the Pope and, "remaining in secret, can give the decision to whom they wish." Nonetheless, "so that the universality may believe that those were pouched who had won [the election], it should be permitted to the Council to send as security two citizens chosen by it, to be witnesses of the pouching" (DF.29). In short, just as in the case of Cosimo de' Medici, things are decided by one but done with the consent of many, making this state a civil principality.

The Cyle of Regimes

Considered as a process, Machiavelli's ideas about political order manifest a distinct sequence. In the beginning, there is a natural condition of license among individuals who struggle for domination on account of ambition and fear. Out of this struggle, a new principality arises as the primary political order, when the individual with the greatest *virtù* succeeds at imposing his will on a number on others by threatening them with violence; in other words, political order as such comes into being by autocratic force.

The subsequent path depends on the new prince. If he chooses the temporary pleasures available to tyrants, he will seek to exploit his subjects and leave the principality to his descendants. If such succession takes place over several generations, the subjects will become habituated to the princely line and a hereditary principality forms. On the other hand, if the princes habituate the subjects to a religious belief and the dominion is subsequently taken over by a cleric, an ecclesiastical principality has come into existence. Further, when a hereditary prince adds a new province to his domain he thereby creates a mixed principality. All of these principalities come to an end when an usurper or founder succeeds at wresting them from their rulers.

A founder is a new prince who has sufficient imagination to understand that the true good consists of perpetual glory bestowed on those who leave behind lasting institutions, and thus establishes a civil way of life by introducing wholly new laws and orders and habituating his subjects to them. Once the ordering principle of such a dominion changes from the will of the founder and his successors to laws and orders, a civil principality or a republic have come into being, depending on whether these institutions are maintained by a prince or magistrates. Civil principalities usually come to an end when ambition drives the prince to break the laws and assume absolute authority, transforming the state into a new principality. Republics come to an end when the corruption of good customs has become so general that institutionalized punishment no longer suffices to hold transgressors in check; then, the people either elevate one man to the position of civil prince or lapse into a condition of complete license, or a new prince takes power which he uses either to his own advantage or to found the republic anew.

This sequence may be considered the true cycle of regimes according to Machiavelli, replacing the classical succession of kingship, tyranny, aristocracy, oligarchy, democracy, and mobrule, which he mentions for comparison at the beginning of the *Discourses*.[82] Furthermore, the alternation from license to political order and back to license gives concrete content to Machiavelli's astrological belief that the circular motions of heavenly bodies impart a cycle of order and disorder on the affairs of men, as

> *virtù* makes regions tranquil: and from tranquility then results leisure: and leisure burns countries and towns. Then, when a province has for a time been in a state of disorder, *virtù* often returns to live there another time. (GA.V.967)[83]

In other words, the *virtù* of a new prince imposes a first political order on a region living in license; but, given the corrupting influence of ambition, the regimes that descend from his founding collapse eventually, giving way to another state of license.

Notes

1. Polybius, *The Rise of the Roman Empire,* trans. Ian Scott-Kilvert (London: Penguin Classics, 1979), VI.5.

2. Leo Strauss, *Thoughts on Machiavelli* (Chicago: University of Chicago Press, 1958), 201; Harvey C. Mansfield, Jr., *Machiavelli's New Modes and Orders: A Study of the* Discourses on Livy (Ithaca: Cornell University Press, 1979), 36.

3. Polybius, *Rise of the Roman Empire,* VI.5.

4. Although Machiavelli seems to say here that changes of sect have human rather than occult origins, he actually shares the astrological belief that the rise and fall of religions is governed by the heavenly cycle; for he claims that "the heavens . . . inspired in the breasts of the Roman Senate the choosing of Numa Pompilius as successor to Romulus," who then founded Roman religion (D.I.11.1). Also, Machiavelli's association of the Christian religion with "heaven disarmed" (D.II.2.2) probably refers to the astrological claim that Christianity originated from the conjunction of Jupiter with the peace-loving Mercury; and his above statement that "sects vary two or three times in five or in six thousand years," that is, have a life span of 1,666 to 3,000 years, seems to draw on the ancient idea that the entry of the vernal equinox (i.e., the sun's position relative to the ecliptic on March 20) into a new sign of the zodiac every 2,148 years causes the violent overthrow of one race of gods by another, followed by a corresponding change of worship. On the astrological meaning of Machiavelli's references to religion, see Anthony J. Parel, *The Machiavellian Cosmos* (New Haven: Yale University Press, 1992), 46-51; on the precessional cycle, see Graham Hancock, *Fingerprints of the Gods* (New York: Crown Trade Paperbacks, 1995), 227-41, 455-56.

5. Cf. D.I.2.2, 2.6, 58.4; FH.IV.9.

6. See DF.26; cf P.I.1.

7. See Thomas Hobbes, *Leviathan: With Selected Variants from the Latin Edition of 1688* [1651], ed. Edwin Curley (Indianapolis: Hackett, 1994), XIII.

8. Cf. AS.III.961, V.967.

9. Cf. P.III.11, VII.33; FH.III.5; DF.31; AS.V.966.

10. See Hobbes, *Leviathan,* XIII.3-4.

11. Cf. FH.III.13; P.XIX.75.

12. Cf. FH.III.22; *Dell'Ingratitudine*, in TO.980-83, at 983.

13. Cf. D.I.7.2.

14. Cf. D.I.2.3.

15. Cf. FH.I.29.

16. Cf. "A Description of the Method Used by Duke Valentino in Killing Vitellozzo Vitelli, Oliveretto Da Fermo and Others," in CW.I.163-69; "Mission to the Duke of Valentinois," in W.III.141-280, at 259-63.

17. See FH.V.13, VI.13, VI.17-22.

18. Cf. P.XVII.65; "Mission to the Duke of Valentinois," in W.III.141-280, at 264.

19. Cf. D.III.6.2; FH.V.13; AG.IV.354.

20. Sheldon S. Wolin, "Machiavelli: Politics and the Economy of Violence," in *Politics and Vision: Continuity and Innovation in Western Political Thought* (Boston: Little Brown, 1960), 195-238, esp. 220-24.

21. See D.I.19.3-4. Note, however, that Machiavelli states the opposite at D.I.11.2.

22. Cf. D.III. 5.

23. See P.XVIII.70-71; P.XIX.72-73, 75, 78; P.XX.83.

24. Cf. D.I.16.4-5, 40.5-6; FH.II.34.

25. The synonymy of these three terms can be seen most directly from their

common opposition to an absolute and tyrannical order at D.I.9.2 and D.I.25; cf. D.I.55.4; FH.III.5; DF.23, 27.

26. Cf. D.I.18.3.

27. Cf. D.I.11.1, 24.1, 37.2, 45.1, 49.2, 55.4; P.XVIII.69; FH.II.21, IV.30, V.6, VIII.6.

28. Cf. FH.II.39.

29. Cf. FH.Pr.

30. For a semantic analysis of Machiavelli's concept of *ordini,* see Hans De Vries, *Essai sur la terminologie constitutionelle chez Machiavel ("Il Principe")* ('S-Gravenhage: Uitgeverij Excelsior, 1957), 8-22; J. H. Whitfield, "On Machiavelli's use of *ordini,"* *Italian Studies* 10 (1955): 19-39.

31. Cf. DF.27-28.

32. Cf. D.I.49.1.

33. On ancient republicanism, see F. E. Adcock, *Roman Political Ideas and Practice* (Ann Arbor: University of Michigan Press, 1959); D. C. Earl, *The Moral and Political Tradition of Rome* (Ithaca: Cornell University Press, 1967); Claude Nicolet, *The World of the Citizen in Republican Rome,* trans. P. S. Falla (Berkeley, Calif.: University of California Press, 1980); Ronald C. Wilson, *Ancient Republicanism: Its Struggle for Liberty Against Corruption* (New York: P. Lang, 1989); Paul A. Rahe, *Republics Ancient and Modern,* vol. I, *The Ancien Régime in Classical Greece* (Chapel Hill: University of North Carolina Press, 1994).

On humanist republicanism, see Hans Baron, *The Crisis of the Early Italian Renaissance: Civic Humanism and Republican Liberty in an Age of Classicism and Tyranny,* 2nd ed. (Princeton University Press, 1966); Eugenio Garin, *Italian Humanism, Philosophy and Civic Life in the Renaissance,* trans. Peter Munz (New York: Harper and Row, 1965); Quentin Skinner, *The Foundations of Modern Political Thought,* vol. 1, *The Renaissance* (Cambridge: Cambridge University Press, 1978), 69-112, 139-44, 152-80; Maurizio Viroli, *From Politics to Reason of State: The Acquisition and Transformation of the Language of Politics 1250-1600* (Cambridge: Cambridge University Press, 1992a), 71-125.

34. On *homonoia* and *concordia,* see Aristotle, *Nicomachean Ethics,* trans. Terence Irwin (Indianapolis: Hackett, 1985), 1167a27-1167b16; Polybius, *The Rise of the Roman Empire,* trans. Ian Scott-Kilvert (London: Penguin Classics, 1979), VI.46, 48; Cicero, *De Re Publica,* trans. C. W. Keyes, Loeb Classical Library 213 (Cambridge, Mass.: Harvard University Press, 1928), I.xxxii, II.xlii; Cicero, *On Duties,* trans. Walter Miller, Loeb Classical Library 30 (Cambridge, Mass.: Harvard University Press, 1913), I.xxv; Sallust, *The War With Catiline,* in *Sallust,* trans. J. C. Rolfe, Loeb Classical Library 116 (Cambridge, Mass.: Harvard University Press, 1985), 1-129, at VI, IX. On friendship in cities, see Aristotle, *Nicomachean Ethics,* 1155a23-1157b23; Aristotle, *The Politics,* trans. Carnes Lord (Chicago: University of Chicago Press, 1984), 1280b37-38.

35. On size, see Aristotle, *Nicomachean Ethics,* 1170b30-35; Aristotle, *Politics,* 1326a26-1327a3. On foreign contacts, see Aristotle, *Politics,* 1327a11-

39; Cicero, *De Re Publica,* II.iv. On education, see Aristotle, *Nicomachean Ethics,* 1179b32-1180a33; Aristotle, *Politics,* 1263b36-1264a1, 1332a40–1342b35; Cicero, *De Re Publica,* I.ii, V.iv; Cicero, *De Legibus,* trans. C. W. Keyes, Loeb Classical Library 213 (Cambridge, Mass.: Harvard University Press, 1928), II.vii, II.xiv-xv.

36. On man as a naturally political or social being, see Aristotle, *Politics,* 1253a2; Cicero, *De Re Publica,* I.i, xxv; Cicero, *De Legibus,* I.v.

37. Cf. FH.VII.1.

38. On sects and partisans in Machiavelli's thought, see also Harvey C. Mansfield, Jr., "Party & Sect in Machiavelli's *Florentine Histories,*" in *Machiavelli and the Nature of Political Thought,* ed. Martin Fleisher (New York: Atheneum, 1972), 209-75; Gisela Bock, "Civil Discord in Machiavelli's *Istorie Fiorentine,*" in *Machiavelli and Republicanism,* ed. Gisela Bock, Quentin Skinner, and Maurizio Viroli (Cambridge: Cambridge University Press, 1990), 181-201.

39. Cf. FH.VII.31.

40. According to Wolin, "the truly novel element in Machiavelli's approach was that it not only converted the problem of interest into the central problem of political theory, but that he sought to accompany this with a theory which indicated both the salutary effects of socio-economic conflicts amd the techniques by which they might be resolved. . . . The upshot of Machiavelli's argument was to recast the notion of political unity in accordance with the new picture of political society as a diagram of interest-propelled forces." See Wolin, "Machiavelli," 232-33.

41. Cf. Aristotle, *Politics,* 1281b26-1282a41, 1293b33-1294b39; Polybius, *The Rise of the Roman Empire,* VI.3, 10-18; Cicero, *De Re Publica,* I.xxix, I.xxxv, II.xxxii-xxxiv; Cicero, *De Legibus,* III.iii-v, vii, x.

42. Cf. P.IX.39; DF.27; FH.II.42, III.1, III.18.

43. Cf. Parel, *Machiavellian Cosmos,* 101-12.

44. See D.I.2.7; Livy, *The Early History of Rome: Books I-V of The History of Rome From Its Foundation,* trans. Aubrey de Sélincourt (London: Penguin Books, 1960), 1.59-II.1.

45. See D.I.3.2, cf. 40.4; Livy, *The Early History of Rome,* II.31-32, cf. III.51-56.

46. See D.II.22.1; D.III.16.1.

47. Cf. Thucydides, *History of the Peloponnesian War,* trans. Rex Warner (London: Penguin Books, 1954), VI.8-9

48. Cf. D.I.12.1; FH.III.1.

49. "Commissions to Pisa and Other Places Within and Without the Florentine Dominion," in W.IV.304-16, at 307.

50. Cf. D.III.34.2-3.

51. Note, however, Machiavelli's claim that "the common utility that is drawn from a free way of life is not recognized by anyone while it is possessed: this is to being able to enjoy one's things freely, without any suspicion, not fearing for the honor of wives and that of children, not to be afraid for oneself" (D.I.16.3).

52. Cf. D.III.8.2.

53. Cf. D.I.16.4; Livy, *Early History of Rome*, II.3-5.

54. Cf. Livy, *Early History of Rome*, IV.13-16.

55. Cf. D.I.8.1, 4; D.III.8.1-2; Livy, *Rome and Italy*, VI.11-20.

56. See Livy, *Rome and Italy: Books VI-X of* The History of Rome from its Foundation, trans. Betty Radice (London: Penguin Books, 1982), VIII.7-8.

57. Cf. Livy, *Rome and Italy*, VIII.30-35.

58. See D.I.29.3; Livy, *Rome and the Mediterranean: Books XXXI-XLV of* The History of Rome from its Foundation, trans. Henry Bettenson (London: Penguin Books, 1976), XXXVIII.50-60.

59. See D.I.24.2; Livy, *Early History of Rome*, II.10-13; Polybius, *Rise of the Roman Empire*, VI.55.

60. See D.II.16.1, III.45; Livy, *Rome and Italy*, VIII.9-10, X.26-29.

61. See D.III.20.

62. See Leslie J. Walker, "Notes," in *The Discourses of Niccolò Machiavelli*, trans. Leslie J. Walker, vol. II (New Haven: Yale University Press, 1950), 150.

63. Livy, *Early History of Rome*, II.14.

64. Marcus Porcius Cato the Elder lived from 234 to 149 BC, Marcus Porcius Cato the Younger from 95 to 46 BC.

65. Cf. D.I.49.3.

66. See D.III. 49.1-3. Cf. Livy, *Early History of Rome*, II.59; Livy, *Rome and Italy*, VIII.18; Livy, *Rome and the Mediterranean*, XXXIX.8-18; Polybius, *Rise of the Roman Empire*, VI.38.

67. Machiavelli here refers to Marcus Junius Brutus, leader of the resistance against Caesar and his party, not Lucius Junius Brutus, who led the rebellion against the Tarquin kings in 510 B.C. Cf. D.I.5, 37.2.

68. See D.III.22.3.

69. According to Strauss, Machiavelli's idea of "foundation is, as it were, continuous foundation; not only at the beginning, but 'every day,' a commonwealth needs 'new orders.' Once one realizes this, one sees that the founders of a republic are its leading men throughout the ages, or its ruling class." See Strauss, *Thoughts on Machiavelli*, 44, cf. 166-67, 228-31, 274, 278. For a recent elaboration of this argument, see Harvey C. Mansfield and Nathan Tarcov, "Introduction," in Niccolò Machiavelli, *Discourses on Livy*, trans. Harvey C. Mansfield and Nathan Tarcov (Chicago: University of Chicago Press, 1996), xvii-xliv, esp. xxiv-xxix.

70. Cf. D.I.25.

71. Cf. FH.IV.15; Mansfield, "Party & Sect in Machiavelli's *Florentine Histories*," 245, 257-58.

72. Note that this phrase is my creation, not Machiavelli's; nonetheless, he would have found it appropriate.

73. Aristotle, *Politics,* 1280b5-1281a3, mt.

74. On the humanist concept of *vivere civile* or *vivere politico* in particular, see J. G. A. Pocock, *The Machiavellian Moment: Florentine Political Thought and the Atlantic Republican Tradition* (Princeton: Princeton University Press, 1975), 49-80; Maurizio Viroli, "Machiavelli and the Republican Idea of

Politics," in *Machiavelli and Republicanism,* ed. Gisela Bock, Quentin Skinner, and Maurizio Viroli (Cambridge: Cambridge University Press, 1990), 143-72.

75. *Discorso o dialogo intorno alla nostra lingua* [Discourse or dialogue internal to our language], in TO.923-30, at 923-24, mt.

76. Cf. D.III.41, 47; FH.III.5, 7, 8; AG.I.302; *Nature di huomini fiorentini et in che luoghi si possino inserire le laude loro* [Natures of Florentine men and in which place their praise can be inserted], in TO.917-918, at 918; L.321.1010; "Mission to the Emperor of Germany," in W.IV.83-154, at 111.

77. On the other hand, love of military leaders can also arise from a "natural conformity," that is, being born in the same province as they; see AG.I.316; cf. D.III.33.1.

78. "Mission to the Duke of Valentinois," in W.III.141-280, at 166, mt.

79. *Discorso o dialogo intorno alla nostra lingua,* in TO.923-30, at 924, mt.

80. *Discorso o dialogo intorno alla nostra lingua,* in TO.923-30, at 928-29, mt.

81. The following account of the regime that Machiavelli proposed for Florence is based on DF.27-29, as well as the translator's annotation in "A Discourse on Remodeling the Government of Florence," in CW.I.101-115, at 108-13.

82. See D.I.2.3-4.

83. Cf. FH.V.1; D.II.Pr.2.

Chapter 6

Struggle for Empire

The dualism of Machiavelli's anthropological assumptions–a first nature tending to ambitious license, a second nature capable of cooperative customs–manifests itself also in two kinds of foreign politics: driven by ambition and fear, cities exist necessarily in a foreign condition of license, which consists of a violent struggle for domination that ends only with the imposition of a system-wide or encompassing empire by the winner; on the basis of cooperative habits, the successor states of such an empire are sometimes able to maintain foreign institutions that mitigate conflict among them.

The Causes of War and Security

Foreign affairs are by nature in a state of license for the simple reason that the license which prevailed among the first human beings–who lived in isolation and were exposed to the rapine of others–continues to exist between the cities that have been built to protect the individuals within. In other words, Machiavelli's notion of license corresponds to what contemporary students of international relations, especially those of the realist persuasion, call "anarchy" and understand as the absence of central protection.[1]

Cities make war on each other for the same two reasons that

lead to conflict among individuals: ambition and fear for one's preservation. In Machiavelli's words, "war is made on a republic for two reasons: one, to become master of it; the other, for fear lest it seize you" (D.I.6.4).[2] Again, his explanation of war from ambition is straightforward: Cities use force against each other in order to attain goods that cannot be enjoyed jointly, such as greatness, empire, and treasure. For instance, Rome "had as its end empire and glory" (D.II.9), and "the intention of whoever makes war through choice—or, in truth, ambition—is to acquire and to maintain the acquisition, and to proceed with so that it enriches and does not impoverish the country" (D.II.6.1).

Machiavelli's innovative account of war from fear for preservation begins with the assumption that the capabilities of states which are close enough to cause harm are threatening in themselves, regardless of the professed or surmised intentions of those who possess them; for, under anarchy, we can never be certain that the others will not use their capabilities to our detriment, either presently or in the future, and therefore tend to imagine the worst. Thus, when the commerce-minded magistrates of Florence wanted to cut military expenditures, arguing that "we are under the [French] king's protection, and our enemies are extinguished, [Cesare Borgia] has no reason to attack us," Machiavelli lectured them that "such an opinion cannot be more temerarious, because every city, every state must consider as enemies all those who can hope to be able to occupy what is hers, and against whom she cannot defend herself."[3]

When faced with such a threat from the capabilities of others, ingenuity and imagination suggest that, at a minimum, we acquire military forces of such a strength that would-be aggressors will think that the risks and costs of attacking us outweigh the possible gains. In other words, the basic way to security in the foreign condition of license consists of a strategy of "deterrence."[4] In his address to the Florentine government, Machiavelli makes the following case for deterrence:

> The remedy is to make the forces be in such order that [the French king] has to have respect for you in each of his decisions, as [he does] for the others of Italy, and not—by remaining disarmed—give spirit to someone powerful to demand you from the King as booty . . . but to act in a mode that he has to esteem you, and that others will not think of subjugating you.[5]

A policy of appeasement or reassurance, in contrast, is bound to fail in a world of limitless ambition: "for he to whom you will have conceded this and uncovered your cowardice will not stand still but will want to take other things away from you and will get more inflamed against you since he esteems you less" (D.II.14). Despite their usual prowess, the Romans once made this mistake: When the Samnites complained that the Latins had attacked them, the Romans "did not wish to forbid such a war to the Latins, desiring not to anger them. This not only did not anger them, but made them become more spirited against [the Romans] and uncover themselves as enemies sooner" (D.II.14). In short, a strategy of deterrence is indispensable to security under anarchy.

Yet, at the same time, deterrence fails to consider the "security dilemma" connected with acquiring weapons and other means for defensive purposes: Since one state can never be certain that the defensive capabilities of another will not some day be used offensively, capabilities acquired for the sake of mere deterrence inherently create a threat to other states as well. In addition, since the latter states are likely to respond to this threat by strengthening their own capabilities in turn, there arises a "spiral" of arms build-up and perception of threat, which erupts into war as soon as one state believes that the likely cost of suffering an attack exceeds that of carrying out a preemptive strike.[6] In Machiavelli's words, "the fear of one power brought the growth of someone weak, and when that one had grown, he was to be feared, and being feared they sought to bring him down" (FH.II.10).[7] In short, the effort to gain security by deterrence generates the insecurity of war as an unintended consequence.

To cope with this problem, Machiavelli first inquires whether a state could avoid war by acquiring enough power to deter, but not so strong as to pose a threat:

> I would well believe that to make a republic that would last for a long time, the mode would be to order it within like Sparta or like Venice. to settle it in a strong place of such power that nobody would believe he could crush it at once. On the other hand, it would not be so great as to be formidable to its neighbors; and so it could enjoy its state at length. (D.I.6.4)[8]

Machiavelli's mention of a "strong place" suggests in particular that the best way to prevent one's capabilities from provoking war is to make it physically impossible to use them offensively, for instance, by relying mostly on natural defenses. However, having made this suggestion, Machiavelli immediately rejects it as a practical impossibility. The sheer contingency of politics makes it impossible

to strike an exact balance between inviting aggression through
weakness and provoking war through strength:

> If the thing could be held balanced in this mode, it would be the true
> political life and the true quiet of a city. But since all things of men are
> in motion and cannot stay steady, they must either rise or fall . . . one
> cannot, as I believe, balance this thing, nor maintain this middle way
> exactly. (D.I.6.4)[9]

In addition, if a city were fortunate enough to keep the peace by
maintaining this "middle way," it would thereby lose its military
prowess or lapse into civil strife from want of external adversity: "on
the other hand, if heaven were so kind that it did not have to make
war, from that would arise the idleness to make it either effeminate or
divided; these two things together, or each by itself, would be the
cause of its ruin" (D.I.6.4). Finally, cities cannot avoid being drawn
into the wars of others by staying neutral, because neutrals make
enemies of the losers, who could have needed their help, and appear
easy prey to the winners: "he who stays neutral comes to be hated by
him who loses, and held in contempt by him who wins, like one who
needs not be taken into account and is estimated to be an useless ally
and an unformidable enemy" (L.233.1184).[10] In short, war as the
unintended consequence of efforts at preservation cannot be avoided
in the foreign condition of license.

The inference with Machiavelli draws from this anarchic fact is
uncompromisingly logical; since war cannot be avoided, the advantage
must be gained by beginning it on one's own terms:

> The Romans, seeing inconveniences from afar, always found remedies
> for them and never allowed them to continue so as to escape a war,
> because they knew war may not be avoided but is deferred to the
> advantage of others. So they decided to make war with Philip and
> Antiochus in Greece in order not to have to do so in Italy. (P.III.12-
> 13)[11]

But merely to defeat an enemy on the battlefield will bring only
temporary relief, since it will rearm sooner or later. To gain lasting
security, the adversary's war-making potential–its people, raw
materials, and manufacturing capacity–must either be destroyed or,
better still, subdued and added to one's own resources. If the defeated
city was used to autocratic rule, the remaining inhabitants can be
subordinated by killing the elite, especially the princely house, and
settling one's own people among them.[12] On the other hand, if the

vanquished were used to a republican way of life, "there is no secure mode to possess them other than to ruin them," for "the memory of their ancient liberty does not and cannot let them rest" (P.V.20-21).[13] What such ruin means more concretely becomes clear from Machiavelli's account of ancient warfare: "then men overcome in war either were killed or kept in perpetual slavery . . . conquered cities were either laid waste or the inhabitants driven out, their goods taken from them and they themselves sent wandering through the world" (AG.II.332).

In sum, in a world where war cannot be avoided, security rests on imperial domination. In Machiavelli's words, "in ordering a republic there is need to think of the more honorable part and to order it so that if indeed necessity brings it to expand [which it always will], it can conserve what it has seized" (D.I.6.4). Fear for preservation thus leads to the same outcome as ambition: a struggle for empire among cities.

Alliance Failure and Bandwagoning

In a condition of license, the only form of cooperation sanctioned by narrowly instrumental reason consists of an alliance against a common threat which is greater than the threat the allies pose to each other; for only fear of destruction or servitude makes it worthwhile to run the risks of cooperation under anarchy, namely to become weaker than one's partner by gaining relatively less from or becoming relatively more dependent on cooperation. Machiavelli understood this logic only too well: "a prince must beware never to associate with someone more powerful than himself so as to attack others, except when necessity presses" (P.XXI.90); for, then, "there will be nothing through which the allies need to doubt one another, for . . . the enemies will be so powerful and dangerous that they will be held together chained" (L.211.1148-49).[14] Conversely, once the common threat has subsided, alliances readily break apart, because "promises are . . . not observed when the causes that made them promise are missing" (D.III.42.1).[15] In short, "alliances between princes are maintained only by arms,"[16] and are "broken for utility" (D.I.59).

While grasping the logic of alliances, Machiavelli has little faith in their effectiveness: "the union of many heads against one is difficult to make, and then, when it is made, difficult to keep" (L.233.1183).[17] This difficulty arises first from lack of foresight:

Powers that are distant and do not have business with [an expanding city] care for the thing as a distant affair that does not belong to them. They stay in that error until this fire comes near them; when it has come, they have no remedy to eliminate it unless with their own forces, which then are not enough since it has become very powerful. (D.II.1.2)

It was such a failure to foresee the expansion of a still distant Rome that doomed the Carthaginians: "their power, together with the distance between their borders and the Roman people, made them never think of assaulting the latter or of succoring the Samnites and the Tuscans [i.e., Etruscans]" in their. wars with the Romans; nor did the Carthaginians "perceive the error they made before the Romans, having subdued all the peoples between them and the Carthaginians, began to combat them over the empire of Sicily and of Spain" (D.II.1.2).

The second cause of alliance failure rests on the "free-rider" problem in the logic of collective action: Seeking to enjoy the benefits of security without having to bear the burdens of war, cities hope that others will eliminate the threat before they have to face it. In contemporary diction, it was such "buck-passing"[18] among the adversaries of the Romans that allowed them to acquire their empire: "while the Roman people was occupied with the other, each of them believed that the other would overcome it and there would be time to defend itself from it either by peace or by war" (D.II.1.2); otherwise, "if two of these powers, when they were fresh, had been combined together intact, one can easily conjecture without doubt that the ruin of the Roman republic would have followed from it" (D.II.1.1).

Both of these causes of alliance failure introduce a significant element of contingency into the quest for empire insofar as success comes to depend on the errors of one's adversaries. Nonetheless, their propensity to pass the buck can be exploited by the Roman strategy of *divide et impera* (divide and rule); for then, is it "almost in the choice of that power to make war with whichever of its neighbors it likes, and to quiet the others with its devices" (D.II.1.2).[19]

In a world where alliances fail, the weak are constrained to seek security by submitting to the strong in exchange for protection; in contemporary parlance, again, they need to "bandwagon."[20] In Machiavelli's words, "weak cities defend themselves by uniting with whoever conquers" (AG.II.333), and men surrender "fear of the enemy nearby being more powerful with them than faith in a friend far away" (FH.V.11).[21] Indeed, Machiavelli elevates bandwagoning to a general rule:

Princes who are assaulted cannot make a greater error, when the attack is made by men very much more powerful than they, than to refuse every accord, especially when it is offered to them. For one will never be offered so base that there is not inside it in some part the well-being of him who accepts it, and there will be a part of victory for him. (D.II.27.4)

Accordingly, once Rome's neighbors had missed the chance to nip the rising republic in the bud, they should have bandwagoned with her, rather than belatedly trying to oppose her: "since Rome had grown to so much power, it was more salutary to seek to appease it and to hold it back with the modes of peace than to make them think about new orders and new defenses with the modes of war" (D.I.33.5).

Modes of Expansion

Machiavelli discusses three strategies that ancient cities used to acquire empire: the Spartan-Athenian, the Etruscan, and the Roman.[22] His assessment of these modes rests on the following principle of proportionality: To maintain the expansion of its empire, a city must maintain a balance between the rate at which additional territories are conquered and the rate at which manpower and economic surplus can be extracted from previously subdued areas, which, in turn, depends on the extent to which their inhabitants have accepted the new rulers.

Sparta and Athens used force to make other cities into "direct subjects" (D.II.4.1). But force, although a highly effective means of conquest, is a poor mode of governance. First, it fails to inspire acceptance by the subjects and thus necessitates sizable forces of occupation that cannot be used to expand the empire elsewhere: "governing cities by violence, especially those accustomed to living freely, is a difficult and laborious thing. If you are not armed and massive with arms, you can neither command nor rule them" (D.II.4.1). Second, this lack of acceptance makes it impossible to recruit manpower from the subjects in order to increase the size of one's forces. As a result, purely coercive empires tend to collapse from imperial overstretch: Sparta, "after it had subjected almost all Greece to itself, showed its weak foundation upon one slightest accident; for when other cities rebelled, following the rebellion of Thebes, caused by Pelopidas, that republic was altogether ruined" (D.I.6.4).

In contrast, the Etruscans established an empire by consent when they formed a "league of several republics together, where none was before another in either authority or rank; in acquiring other cities they made them partners" (D.II.4.1). Given their consensual character, leagues are readily accepted by their members and are defensively strong. Thus, the Etruscan league "was secure for a great time, with the highest glory of empire and of arms and special praise for customs and religion"; for with a league "you easily keep as much as you take" (D.II.4.2). Nonetheless, just like alliances, leagues will fail to defend themselves against adversaries who know how to divide and rule. But the greatest shortcoming of a league rests with its inability to expand beyond a certain number, due to various problems of collective action:

> The cause of its inability to expand is its being a republic that is disunited and placed in various seats, which enables them to consult and decide only with difficulty. It also makes them not be desirous of dominating; for since there are many communities to participate in dominion, they do not esteem such acquisition as much as one republic alone that hopes to enjoy it entirely. Besides this, they govern themselves through a council, and they must be slower in every decision than those who inhabit within one and the same wall. (D.II.4.2)

As a result, leagues are limited in size to a "small group," where one's share in the common good is large enough to induce cooperative behavior.[23] In Machiavelli's words, a league "is to reach twelve or fourteen communities and then not to seek to go further. For having arrived at a rank that seems to enable them to defend themselves from everyone, they do not seek larger dominion" (D.II.4.2). In other words, a league functions like an alliance that remains cohesive in the presence of a common threat, but tends to dissolve when it is absent. At most, leagues can expand their influence beyond the critical number by offering protection to weak cities in exchange for tribute or by making their armed forces available for hire.[24]

In a world where struggle for the most powerful empire is a necessity, strategies that cannot expand an empire beyond a certain limit–such as the Spartan-Athenian and Etruscan modes–are obviously doomed to failure. Now, their limitations result from their one-sidedness: Coercion by itself resolves the problem of collective action, but fails to generate loyal manpower; consent by itself generates loyal manpower, but founders on the problem of collective action. To solve both of these problems in one stroke, one needs to combine coercion and consent in the Roman mode, which, after all, produced the largest and most durable empire the Western world has seen.

Having used massive force to defeat an adversary on the battlefield, the Romans made a conscious choice between killing and enslaving the vanquished or offering them the status of partners (*socii*), for they knew that "men should be either caressed or eliminated, because they avenge themselves for slight offenses but cannot do so for grave ones" (P.III.10).[25] Addressing the Senate, the consul Camillus put this choice as follows:

> You can provide perpetual peace for yourselves, as far as pertains to the Latins, either by raging or by forgiving. Do you wish to make very cruel decisions against those who have surrendered and been conquered? You may destroy all Latium. Do you wish to increase the Roman republic on the example of your forefathers by accepting the conquered into citizenship? Matter is at hand for growing by means of the greatest glory. That rule is certainly the firmest that is obeyed gladly. (D.II.23.2)

Usually taking the second option, Rome "got many partners throughout all Italy who in many things lived with it under equal laws," but, at the same time, "always reserved for it itself the seat of empire and the title of command" over the auxiliary troops the partners had to supply (D.II.4.1). To maintain their consent, the Romans resorted to fraud as well: They planted colonies of Roman veterans among the partner cities and kept the outer provinces of the empire under direct rule; thus, when the partners rebelled at last, the Romans crushed them with ease.[26] Thus, "a republic that wishes to expand [cannot] take another mode, for experience has not shown us any more certain or more true" (D.II.4.1).

Foreign Constraint on Domestic Order

To compete in the foreign struggle for domination, cities must organize their domestic affairs for war. Hence, the pacifist opinion "that there is no thing that has less conformity with another, nor is so dissimilar, than the civil life from the military one" is dangerously mistaken; for a prosperous city like Florence whose humanist leaders neglected its defenses is like "the residences of a proud and regal palace, which, although ornamented with gems and gold, being without cover, have nothing to defend them from the rain" (AG.Pr.301).[27] In short, "without forces cities do not maintain themselves but come to their end; the end is either desolation or servitude."[28]

Since continued expansion is necessary for preservation and

prosperity, the forces of a city should not merely be adequate to the current threat, but as large as possible: "any king or any republic should . . . form in their country as many brigades as it can support" (AG.II.325). Forming many brigades, in turn, requires that "those who plan for a city to make a great empire should contrive with every industriousness to make it full of inhabitants" (D.II.3)."Having thickened the body of its city," Rome thus kept conquering because it "could already put in arms two hundred eighty thousand men," whereas Sparta and Athens went under because they "never passed beyond twenty thousand each" (D.II.3). To increase the number of their inhabitants, cities should promote immigration either by consent, that is, "through keeping the ways open and secure for foreigners . . . so that everyone may inhabit it voluntarily," or by coercion, that is, "through undoing the neighboring cities and sending their inhabitants to inhabit your city" (D.II.3). Further, cities should promote child-bearing by allowing a free way of life that rewards individual achievement:

> [In] all cities and provinces that live freely in every part . . . larger peoples are seen there, because marriages are freer and more desirable to men since each willingly procreates those children he believes he can nourish. He does not fear that his patrimony will be taken away, and he knows not only that they are born free and not slaves, but that they can, through their *virtù,* become princes. (D.II.2.3)

While recognizing the importance of numbers to military power, Machiavelli denies the significance of economic surplus: "not gold, as the common opinion cries out, but good soldiers are the sinew of war; for gold is not sufficient to find good soldiers, but good soldiers are quite sufficient to find gold" (D.II.10.2). In his eyes, this fact is shown by "every history . . . in a thousand places," such as Greece during the Peloponnesian War, when "the counsel and good soldiers of Sparta were worth more than the industry and the money of Athens" (D.II.10.3).

In addition to quantity, the armed forces of a city must also possess quality. Since martial *virtù* is an acquired characteristic–as the "spirited army is not made so by spirited men being in it, but by its orders being well ordered" (AG.II.326), republics should maintain military exercises with the "highest seriousness" (D.II.19.1), and princes should have "no other object, nor any other thought, nor take anything else as his art but the art of war" (P.XIV.58).[29] In promoting soldierly excellence, republics have an advantage over princes as "republics usually honor *virtù,* kingdoms fear it" (AG.II.332); for princes cannot at all tolerate subjects with the power to dethrone them, whereas republics have institutions that can check ambitious individuals.[30] Being able to change their leaders far more readily, republics have a further advantage in matching the humor of their commander to the quality of the times; thus, the Romans defeated Carthage in the Second Punic War because they made the cautious Fabius Maximus their commander when times were difficult and relied on the bold Scipio when it was time to go on the offensive.[31]

Large numbers of capable soldiers are useful only to the extent of their loyalty to the state. Consequently, Machiavelli rejects mercenaries in favor of arming one's own people: "Mercenary and auxiliary arms are useless and dangerous. . . . The cause of this is that they have no love nor cause to keep them in the field other than a small stipend, which is not sufficient to make them want to die for you" (P.XII.48-49); whereas "the best armies that can be, are those of armed peoples" (L.214.1156).[32] In this, hereditary princes are better off than new ones, who may still be resented by their subjects for the injuries from the usurpation; but best off are republics, for they are participatory regimes capable of fostering customs that tie men to the common good.

In sum, the foreign condition of license rewards cities that are open, law-governed, and give the people a share in authority; for it is under such a political order that immigrants will swell the population, marriages will produce soldiers, armed masses will be loyal, excellence will be rewarded, and leadership will accord with the quality of the times. Driven in addition by the necessity to despoil foreigners to keep peace at home, such a regime will be the best for man's natural pursuit of imperial greatness. Historically, the city that most obeyed these selective constraints was obviously the Roman republic, which thus shows "the true way of to make a republic great and to acquire empire" (D.II.19.1).

Further, this foreign constraint to organize domestic affairs for war and conquest entails Machiavelli's most compelling critique of the classical tradition. According to Plato, a city should be small so that its citizens can be made virtuous, it ought to be isolated from the corrupting influences of foreign commerce, and its arms should be borne by the ruling class only.[33] According to Machiavelli, such a city belongs precisely to the kind of "imagined republics and principalities that have never been seen or known to exist in truth" and will learn their ruin rather than their preservation (P.XV.61); for in a condition where struggle for domination is inescapable, virtuous cities that are small, isolated, and keep the people disarmed will readily fall prey to vicious cities that are large, open, and arm the masses–such as Rome. The small, xenophobic, and aristocratic Sparta, which served Plato as a model, thus "showed its weak foundation upon one slightest accident" (D.I.6.4) because of its failure to grow stronger by learning from foreigners and admitting them to citizenship:

> Since Lycurgus, founder of the Spartan republic, considered nothing could dissolve his laws more easily than the mixture of new inhabitants, he did everything so that foreigners should not have to deal there. Besides not admitting them into marriages, into citizenship, and into the other dealings that make men come together, he ordered that leather money should be spent in his republic to take away from everyone the desire to come there, to bring merchandise there, or bring some art there, so the city never could thicken with inhabitants. (D.II.3)[34]

Aristotle also wanted the city to be small enough for the citizens to know each other's characters, but, being more empirically inclined than Plato, accepted the fact that its forces must be fitted to the threat at hand and that supplies need to be obtained by foreign trade.[35] At the same time, he advocated a middle way between having too much and too little strength–in direct contrast to Machiavelli:

> Possessions . . . should be adequate not only for political uses but also for foreign dangers. Hence the extent of them should neither be so much that those near at hand and superior will desire them and those having them will be unable to ward off the attackers, nor so little that they will be unable to sustain a war even against those who are equal and similar.[36]

Thus, Machiavellli's above statement that "if the thing could be held balanced in this mode, it would be the true political life [*vero vivere politico*] and the true quiet of a city" but that "one cannot . . . balance this thing, nor maintain this middle way exactly" (D.I.7.4) may be taken as a direct reference and rejection of this passage from Aristotle's *Politics,* which Machiavelli knew to be one of the principal sources for the humanist notion of *vivere civile/politico.*[37]

In a remarkable conclusion, Leo Strauss, who otherwise condemns Machiavelli, seems to agree with his repudiation of the classical tradition on this ground:

> The moral-political supervision of inventions by the good and wise city is necessarily limited by the need of adaptation to the practices of morally inferior cities which scorn such supervision because their end is

acquisition or ease. . . . Only in this point does Machiavelli's contention that the good cannot be good because there are so many bad ones prove to possess a foundation.[38]

Indeed, it is, according to Strauss, the "use of science for [inventions pertaining to the art of war] which renders impossible the good city in the classical sense."[39]

The classical rejoinders to this critique of virtue were already voiced by Plato. First, if there is unity to the virtues, then those who have more wisdom, justice, and moderation, will also have more courage and cleverness in war, making up for smaller numbers and fewer resources; or, as Plato asked somewhat comically, "wouldn't one boxer with the finest possible training in the art easily fight with two rich, fat nonboxers?"[40] Second, and far more radically, Plato postulated that "we do not hold, as the many do, that preservation and mere existence are what is most honorable for human beings. What is most honorable is for them to become as excellent as possible and to remain so for as long a time as they may exist."[41] Indeed, "for a corrupt person it is better not to be alive, for he necessarily lives badly."[42] Better to suffer death in consequence of having lived a good life than to survive, let alone prosper, by violating what is right—which ought to make sense to non-philosophers if they believed the soul to be immortal and thus capable of carrying their merits and demerits forward forever.[43]

Encompassing Empire and *Virtù*

In a world where alliances tend to fail and the weak bandwagon with the strong, cities that observe Machiavelli's maxims—to pursue a mixed strategy of coercion and consent, arm the people, admit foreigners, maintain military readiness, etc.—will tend to win the foreign struggle for domination. They will destroy, subdue, or assimilate the weak and establish empires that subsume the entire regional system of states—as famously accomplished by the Assyrians, Persians, and Romans. Once such an empire has been securely established, however, *virtù* tends to decline from the corruption that befalls men who lack the invigoration competition of war; for "men become excellent and show their *virtù* according to how they are employed and brought forward by their prince or republic or king. . . . Hence it follows that where authorities are many, many capable men arise; where they are few, few" (AG.II.332).[44] For instance, "when the

Roman Empire had grown and extinguished all the republics and principalities of Europe and Africa and for the greater part those of Asia, no road to *virtù* was left except through Rome; whence it arose that men of *virtù* began to be few" (AG.II.333).

These tendencies result in a cyclical alteration between peaceful order based on the *virtù* that comes to the fore in the prior time of war, and warlike disorder that results from the loss of *virtù* during the prior time of order:

> *Virtù* makes regions tranquil; and from tranquility then results idleness; and idleness burns countries and towns. Then, when a province has for a time been in a state of disorder, *virtù* often returns to live there another time. (AS.V.967)[45]

On a world-historical scale, this cycle can be understood as concentrations of *virtù* that move from region to region:

> Where [the world] had first placed its *virtù* in Assyria, it put it in Media, then in Persia, until it came to be in Italy and Rome. And if no empire followed after the Roman Empire that might have endured and in which the world might have kept its *virtù* together, it is seen nonetheless to be scattered in many nations where they lived *virtuosamente,* such as was the kingdom of the Franks, the kingdom of the Turks, that of the sultan, and the peoples of Germany today. (D.II.Pr.2)[46]

In other words, the city with the greatest *virtù* wins the struggle for domination and forms an encompassing empire, whose size depends on how much greater the imperial power's *virtù* is relative to the other states. Then, *virtù* gradually declines because of imperial peace, leading to the eventual collapse of the empire from within, and its fragmentation into a number of successor states. Among them, a struggle for domination naturally resumes and drives them to regenerate *virtù*, until the city with the greatest amount imposes another empire.

In Machiavelli's day, as he states above, the world's *virtù* was dispersed among many nations, with the result that none of them attained to the superior greatness, power, and riches of an encompassing empire. To teach his Italian readers how to found and expand a state that would bring the world's scattered *virtù* back together again, was the practical goal of Machiavelli's writings. Thus, he wrote the *Prince* so that its reader would "introduce a form [in Italy] that would bring honor to him and good to the universality there" (P.XXVI.102), in clear imitation of such founders as Moses, Cyrus, Romulus, and Theseus.[47] He composed the *Discourses* "so that the spirits of youths who may read these writings of mine can flee [our times] and prepare themselves to imitate [the times of the ancient Romans]" (D.II.Pr.3). He wrote the *Florentine Histories* to show "the causes of the hatreds and divisions in the city, so that when [the citizens who govern republics] have become wise through the dangers of others, they may be able to maintain themselves united" (FH.Pr). And he prepared the *Art of War* to "bring [military orders] back to ancient modes and to give them back a form of past *virtù*," so that the ruler who "first enters this road" will be like Philip of Macedon, who "became, with this order and with these practices, so powerful that in a few years he could occupy all [of Greece], and leave to his son such a foundation that he could make himself prince of the whole world" (AG.Pr.302, VII.389).[48]

Postimperial Institutions

When arguing that cities cannot escape war and must acquire empires, Machiavelli comes across a fact that seems to falsify his thesis: the attenuation of warfare among the principalities and towns of Germany, which had become independent when the Holy Roman Empire disintegrated during the thirteenth century. To explain this peace in the absence of central authority, he refers to their common recognition of the German emperor (who had retained his nominal authority) as a mediator:

> This province was divided into the Swiss, republics (whom they call free towns), princes, and emperor. And the cause why wars do not arise among so much diversity of ways of life, or if they arise they do not long endure, is that sign of the emperor, who, should he happen not to have forces, nonetheless has so much reputation among them that he is a conciliator for them, and extinguishes every scandal with his authority by interposing himself as a mediator. (D.II.19.2)

This mediatory institution lessens the anarchic constraint to acquire one's own empire in order to be secure. In Machiavelli's words, "those communities can thus live content with their small dominion, because, thanks to the imperial authority, they do not have cause to desire more" (D.II.19.2).

However, Germany is a special case that cannot be generalized: "Since there are no such conditions elsewhere, one cannot take this mode of living and needs either to expand by way of leagues or to expand like the Romans. Whoever governs himself otherwise seeks not his life but his death and ruin" (D.II.19.2). Since the German emperors were often hereditary princes, we may surmise that their continued recognition by the cities of Germany rests on habituation, that is, the customary order that had grown up around them and demanded peace in the land.

The second fact suggestive of foreign institutions occurs with regard to Machiavelli's argument that warlike competition among a number of political units promotes *virtù*. Accordingly, the fragmentation of the Roman Empire into separate kingdoms should by his time have led to a regeneration of the ancient *virtù* that had been lost under *pax Romana*. In reality, however, "though . . . that empire, through inundation by the barbarians, was divided into several parts, this *virtù* was not reborn there" (AW.II.323). Machiavelli offers two explanations: simple inertia and the pacific effects of Christianity. "It takes a little to resume orders when they are spoiled"; and "today's mode of living, thanks to the Christian religion, does not impose that necessity to defend oneself as it anciently was" (AW.II.333). Since military defeat among Christians does not lead to wholesale slaughter and enslavement, men no longer uphold military orders that breed *virtù*:

> Today . . . of the vanquished, few are killed; no one is long held a prisoner, because with facility are they freed. The cities, even though having a thousand times rebelled, are not undone, men are left their goods, in a mode that the greater evil to be feared is a tax. thus, men do not wish to submit to military orders and to labor under them, in order to flee dangers which they fear little. (AW.II.333)

Since Machiavelli considers religion a custom, this mitigation of European warfare by Christianity can be understood as another institution based on habituation. In particular, whereas the bloody rituals of the pagans made men fierce, the pacific ceremonies of the Christian "mode of life . . . seems to have rendered the world weak," glorifying "humble and contemplative more than active men" and wanting "you to be capable more of suffering than of doing something strong" (D.II.2.2). In other words, a change in religious practices led to a corresponding change in men's second nature.

According to Machiavelli, the empire which generated these customs was that of the Franks; for after "the pope and the Roman people made [Charlemagne] emperor" in 800 A.D., and "as the Empire was coming to lose its privileges, the Church acquired them, and by these means it kept increasing its authority over the temporal princes" (FH.I.11). In the centuries to follow, the popes, "sustained and defended by spiritual power and reputation" (FH.VIII.17), "with their censures made the whole West tremble" (FH.I.14).[49] For instance, when the German king Otto endangered the interests of the Holy See, "the pope excommunicated him so that he was abandoned by everyone" (FH.I.20).[50]

Hence, the institutions that may mitigate foreign anarchy according to Machiavelli are postimperial in the sense that they arise when an encompassing empire passes away and bequeaths cooperative customs to its successor states. These cities are then able to maintain the corresponding institutions because their habits prevent them from fully realizing that they exist once more in the absence of a common power and that preventive war and imperial domination are again the best means of being secure and satisfying one's ambition–just as the habits which a founder leaves to the citizens of a republic prevent them from calculating their individual costs and benefits.

Given the contingency of good customs and the necessary growth of ambition, postimperial institutions should be epiphenomena of limited duration: Sooner or later, an opportunity to take advantage of the peaceful habits of the others will present itself to a prince capable of imagining the fruits of domination and devising means to reap them; stimulated by his example, other rulers let their ambition corrupt their good customs in like manner; fearing the threat posed by their advances, the remaining cities then take warlike measures for their own protection, bringing about the collapse of the pacific institution and the return of the foreign realm to its fundamental condition–struggle for empire.

Notes

1. See Kenneth Waltz, *Theory of International Politics* (New York: Random House, 1979), 88-89, 93, 102-04.

2. Cf. D.I.1.4; D.II.9.1; D.III.12.1, 16.2.

3. *Parole da dirle sopra la provisione del danaio, facto un poco di proemio et di scusa* [Words to be spoken about the provision of money, having given a little preface and excuse], in TO.11-13, at 12, mt.

4. On deterrence, see Glenn H. Snyder, "Deterrence and Defense," in *The Use of Force,* 2nd ed., ed. Robert J. Art and Kenneth N. Waltz (Lanham, Md.: University Press of America, 1983), 123-41; John J. Mearsheimer, *Conventional Deterrence* (Ithaca: Cornell University Press, 1983), 13-66.

5. *Parole da dirle sopra la provisione del danaio,* in TO.11-13, at 12, mt.

6. On the security dilemma and the spiral of perceived aggression, see John Herz, "Idealist Internationalism and the Security Dilemma," *World Politics* 2, no. 2 (January 1950): 157-80; Robert Jervis, "Deterrence, the Spiral Model, and the Intentions of the Adversary," chap. in *Perception and Misperception in International Politics* (Princeton: Princeton University Press, 1976).

7. Cf. P.III.16; L.214.1156.

8. Cf. D.II.19.1.

9. Cf. D.II.19.1.

10. Cf. L.235.1187.

11. Cf. P.III.15.

12. See P.III.9-12; P.IV.17-18; P.V.21.

13. Cf. D.I.16.5.

14. Cf. "Mission to the Duke of Valentinois," in W.III.141-280, at 216.

15. Cf. "Third Mission to the Court of France," in W.IV.220-76, at 251.

16. "Mission to the Duke of Valentinois," in W.III.141-280, at 202; cf. "Mission to the Court of Rome," in W.III.283-388, at 290; *Rapporto delle cose della Magna, fatto questio di 17 giugno 1508* [Report on the affairs of Germany, made on 17th June 1508], in TO.63-68, at 63.

17. Cf. "Mission to the Duke of Valentinois," in W.III.141-280, at 216.

18. See Barry R. Posen, *The Sources of Military Doctrine: France, Britain, and Germany Between the World Wars* (Ithaca: Cornell University Press, 1984), 63-64, 232.

19. Cf. D.III.11.1; L.233.1183.

20. See Waltz, *Theory of International Politics,* 125-27; Stephen M. Walt, *The Origins of Alliances* (Ithaca: Cornell University Press, 1987), 32, cf. 17-33, 147-80.

21. Cf. D.II.30.1.

22. Cf. Hannah F. Pitkin, *Fortune Is a Woman: Gender and Politics in the Thought of Niccolò Machiavelli* (Berkeley, Calif.: University of California Press, 1984), 257-61.

23. On small-group logic, see Mancur Olsen, *The Logic of Collective Action: Public Goods and the Theory of Groups* (Cambridge: Harvard University Press, 1965), 22-36; Russell Hardin, *Collective Action* (Baltimore: Johns Hopkins University Press, 1982), ch. 3.

24. See D.II.4.2.

25. In contrast, the Florentines made the inhabitants of Arezzo into worse enemies than before when putting down their rebellion; for "they used that middle way which is very harmful in judging men: they exiled part of the Aretines, fined part of them, took away from all of them their honors and former ranks in the city, and left the city intact"; see D.II.23.3.

26. See P.III.10-12; D.II.4.1, 13.2.

27. Cf. "Mission to the Duke of Valentinois," in W.III.141-280, at 225; "Mission to Mantua on Business With the Emperor of Germany," in W.IV.195-219, at 214.

28. *Parole da dirle sopra la provisione del danaio,* in TO.11-13, at 11-12;

cf. 11. Cf. P.XII.50; D.I.2.4; FH.II.5.

29. Cf. D.I.21.

30. See D.I.29-30.

31. See D.III.9.1-2.

32. Cf. D.I.43; Felix Gilbert, "Machiavelli: The Renaissance of the Art of War," in *Makers of Modern Strategy from Machiavelli to the Nuclear Age,* ed. Peter Paret (Princeton: Princeton University Press, 1986), 11-31, at 26.

33. Plato, *Plato's Republic,* 2nd ed., trans. Allan Bloom (New York: Basic Books, 1968), 422b-423c; Plato, *The Laws of Plato,* trans. Thomas L. Pangle (Chicago: University of Chicago Press, 1980), 704a-707c.

34. Note how Plato's demand that citizens should "possess a kind of coin that carries value among themselves, but is valueless among other human beings" emulates the leather money of Lycurgus; see *Laws of Plato,* 742a; cf. 743d.

35. Aristotle, *The Politics,* trans. Carnes Lord (Chicago: University of Chicago Press, 1984), 1325a, 1326a-1327b, 1330b-1331a.

36. Aristotle, *Politics,* 1267a21-28.

37. That Machiavelli had read Aristotle's *Politics* in translation is further evident from D.III.26.2; L.214.1156; and DF.30. See also Friedrich Mehmel, "Machiavelli und die Antike," in *Antike und Abendland: Beiträge zum Verständnis der Griechen und Römer und ihres Nachlebens,* ed. Bruno Snell, vol. 3 (Hamburg: Marion von Schröder, 1948), 151-86, esp. 153-62; Bernard Guillemin, "Machiavel, lecteur d'Aristote," in *Platon et Aristote à la renaissance: XVIe Colloque International de Tours, De Petrarque à Descartes,* vol. XXXII (Paris: Librairie Philosophique J. Vrin, 1976), 163-73.

38. Leo Strauss, *Thoughts on Machiavelli* (Chicago: University of Chicago Press, 1958), 298-99.

39. Strauss, *Thoughts on Machiavelli,* 299.

40. *Plato's Republic,* 422b.

41. *The Laws of Plato,* 707d; cf. 705e-706a, 742d.

42. Plato, *Gorgias,* trans. Donald J. Zeyl (Indianapolis: Hackett, 1987), 512b.

43. See *Plato's Republic,* 608c-621d; Plato, *Gorgias,* 522b-527d.

44. Cf. FH.VII.28.

45. Cf. FH.V.1.

46. Cf. F.978-79.

47. To see this, compare P.XXVI.102-103 with P.VI.22-23.

48. Cf. P.XXVI.104-105. Philip's son was Alexander the Great.

49. Cf. FH.I.9-11, I.19, I.31.

50. Cf. FH.I.15.

Chapter 7

Intentions, Insights, and Errors

The Break with the Classical Tradition

Insofar as Machiavelli's thought was new, it moved the West toward modernity. As we have seen, he denied that the world was a *cosmos* in the classical and Christian sense, ommitting natural law and replacing the providence of God with the occult but immanent influence of the heavens and Fortune. Human beings are consequently exposed to large-scale contingency and bereft of cosmic support for living an ethical moral life. In the absence of final causes, they must learn how to manipulate efficient causes that are known from experience in order to bring about desired consequences most of the time. In short, Machiavelli was instrumental to modernity's rejection of classical teleology and its concomitant emphasis on empirical relationships of cause and effect.

He also denied the traditional assumption that human beings have a natural capacity for certain virtues, such as justice or temperance, which they develop in political community. Rejecting in addition that the will is free and that the few are ethically superior to the many, Machiavelli assumed all men to be self-seeking individuals who use their mental faculties to satisfy natural desires for self-preservation, glory, power, and wealth. With everyone looking out for himself, leaderless multitudes readily fail to provide for the common good, succumbing to what nowadays are called problems of collective action.

Here, Machiavelli obviously blazed the trail for the modern view that takes human beings to be individuals who use instrumental reason to maximize their own utility, which had its systematic beginning in Hobbes, was elaborated by Hume, Bentham, and Adam Smith, and is now most generally known as rational-choice theory.

Since human beings are incapable of virtue, the good of political order needs to be lowered to the collective provision of what human beings crave by nature: security, greatness, empire, and treasure, with liberty being appreciated as a means to the former. Thus, the ground has been broken for the modern excision of the soul's salvation from the purview of the state, soon to be championed by liberalism as the best way to end the wars of religion that issued from the Reformation. Further, actions to attain the political good are evaluated according to their consequences, allowing for the use of evil means to bring about good effects. In making this claim, Machiavelli abrogated the Pauline principle that "evil must not be done that good may come" (Rom. iii.8), and planted an important seed for the utilitarian approach to morality, epitomized by Bentham's claim that right is what causes the greatest happiness of the greatest number.[1] Moreover, Machiavelli's belief that the political good normally requires the commission of evil deeds, when coupled with his retention of traditional notions of right and wrong, shows what the absence of a *cosmos* means concretely: one can either be successful or moral–but not both. And this claim denies nothing less than that the world is a single intelligible structure, the axiom on which Western thought had been based since Plato.

Human beings are by nature individuals who exist in a condition of license, where conflict erupts from both ambition and fear–akin to Hobbes's state of nature. Out of this condition, the first political order arises when the most *virtuoso* men become princes, whose willful rule is tempered only by considerations of expediency, such as benefiting subjects to gain their support against rivals or establishing a republic or law-governed kingdom to gain the glory of a founder. Those of lesser ability can be habituated by their princes to a *vivere civile,* whose laws and orders organize people's self-seeking efforts in such a way that they cooperatively gratify their ambitions more effectively than proceeding individually. Although this conception of political life reinstates the ancient celebration of glory as the highest good, it repudiates classical political theory in fundamental ways. First, it understands domestic politics as nonviolent conflict rather than concord, foreshadowing the modern definition of politics as a struggle of interests. Second, it defines the central function of the city as the satisfaction of the desires of the multitude, rather than the cultivation of virtue by the few, preparing the ground for the modern view of the state as a convenience for individuals equal in worth, and making law a purely positive construct. Third, it argues that cities must be large, open, and organized for war in order to prevail in the inescapable struggle for domination that rages in foreign affairs, repudiating the ancient idea that cities should remain small and closed in order to be virtuous, and anticipating the liberal idea that free enterprise generates not only opulence but national power as well.

Whether Machiavelli's manifold break with the classical tradition was a blessing or a curse depends on one's perspective. Those impressed with the pleasures, equality, and freedom presently enjoyed by so many, might want to thank Machiavelli for loosening the grip of classical teleology, which disregarded not only the needs of individuals and the wants of the common man, but stifled innovation, enterprise, and inquiry into the cause-effect relationships that now allow us to control nature. On the other hand, those alarmed by the loss of community, the removal of the good life (*eu zen*) from public purview, and the rampant pursuit of material and bodily goods might want to curse Machiavelli for having subverted the virtues that gave complementary meaning to the lives of all, and for having undermined the belief that certain things ought never be done, however advantageous the effect. Indeed, they might hold Machiavelli to some extent responsible for the crimes of a Lenin, Hitler, Mao, or Pol Pot, who had learned from him to excuse the murder innocents by its supposed benefits for humanity. And this education may be more direct than one might think; for at least Hitler was reported to have said that reading Machiavelli's *Prince* had a "cleansing and liberating effect" on him, freeing him from "sentimental conceptions" and "prejudices" and teaching him "what politics was in its proper sense."[2] In other words, Machiavelli's contribution to what may be good about modernity has come at a high price.

Machiavelli's Project

But did Machiavelli actually intend to break with what had come before and inaugurate an entirely new way of life? It may seem so from the first paragraph of the *Discourses,* where he claims to have taken "a path as yet untrodden by anyone" and found "new modes and orders," comparable to the "unknown waters and lands" that had been reached by the great seafarers of his age (D.I.Pr.1). However, in the second paragraph he elaborates this claim to innovation as doing for politics what the humanists had done for the arts and letters since the fourteenth century, namely to recover and imitate the superior ways of the ancients: "Considering thus how much honor is awarded to antiquity" in the imitation of ancient sculptures, in the practice of Roman law, and in medicine, "and seeing on the other hand, that the most *virtuoso* works the histories show us, which have been done by ancient kingdoms and republics, by kings, captains, citizens, legislators, and others who have labored for their fatherland, are admired rather than imitated . . . I can do no other than marvel and grieve" (D.I.Pr.2). This grievous failure to extend the Renaissance–or "rebirth of antiquity"–to political life has been caused to some extent by "the weakness into which the present religion [i.e., Christianity] has led the world," but, more importantly, it results from "not having a true knowledge of histories, through not getting from reading them that sense nor tasting that flavor that they have in themselves" (D.I.Pr.2). To mend this interpretive shortcoming is the avowed purpose of Machiavelli's *Discourses on Livy:*

> Wishing . . . to turn men from this error, I have judged it necessary to write on all those books of Titus Livy that have not been intercepted by the malignity of the times whatever I shall judge necessary for their greater understanding, according to knowledge of ancient and modern things, so that those who read these statements of mine can more easily draw from them that utility for which one should seek knowledge of histories. (D.I.Pr.2)

But what precisely did Machiavelli mean by the "true knowledge" or "greater understanding" of history? None other than what we have recognized as the central and most radical idea of his political theory: that rulers must commit wicked deeds on a regular basis to make their cities secure, glorious, imperial, and prosperous.

According to Machiavelli, the ancient writers had known this harsh truth, but had chosen to express it only surreptitiously. Thus, after claiming that a prince must be both a law-abiding man and a violent beast, he argues that

> this role was taught *covertly* to princes by ancient writers, who wrote that Achilles, and many other princes, were given to Chiron the centaur to be raised, so that he would look after them with his discipline. To have as teacher a half-beast, half-man means nothing other than that a prince needs to know how to use both natures. (P.XVIII.69, ea)

Even the authors of Scripture practiced this deception: "whoever reads the Bible *judiciously* will see that since he wished his laws and his orders to go forward, Moses was forced to kill infinite men who, moved by nothing other than envy, were opposed to his plans" (D.III.30.1, ea). In other words, the story of the golden calf only seems to teach us that those who sin against God shall be justly punished; in truth, it suggests that founders need to murder those who fail to agree with their vision in order to be effective.

In similar fashion, Machiavelli reads between the lines of Roman historians and moralists, turning accounts given in terms of right and wrong into maxims of expediency.[3] Take his reading of Livy for example.[4] According to Machiavelli, Romulus murdered his brother Remus and consented to the murder of Titus Tatius in order to found Rome. But Livy reports that he killed Remus either from "jealousy and ambition" or a "fit of rage" about a perceived slight, and writes with regard to Titus Tatius that "Romulus is said to have felt less distress at his death than was strictly proper: possibly the joint reign was not, in fact, entirely harmonious; possibly he felt that Tatius deserved what he got," for he had provoked a riot by favoring his kinsmen when dispensing justice.[5] Likewise, when Livy tells the story of the Caudine Forks, where the Romans reneged on their peace guarantee to the Samnites on the dubious ground that neither the Senate nor the people of Rome were bound by agreements made by their consuls in the field, he stresses the Roman effort at showing that justice was served;[6] according to Machiavelli, on the other hand, this event suggests that "it is not shameful not to observe the promises that you have been made to promise by force," and that there "ought not to enter any consideration of either just or unjust, merciful or cruel" when the safety of the fatherland is at stake (D.III.42). Then, Machiavelli rips Sallust's famous claim about the salutary effect of glory–that republics rise to greatness because they allow men to win glory and thus motivate them to work for the common good–from its context of concord and justice, and turns it into another maxim of *raison d'état* (reason of state): republics are better at providing for the common good because the majority can easily "crush" the minority, regardless of the fact that "it may turn out to harm this or that private individual" (D.II.2.1).[7] Further, whereas Sallust deplores the conspiracy of Catiline as an instance of corruption, Machiavelli cites his brazen appearance before the Senate after having been exposed as evidence for how little danger is incurred by those who conspire against republics (as opposed to principalities).[8] Finally, when importing the duality of human and beastly action from Cicero, Machiavelli completely ignores the fact that Cicero permitted the beastly course of violence only when a just cause–such as prior injury by the other side–was present, and thus severs the link between the "truly expedient" (*vero utile*) and "morally right" (*honestum*) that the Roman moralist had striven so hard to maintain.[9]

Hence, the "path as yet untrodden by anyone" that Machiavelli takes in the *Discourses* leads in the same direction as his endeavor to "depart from the orders of others" in the *Prince:* namely, to go to the consequentialist truth of politics. In other words, Machiavelli did not mean to suggest that he was the first to exhort his contemporaries to emulate the political life of the ancients; indeed, he could not, for such well-known humanists as Colluccio Salutati, Leonardo Bruni, Pier Paolo Vergerio, Poggio Bracciolini, Leon Battista Alberti, Francesco Patrizi, and Giovanni Pontano, had already done so at length.[10] Rather, whereas the humanists took the moralizing aspects of the ancient works to be their true message, Machiavelli was the first to claim that, between the lines, the ancients had taught that political good rests on evil means. In particular, whereas the ancients maintained the classical belief that princes could and should uphold such virtues as justice, liberality, charity, and faith, Machiavelli advised the fashion to enter into the corresponding vices; whereas the humanists conceived republics as communities that rest on concord and make the citizens virtuous, Machiavelli described them as war machines propelled by domestic conflicts of interest. To understand that this was the real message of the ancients is thus to have "true knowledge of histories," according to Machiavelli.

To "turn men from this error" of reading the ancients in a moralizing way, Machiavelli must replace the Christian (and humanist) "education" (D.II.2.2)[11] with one of his own; for the fact that men's "works are more *virtuoso* now in this province than in that" depends on "the form of education in which those people have taken their mode of life" (D.III.43). To return to a political life that realizes man's actual ambitions, Christian scruples about injuring innocents must be cast aside and men's strength must be renewed by habituating them to ferocious rituals Moreover, to remedy the fact that "no sign of that ancient *virtù* remains with us" implies to bring together the *virtù* that had been scattered by the fall of the Roman Empire, and thus to create another peak of the cycle of history after the trough during the age of faith. In fact, to bring *virtù* back to Italy means nothing less than to imitate the Romans in their imperial conquest. Thus, Machiavelli instructs the Italian youths not only in the "decisions made by the Romans pertaining to the inside of the city," but also in "those that the Roman people made pertaining to the increase of its empire" (D.II.Pr.3), as well as "how much the actions of particular men made Rome great" (D.III.1.6).

Accordingly, Machiavelli did not wittingly attempt a revaluation in the Nietzschean sense, whereby a superior thinker steps outside all prior horizons and consciously constructs reality anew.[12] Apart from such an idea lying far in the future, Machiavelli was prevented from thinking in this way by his assumption that history proceeds in cycles and that the basic order of things remains the same. Thus, he thought he had found the timeless truth about politics by reading the ancients in a new way, which, moreover, agreed with how he understood the political actions of his contemporaries.

But Machiavelli's reading of the ancients was largely wrong, for the classical authors had ultimately been serious about exhorting men to take the path of virtue and to live in ethical community. True, they described ruthless practices and openly discussed a strand of Greek thought that *did* exalt glorious violence and the sacrifice of human beings to the city, namely the heroic ethos of Homer and the agonistic views of sophists like Thrasymachus and Callicles, but they did so in order order to refute them and to exhort men to act morally instead. Machiavelli undoubtedly sensed this ruthless sidecurrent of the classical tradition, and–being ignorant of its separateness and inclining to it from his own experience–mistook it for covertly expressed truth. Since it was this peculiar reading that led Machiavelli to depart from the classical tradition in such a radical way, his contribution to modernity comes to light as a sleight of hand: He intended to return his contemporaries to the political ideas and practices of the ancients, whom he thought to have understood correctly for the first time; but since his understanding was actually very different from what classical thinkers had always maintained, Machiavelli thereby created a fresh vision of political life, which propelled the West toward modernity.

Ambition and Autonomy

Machiavelli's conception of the human essence as a capacity for ambition developed by mental activity illumines what may well be the fundamental predicament of our species: that we have minds capable of expanding awareness far beyond the concrete moment; for it is above all our faculty of imagination that makes us forever fearful of future pain and desirous of future pleasure–even though our bodies may presently be satisfied. Or, as Machiavelli put it, "since the desire is always greater than the power of acquiring, the result is discontent with what one possesses and a lack of satisfaction with it" (D.I.37.1)[13] Better to remain an animal that finds contentment in the pleasure of the moment, such as Circe's porker, who declines her offer to regain his human form "because in this mud I live more happily; here without anxiety I bathe and roll myself" (AS.VIII.976).

But if Machiavelli realized the impossibility of enduringly satisfying our ambitions, why did he nonetheless teach us how to pursue them more effectively? Why make us construct a political order that seeks to satisfy our desires for glory, power, and wealth as much as publicly possible, if the very effort will make us even more desirous, thus keeping a steady state of contentment out of reach forever? Machiavelli could have responded to this charge with a reference to the peculiar nature of glory–which, as we know, he takes to be the highest good. Power and wealth will cease to be ours either while we live or, for sure, when we die; but the praise of our deeds might be sung for millenia.[14] True, our awareness of being celebrated ends as well the moment we die (assuming there is no immortal soul), but we can imagine our future glory while we live, and if we have grounds to believe that it will be great and lasting, the present satisfaction may be so immense that it quenches the corresponding thirst. In a famous speech reported by Thucydides, Pericles thus told his fellow Athenians that "mighty indeed are the marks and monuments of our empire which we have left. Future ages will wonder at us, as the present age wonders at us now," and exhorted them to "fix your eyes every day on the greatness of Athens as she really is, and become her lovers," and to die for her knowing that "one's sense of honor is the only thing that does not grow old."[15] In other words, our capacity to expand consciousness beyond the moment not only causes us great anxiety about future contingency, but also provides us with a partial remedy insofar as we belong to a population whose memory stretches across generations. Ultimately, it is not so much the political orders or "dams and dikes" that overcome Fortune, for her "violent rivers" will undermine them sooner or later, but the memories of really great ones–Egypt, Persia, Athens, Rome–that vanquish contingency.

But even if glory is a more enduring good than preservation, power, and wealth, it is problematic to elevate it to the highest good; for classical thinkers like Aristotle surely had a point when they argued that happiness comes from cultivating goods which are internal to one's actions, that is, virtues such as wisdom or justice[16]–rather than from chasing after external goods, such as wealth and glory; for the latter give pleasure only after the drudgery of acquiring them has been endured, which, in Machiavelli's world, includes ceaseless competition, the danger of injury, and the risk of violent death. Moreover, the man who pursues glory, power, and wealth will evaluate these hazards in entirely negative terms–as costs he would gladly dispense with–for he judges everything from a purely self-regarding point of view. In contrast, the man who cultivates such virtues as justice or courage may view the concomitant hardships in positive terms, since overcoming them while acting for the sake of the good is what virtue is all about.[17] In other words, whereas facing adversity for the sake of goods external to the soul (i.e., glory, power, wealth) detracts from happiness because it is merely a means to it, braving the same adversity for the sake of internal goods (i.e., the virtues) inherently augments happiness because it is an end in itself.

Further, insofar as external goods are scarce and exclusive, they goad their lovers into a competition that makes them forever restless and anxious. In particular, since the glory of one man tends to diminish that of another, the glory-seeker feels the thorn of envy as long as he ranks below and the dread of being outshone as soon as he is on top. In contrast, goods of the soul can be enjoyed jointly because they are spiritual in nature. One person's happiness of being knowledgeable, just, or loving is not diminished by the like virtues in another; indeed, recognizing their own virtue in the other makes them capable of the highest form of friendship. Also, insofar as external goods depend on circumstances beyond our control, their enjoyment is not truly our own. Since glory is bestowed by others, the glory-seeker makes his happiness dependent on their opinions, so that people may be celebrated in one age and reviled or forgotten in another.[18] Finally, the quest for glory leads to alienation, as confirmed by the inventor of the concept–Jean-Jacques Rousseau–who had this to say about people who make "*power* and *reputation*" their preoccupation in life:

> there is a type of men . . . who know how to be happy and content with themselves on the testimony of others rather than their own . . . the man accustomed to the ways of society is always outside himself and knows how to live only in the opinion of others. And it is, as it were, from their judgment alone that he draws the sentiment of his own existence.[19]

In contrast, goods of the soul can neither be taken from us nor depend so readily on others, because we realize them by cultivating our own thoughts and feelings. In other words, developing the virtues make us self-sufficient because they become part of our character.[20] But

Machiavelli, as we know, did not believe that human beings had a soul which could be developed in this way. Having a shallow image of man, he grasped only his more primitive urges for power, reputation, riches, and lust.

One might argue against this that Machiavelli's doctrine of *virtuoso* action aims at autonomy[21]–which could be considered the characteristically modern good of the soul. For Machiavelli's very definition of *virtù* assumes independence from the arms and goodwill of others, and those with the greatest *virtù* are founders endowed with a brain that "understands by itself" and thus can introduce "new orders [that] are altogether alien to past ones" (D.I.25). Indeed, Machiavelli repeatedly ascribes the faculty of creation to human beings–but nowhere to God–as when he writes that "a state has been created by that prince" (P.V.20) or that "new necessities in managing [Rome] were always discovered, and it was necessary to create new orders, as happened when they created the censors" (D.I.49.1).[22] In other words, Machiavelli freed man from his medieval subordination to the divine order and turned the resultant contingency into opportunities for self-directed action. More precisely, Machiavelli estimated that *virtuoso* action succeeds almost half of the time, as "fortune is arbiter of half of our actions, but also . . . leaves the other half, or close to it, for us to govern" (P.XXV.98).

In this assertion of human action, Machiavelli was surely influenced by the humanists, who had rejected the pagan notion of fate and claimed that human beings can achieve excellence on their own, composing impassionate orations on the "dignity of man."[23] But he seemed to go much farther than the humanists; for they upheld the traditional belief that the universe is guided by divine providence, whereas Machiavelli rejected any such transcendental order and put in its place the contingency of Fortune and the necessity of the heavens. Thus, whereas the humanists named *virtus, fortuna,* and *providentia Dei* as the three determinants of human action, Machiavelli cast them as *virtù, fortuna,* and *necessità.*[24]

In truth, however, this substitution of heavenly necessity for divine providence actually *diminishes* human autonomy. For the heavens and Fortune reintroduce the pagan belief that fate (*moira, fatum*) and the gods determines human affairs events with a necessity that is external to us, whereas the Christian idea of divine providence assumes merely that God has perfect foresight of the decisions that human beings make by internal acts of free will. In other words, the pagans located the efficient cause of human action in the objective entities of fate and divine will, whereas the Christians placed it in the subjectively existing will of our rational soul. That Machiavelli sided with the pagans on this issue can be most clearly seen from his denial of the soul and its free will. Whereas the humanists exalted free will (*libero arbitrio*) as the source of man's superiority,[25] Machiavelli claimed that "our mind . . . grants no defense against habit or nature" (AS.956). Indeed, he subverts the traditional meaning of *libero arbitrio* by making it signify nothing more than freedom from external constraint: only to wise counselors should a prudent prince "give *libero arbitrio* to speak the truth to him, and of those things only that he asks about and nothing else" (P.XXIII.94); and Fortune leaves close to half of our actions for us to govern "so that our *libero arbitrio* not be eliminated" (P.XXVI.98). In other words, Machiavelli understood free will not as the capacity to overcome one's own desires and dispositions, but merely as the ability to gratify one's ambition without interference from outside forces, such as a prince or Fortune–akin to Hobbes's definition of liberty as the absence of external impediments.[26]

Hence, the freedom of *virtuoso* agents does not deserve to be called autonomy–the ability to give a law to oneself and follow it. For *virtù* merely gives us the power to determine our relations with others, in essence, to decide who dominates whom; but it does not grant us the capacity to shape ourselves, that is, to remake our nature by acts of free will. Ignorant of subjectivity, Machiavelli limits human freedom to the immanent level where individuals compete for the goods of Fortune and Venus. In other words, without a freely willing soul that enables us to transcend the passions, our freedom reduces to license.

The Doctrine of Necessary Evil

Does Machiavelli's stress on the necessity of unjust force and fraud capture any permanent truth about politics? To sketch an answer to this difficult question, we may begin with the simple observation that unjust force and fraud have been remarkably common and successful throughout history. Hence, as long as despots and demagogues abound, Machiavelli remains required reading for those who have to deal with them. For instance, when Saddam Hussein (a known admirer of Machiavelli) baffled Western audiences during the Gulf War by displaying the bruised faces of captured pilots on television, a quick turn to the *Prince* suggested that he observed the maxim that it is better "to be feared than loved" (P.XVII.66). And when democratic leaders make a show of holding hands with their wives, kissing toddlers, and attending church, we know that they follow the precept that a prince should "appear merciful, faithful, humane, honest, and religious" (P.XVIII.70).

But Machiavelli did more than illumine the less than virtuous ways by which ambitious individuals have always sought to succeed in politics. He claimed that the good that comes from political order rests in fundamental ways on the commission of evil, rendering human reality deeply incoherent. To assess this radical claim, let us make an analytical distinction between evil deeds needed to create political order from those that pertain to its preservation, and, within the latter category, let us further distinguish acts that injure subjects and fellow citizens from those that harm foreigners. In short, let us discuss Machiavelli's doctrine of necessary evil with regard to founding, maintaining the state, and foreign security.

Founding

At first sight, history suggests that Machiavelli had a point with regard to founders. For civilization itself began with the rise of the first states in Mesopotamia and Egypt, which were highly coercive; Europe owed much of its civilization to the Roman conquest, which brought law and urban life to many barbarian tribes; the Frankish conquests made possible the Carolingian Renaissance in learning and the arts; and the revival of law and commerce in the late middle ages and the beginnings of science in early modernity rested on the centralization of authority by nation-building monarchs, who used force to end the anarchy reigning among the castle-lords. Thus, according to Hobbes, "there is scarce a commonwealth in the world whose beginnings can in conscience be justified," for they all find their origin in some form of usurpation; and yet it is rational to obey conquerors and tyrants as long as they protect us from each other, for the ravages of the natural condition are far worse than what we could ever suffer at the hands of our rulers.[27] According to Hegel, "world-historical individuals" like Napoleon (another admirer of Machiavelli) have to engage in "conduct which is indeed obnoxious to moral reprehension," for "so mighty a form must trample down many an innocent flower–crush to pieces many an object in its path," in order to carry the world spirit forward.[28] According to Hegel, such conduct is permissible because "the History of the World occupies a higher ground than that on which morality has properly its position," so that "crimes have been turned into the means–under the direction of a superior principle–of realizing the purpose of that principle."[29] Above all, it is the "consideration that what has happened could not be otherwise" that enables us to endure the picture of "history as the slaughter-bench at which the happiness of peoples, the wisdom of states, and the virtue of individuals have been victimized."[30] In other words, since history advances dialectically, that is, by negation and supercession of what came before, violations of extant morality are justified insofar as they are a necessary moment in the progressive realization of rational freedom.

However, this historical argument for necessary evil can be challenged in at least two ways. First, it overlooks that the good consequences of evil deeds have to be weighed against the bad ones they give rise to as well–especially in the long term.[31] For instance, Napoleon undoubtedly had a hand in advancing rational freedom by introducing a law code that enshrined the liberty of individuals, their equality before the law, and the lay character of the state; but his exploits also triggered the militarization of Europe, which led directly to the carnage of World War I and set a precedent for would-be world-historical individuals like Lenin and Hitler. The French Revolution not only made equality and liberty into the axiomatic values of modern life, but also pioneered the totalitarian reshaping of society by means of terror, name changes, and class war, soon to be perfected by communists and national socialists. Second, the historical argument can be accused of the logical fallacy of *post hoc ergo propter hoc;* for, as Alan Donagan put it, "that good has come about through crime does not show that it could only have come about by crime."[32] Thus, something like the Napoleonic Code would probably have been introduced by any intelligent leader rising in the wake of the French Revolution, including some who would not have perverted its ideals by embarking on a vainglorious career of conquest that harmed millions. And, the advances of the French Revolution itself could have been achieved without guillotine and *terreur*: Better organized and more enlightened revolutionaries could have restrained the anger of the masses and brought about a negotiated change, as suggested by England's Glorious Revolution of 1688 and the recent collapse of communism in Eastern Europe.

Nonetheless, it seems a plausible assumption that humanity would still live on the tribal level–and thus lack a complex division of labor and sustained advances in the arts and sciences–if ambitious leaders had not used coercive means to unite the countless groupings that had arisen from geographic dispersal of humanity and the attendant differentiation of languages and customs. For there are at least two problems of collective action that mitigate against a consentaneous generation of more inclusive units. First, dispersed groups face a "prisoner's dilemma": Although all parties would be better off by coming together and agreeing to establish a sovereign, the fact that they are not yet protected from each other makes it rational to remain at a distance, rather than running the risk of their cooperative effort being abused by the others. Second, such groups suffer from a "coordination problem": Lacking a shared set of norms or even words that could govern their interaction, they find it difficult to convey their willingness to participate in a social contract, let alone agree on the political order it would establish.[33] In addition to these collective-action problems, cooperation is limited by ethnocentric sentiment. As William Graham Sumner argued long ago, human beings naturally feel that the folkways of their "in-group" are the only right ones and that those of the "out-group" are strange and sacrilegious, a threat to one's own identity that must be met with hostility.[34] Indeed, recent anthropological thought suggests a genetic basis for such ethnocentrism: Since helping those who share our genes makes the latter proliferate, we have been selected by evolution to feel cooperative toward people who are familar and like ourselves and to respond with distrust and hostility toward strangers, given the fact that we are more likely to be related to the former than the latter.[35]

For all these reasons, human beings naturally differentiate into competitive groups of clan or tribe-size, rather than spontaneously integrating into entities large enough to bring forth civilization. Hence, to generate the latter and realize its good, some form of centralized coercion seems indeed necessary.

But doesn't this mean that Machiavelli was right when he claimed that the good of a civil way of life rests on evil deeds? Not necessarily, for no less a moral philosopher than Kant argued that the constraint exercised by a founder can be just under truly anarchic conditions. According to Kant, individuals or groups coexisting in a lawless state of nature have a "coercive right . . . to subject [others] to a wider legal constitution in accordance with their conception of right," because they "are a standing offence to one another by the very fact that they are neighbors"; more precisely, "man (or an individual people) in a mere state of nature . . . may not have injured me actively (*facto*), but he does injure me by the very lawlessness of his state (*statu iniusto*), for he is a permanent threat to me."[36] In other words, men that exist without central authority violate the rights of others by merely being close enough to pose a threat to their life, liberty, and property, regardless of intentions. And since those who commit aggression forfeit their own right to be free from constraint, "anyone may thus use force to impel the others to abandon this state for a state of right."[37] Accordingly, the founder does not enter into evil when he uses force to impose his order in a condition of license, for those who resist him to maintain their independence violate the law of nature by wilfully prolonging anarchy, and thus can justly be forced to comply–in analogy to breakers of civil laws. Accordingly, Machiavelli was wrong when he thought that Moses committed a crime by killing the worshippers of the golden calf because they "were opposed to his plans" (D.III.30.1); for by lapsing into license and undermining the prophet's endeavor to introduce a lawful way of life, they committed an aggression under natural law and could be justly punished. Hence, the Torah–as should be expected from the document that founded the Hebrew-Christian *cosmos*–in truth upholds the moral coherence of the world with regard to founding, since what is politically necessary accords with what is morally permissible.

However, this coercive right of the founder applies only to cases where human beings truly live in a licentious condition; once they are organized into a law-bound order, its autonomy must be respected. In Kant's words,

> while natural right allows us to say of men living in a lawless condition that they ought to abandon it, the right of nations does not allow us to say the same of states. For as states, they already have a lawful internal constitution, and have thus outgrown the coercive right of others to subject them to a wider legal constitution in accordance with their conception of right.[38]

Such a "lawful internal constitution" is not merely a matter of living under rules that are enforced, for then a household or hamlet might have outgrown the founder's coercive right already, but a matter of belonging to an order that enables human beings to develop the full range of their faculties. Kant hints at this when he writes that "the highest purpose of nature–i.e. the development of all natural capacities–can be fulfilled for mankind only in society"; only there can "the culture and art which adorn mankind" flourish.[39]

But which level of aggregation makes such flourishing possible? According to Aristotle, a city comes into existence for the sake of "mere life," that is, security and economic exchange based on division of labor; but then its members discover that living in a city prompts them to develop higher capacities and thus to live the truly "good life" (*eu zen*):[40] Making and executing laws in a city requires more intelligence than the shrewdness sufficient to run a village; administering justice in a larger and more complex society takes ethical judgment beyond such rough maxims as "an eye for an eye, a tooth for a tooth"; serving in an army calls for a courage far more disciplined than the violent outbursts of tribal peoples. On the other hand, the possibility of the good life diminishes as the city grows into a large kingdom, empire, or nation; for soon the number of the citizens becomes such that their networks of friendship begin to fray and they no longer have personal acquaintaince with the character of those they elect to public office.[41] Thus, it is at the level of the city-state that the virtues can be cultivated and that human flourishing (*eudaimonia*) is attained.

According to this criterion, Moses, Romulus, and Theseus were justified in using force to constrain the multitude. However, there are deeds that even founders must never do. Cesare Borgia, for instance, may have been right in using harsh measures to pacify the Romagna, but surely went wrong when he cut to pieces his loyal servant Remirro de Orco in order to pacify the crowd.[42] The successors of Romulus and Theseus did wrong when they used force to acquire empires that generated glory, power, and wealth, but did little for the goods of the soul. Likewise, it was permissible for the princes of late medieval Europe to subjugate the local castle-lords in order to create duchies and small kingdoms, such as Scotland, Burgundy, Aragon, or Bavaria, where people could live with a measure of security and justice, develop law-abiding habits, and cultivate the arts and sciences. But their early modern successors were hardly justified in using force to incorporate these entities into national monarchies, such as Great Britain, France, Spain, and Germany; for the fact that these became glorious states with markets large enough to multiply material well-being does not warrant the "infinite . . . injuries that the new acquisition brings in its wake" (P.III.8) and the concomitant reduction of the victims to mere means to the opulence of later generations.

Finally, to bring Kant's rights ethic closer to Aristotle's virtue ethic, the duty to respect rational beings as ends in themselves and permit them to live in liberty can be considered modernity's contribution to the goods of the soul, but only to the extent that this liberty is not construed as the radical freedom to do anything one lists, including the creation of a wholly new self, as long as one does not infringe the rights of others; for such autonomy ultimately destroys the community of the good life (*eu zen koinonia*) that human beings need to be truly happy. Thus, we may conclude that the coercive right of the founder extends to that level of aggregation where human beings can cultivate the virtues in liberty, but becomes void when it serves only to increase glory, power, and wealth.

Maintaining the State

Some of the deeds that Machiavelli commends to rulers who seek to preserve an existing order can also be subsumed under the category of just violence, such as the "excessive and notable" punishments that republics should administer in regular intervals to maintain the good customs of their citizens (D.III.1.3). Indeed, Machiavelli suggests as much when he instantiates such punishments with the fact that the Romans were "accustomed to punish multitudes of the erring" and "killed by way of justice an entire legion" (D.III.49.1).

However, there is a significant number of deeds endorsed by Machiavelli which clearly cannot be justified in this way. For instance, he is wrong to praise the fact that republics procure the common good more effectively because dissenters can be "crushed ordinarily," so that "there follows little or no disorder . . . even though [this or that citizen] has been done a wrong" (D.I.7.2). And he is wrong when he states as a general rule that "where one deliberates entirely on the safety of his fatherland, there ought not to any consideration of either just or unjust, merciful or cruel" (D.III.41); for, as we shall discuss below, a political order that injures innocents is not worth having. But, before we get to this point, let us ask whether unjust actions are actually necessary for maintaining a state? In other words, is there really a need for *raison d'état*?

Again, we can draw on history to sketch an answer. Over the last two to three hundred years, the growing acceptance of the idea of constitutional government and the liberal concept of rights has given rise to a number of political orders, located mainly in Europe and North America, that have been able to maintain themselves without injuring their citizens on a regular basis. Of course, unjust violence by the state continues to occur, but it has become clear that such acts are detrimental to the stability of the regime, rather than necessary. For instance, the occasional use of excessive force by the police against members of the lower classes no longer terrorizes them into submission, but increasingly rouses them to vigorous protest, which succeeds because of support from members of the elite; and while the former could be said to pursue their self-interest, most of the latter act from the principles of respect for persons, rule of law, and equality before the law. Consequently, just violence, administered by the police in accordance with laws and court rulings, has proven quite sufficient to maintain order in liberal societies. Liberal societies may neglect the good from an excessive concern with procedural justice, but they seem to have solved the problem of popular compliance.

To explore this historical phenomenon more deeply, there is again no better guide than Kant. According to Kant's teleological view of history, the fact that human beings have a natural capacity for moral conduct implies that they will develop it sooner or later,[43] for positive developments have a more lasting effect on such a capacity than negative ones. A moral advance in the understanding may fail to be realized for a long time, but once proclaimed "can never be forgotten, since it has revealed in human nature an aptitude and power of improvement."[44] In other words, "the moral principle in man is never extinguished, and reason, which is pragmatically capable of applying the ideas of right according to this principle, constantly increases with the continuous progress of culture, while the guilt attending violations of right increases proportionately."[45] Of course, there will also be moral reverses and confusions, but, over the long run, it simply had to happen that thinkers like Moses, Socrates, Jesus, and Kant himself arose at some point to improve our moral awareness, and that their ideas eventually became more influential than those of Thrasymachus, Genghis Khan, Nietzsche, or Hitler.

More concretely, Kant argues that people who live for generations under an authority that forces them to follow rational laws under dread of punishment, will eventually develop their moral capacity to a point where they begin to appreciate the law for its own sake:

> Within each individual state . . . the citizen's inclination to do violence to one another is counteracted by a more powerful force–that of the government. This not only gives the whole a veneer of morality (*causae non causae*), but by putting an end to outbreaks of lawless proclivities, it genuinely makes it much easier for the moral capacities of men to develop into an immediate respect for right. For each individual believes of himself that he would by all means maintain the sanctity of the concept of right and obey it faithfully, if only he could be certain that all the others would do likewise, and the government in part guarantees this for him; thus a great step is taken *towards* morality (although this is still not the same as a moral step), towards a state where the concept of duty is recognized for its own sake, irrespective of any possible gain in return.[46]

As a result, "violence will gradually become less on the part of those in power, and obedience toward the law will increase."[47]

Of Kantian liberalism Machiavelli obviously knew nothing. Moreover, the deceit, violence, and reversals of fortune he witnessed in Renaissance Italy were indeed prone to suggest to him that extreme measures were needed on a regular basis to maintain political order. Nonetheless, this does not exonerate him from failing to comprehend on a deeper level that moral modes are at least as fundamental to order as unjust force and fraud. For some of his own ideas–if thought through consistently–lead to that very conclusion.

Above all, Machiavelli's maxim that princes should feign the virtues to obtain the support of the people implies that morality belongs to the effectual truth of politics; for if subjects are moved to obey a prince because they believe to recognize his virtue, then their support is a moral phenomenon. The objection that the people may support the apparently virtuous prince only because they expect benefits in return lessens the force of this argument, but does not extinguish it; for even such a self-interested exchange presupposes that the people trust the prince to keep the bargain, and this trust represents a moral ground for political order. More generally, the fact that usurpers and aggressors usually lay claim to some just cause, however contrived, equally suggests that morality matters to politics in an irreducible way.[48] For instance, when Hitler announced his assault on Poland with the words "from this day onward we shall shoot back," he did more than utter a lie: He acknowledged the relevance of justice to foreign affairs, presumably thinking that such a claim might bolster his regime at home, lessen the likelihood of Western intervention, and make him look better in the eyes of history. And however untruthful, the Führer thereby entered into the domain of moral discourse. In short, hypocrisy is the tribute that vice pays to virtue.

Further, Machiavelli himself stated several times that political order rests on justice. When composing memoranda as Secretary of the Florentine Chancery, he wrote: "everyone knows that he who says empire, kingdom, principality, republic, who says men that command, beginning from the first rank and descending finally to the master of a brigantine, says justice and arms."[49] True, Machiavelli had a positivist notion of justice, a convention that has proven useful for stable government and thus lends itself to being cast aside whenever injustice promises to be even more effective. But even such an expedient idea of justice implies that citizens and subjects obey their rulers at least in part because they feel that justice is done.

To all this, Machiavelli would probably reply that however useful the virtues may be in maintaining the state, they will always remain secondary to coercion based on fear; for Numa was able to govern Rome with the arts of peace only because Romulus had ruled it first through the arts of war,[50] and it is "much safer to be feared than loved" because "love is held by a chain of obligation, which, because men are wicked, is broken at every opportunity for their own utility, but fear is held by as dread of punishment that never forsakes you" (P.XVII.66-67). In other words, only physical coercion is a nearly objective means of maintaining political order, as almost everyone prefers submission to injury and death.

But this argument for the objectivity of force overlooks a crucial fact, which David Hume once put memorably as follows:

> The soldan of Egypt, or the emperor of Rome, might drive his harmless subjects, like brute beasts, against their sentiments and inclination: but he must, at least, have led his mamalukes, or praetorian bands, like men, by their opinion. Opinion is of two kinds, to wit, opinion of interest, and opinion of right.[51]

In other words, since a ruler cannot personally coerce numerous and remote subjects, he must rely on a number of subordinates to do the job; and since he cannot personally coerce all of the latter–because he has to sleep, may be weaker than they, and cannot reach them once they have left his sight–he must trust that they will carry out his orders because they consent to his rule; this consent in turn rests either on expectation of benefits in exchange for service or belief in the rightness of his cause. Hence, any coercive order beyond the small group a strongman might be able to control by personal force rests by necessity on a moral relationship. Hence, morality is logically prior to force as a cause of political order.

Again, Machiavelli should have grasped this fact, for he states that princes and their ministers must be able to "trust one another," counseling the former to satisfy the desires of the latter to make them dependent (P.XXII.93). Similarly, he asserts that soldiers obey because they expect benefits, since "if those whom you arm are benefited, one can act with more security toward the others. The difference of treatment that they recognize regarding themselves makes them obligated to you" (P.XX.83).[52] Indeed, he realizes that it

> is not reasonable that whoever is armed obey willingly whoever is unarmed, and that someone unarmed be secure among armed servants. For since there is scorn in the one and suspicion in the other, it is not possible for them to work well together. (P.XIV.58)

But in the subsequent sentence, Machiavelli suggests that this problem can be solved by making the prince well armed:

> And therefore a prince who does not understand the military, besides other miseries, cannot . . . be esteemed by his soldiers nor have trust in them. Therefore, he should never lift his thoughts from the exercise of war, and in peace he should exercise it more than in war. (P.XIV.58-59)

In other words, Machiavelli was so impressed with the violent and deceitful ways of Renaissance politics, and the seemingly successful wickedness of men like Cesare Borgia, that he simply could not see what had been clear to most other political thinkers: namely, that a minimally stable order–principality, republic, firm, family, or gang–cannot rest on coercion as the primary cause on all levels of hierarchy, but requires a modicum of morality at least among the elite.

But if morality is thus essential to political order, then it should be undermined by necessary evil rather than strengthened, especially in the long run. For instance, the fact that an apparently virtuous prince actually uses vicious means will eventually become known as the number of his victims rises, for the latter and those who know them well will not be deceived for long and spread the word. And even if public deception can be maintained, the prince's closest subordinates must realize at some point that his cause is wrong or, at a minimum, that they cannot trust him with their lives Thus, the Soviet Union collapsed when its fraudulent claim to a worker's paradise could no longer be maintained and the elite had lost the nerve for the bloodbath that could have kept them in power a while longer.

In other words, there is a deep tension in Machiavelli's thought between the inescapable fact that political order rests on moral relationships and his counsel that rulers must use immoral means to maintain it. Formally, he manages to resolve this tension by assuming that these means can be hidden from the subjects through fraud. But as soon as this fraud fails–and we have argued that eventually it must–the tension becomes a wholesale contradiction that destroys the order. In the words of Jacques Maritain, "it is impossible that the use of . . . a thoroughly immoral art of politics should not produce a progressive lowering and degeneration of moral values and moral beliefs in the common human life," and that, therefore, "such an art wears away and destroys its very matter, and, by the same token, will degenerate itself."[53]

And even if unjust force and fraud were capable of maintaining order in the long run, this order would not be a truly political one; for the political entails justice not merely as a means to peace and stability, but as an end in itself. For human beings truly flourish in a context that enables them to cultivate the virtues and constrains them to respect persons. Politics cannot be put on a purely consequentialist footing because happiness consists of more than satisfying one's desires by the most effective means. Thus, the true contradiction in Machiavelli's thought lurks in the dictum that evil deeds have good political effects: For once the political good is understood to include justice as an ultimate end, Machiavelli's claim that its means include evil says in effect that rulers must commit injustice in order to uphold justice.

With this contradiction we have reached the moral core of the Western tradition. For the principle that directly opposes Machiavelli's doctrine of necessary evil–St. Paul's injunction that "evil must not be done that good may come" (Rom.iii.8)–rests precisely on the idea of the city as an ethical community. Accordingly, it is absolutely prohibited to harm innocents even for the sake of maintaining the state, because the essential purpose of the state is to protect innocents from harm. In the words of Thomas Aquinas, "the life of righteous men preserves and forwards the common good, since they are the chief part of the community. Therefore it is in no way lawful to slay the innocent."[54] An ethical community can require in general that its members part with their possessions or risk their lives in order to preserve its existence, but it cannot single out any number of innocents to be expropriated or put to death without thereby terminating itself as a community.[55] When a sheriff hands over a prisoner to a lynch mob in order to prevent them from burning down the town and raping and killing its inhabitants, he may thus preserve the physical existence of their houses and bodies, but he thereby destroys their existence as a political community whose essence is justice.

This argument against Machiavellian politics is most significant with regard to the progress of civilization, which consists not only of sophisticated living but, more importantly, of advances in telling right from wrong.[56] Thus, the Roman Empire may have brought laws and urban living to barbarians, but its cult of glory and violence delayed the spread of Socratic and Mosaic ethics for centuries. The rampant use of evil means for supposedly good ends by a Hitler or Lenin halted the eastward spread of the liberal principle of respect for persons for several generations, and, after communism's collapse from its contradictions, left behind societies with their civic fabric thoroughly rent.

Foreign Security

According to Machiavelli, cities must wage preventive war and acquire empire in order to make themselves secure, glorious, and wealthy. This maxim falls under the category of necessary evil because it pursues good consequences through unjust means. Preventive war is unjust because it attacks a state merely from fear of its capabilities, without the latter having committed an aggression;[57] empire is unjust because it deprives rational beings of the opportunity to govern themselves.

But are preventive war and imperial domination indeed necessary to provide security, glory, and wealth? Regarding glory, it is hard to deny that major imperial powers have indeed garnered much of mankind's recognition; for, however unjust we may find the deeds of the Assyrians, Persians, Romans, Mongols, and Turks, we cannot help being impressed with their achievement and daring. The generation of wealth by conquest, on the other hand, seems historically contingent: conquering territory and subduing its inhabitants procures riches in agrarian times, when land and labor are the predominant factors of production, but tends to decrease output in industrial times, when capital has become the decisive element.[58]

Concerning security, Machiavelli's argument for preventive war and imperial domination assumes first of all that the contingency of human affairs makes it impossible to balance an opponent's power with such precision that he is neither tempted to take advantage of one's weakness nor provoked to attack from fear of one's strength. Again, this assumption may have held to some extent for ancient and medieval times, when primitive communications and poorly organized efforts at gathering intelligence made it exceedingly difficult to assess the relative power and intentions of other states–which can be readily seen from Machiavelli's own mission reports to the Florentine government.[59] But it holds far less to modern times, when vastly improved means of surveillance and communications, publicly available statistics, and the size of plants and weapons systems make balancing the power of one's opponents a far more viable strategy than Machiavelli believed. And if we lack the resources to match our adversary's capabilities, we can form countervailing alliances with others that face the same threat. True, Machiavelli discounts the effectiveness of alliances because of their inherent problems of collective action–epitomized by the failure of Carthage, Macedon, and the Seleucid Empire to check the rising power of Rome. But, again, it can be argued that his pessimism was historically conditioned, as the difficulty with assessing power and intentions in premodern times was compounded by the inability to communicate with allies and move troops in concerted fashion. Thus, it has been shown that Europe's rulers became capable of forming effective alliances only after a regular diplomatic system had been established during the Renaissance.[60]

Thus, whereas foreign affairs in ancient and medieval times were marked by a succession of great empires, such as the Akkadian (ca. 2350-2300 and 2050-1950 B.C.), Assyrian (ca. 1800-1047 and 883-626 B.C.), New Babylonian (625-539 B.C.), Persian (529-331 B.C.), Roman (198 B.C.-476 A.D.), Byzantine (395-1453 A.D.), Carolingian (751-880 A.D.), and German (962-1231 A.D.), the modern tendency has been for drives for domination to be checked by countervailing coalitions that restored an equilibrium of power. Spain's attempt under Philip II was defeated by France and England (1556-98), the French bids for hegemony under Louis XIV (1661-1715) and Napoleon (1799-1815) were thwarted by Britain, Austria, Prussia, and Russia, and the German efforts under Wilhelm II (1890-1918) and Hitler (1933-45) were repulsed by Britain, France, Russia, and the United States.[61] In short, balancing against power has been quite sufficient to secure the major powers in the modern era.

Second, Machiavelli argues for preventive war and empire because he assumes that eliminating the threat posed by the mere capabilities of others makes a state more secure, since it can never be certain of their future intentions. However, this argument from uncertainty is quite one-sided: While preventive war reduces the risk of becoming the object of an aggression in the future, it provokes the uncertainty of outcome that is inherent to war itself, caused by the multitude of chance events that Clausewitz called "friction."[62] Thus, it is quite possible that preventive war begun with an expectation of victory may end in defeat, and that security is lost rather than enhanced. Moreover, whereas the risk of preventive war is incurred in the present, that of an adverse shift in the balance of power lies in the future; and future risk must be discounted because unexpected events may yet come to our aid. In short, deterrence is the more prudent strategy.

Third, the use of wicked means in foreign condition of license tends to corrupt the morality needed to maintain domestic order; for those who become used to mistreating foreigners in the interest of the state or for personal gain will sooner or later abuse their fellow citizens. The fate of the Athenians provides the classical example: Acting on the maxim that "it is a general and necessary law of nature to rule whatever one can," they lost their empire because "they were so busy with their own personal intrigues" that they "destroyed themselves by their own internal strife," according to Thucydides.[63] Thus, Machiavelli's idea that a republic can maintain a civil way of life by satisfying the ambitions of its members abroad is deeply problematic; for the license they enjoy in lording it over foreigners will corrode the law-abiding habits they need to be good citizens. Thus, the sober Romans began their long slide into corruption during the first half of the second century B.C.,[64] not long after they had become the undisputed masters of the Mediterranean world and could indulge in the delights and riches of the East.

In sum, preventive war and imperial domination diminish the security of a state at least as much as they enhance it, especially under modern conditions. But Machiavelli's argument can be challenged on even deeper grounds; for the peace that has prevailed among liberal states for almost two centuries suggests that the pervasive insecurity of foreign affairs in the past–which political realists like Machiavelli take to be a natural necessity–may have been historically contingent after all.

Again, there is no better guide than Kant on this momentous matter. According to Kant, "perpetual peace" becomes possible or even probable as men become more enlightened and transform their regimes into constitutional republics. First, in a representative form of government, the rulers need the consent of the citizens to wage major wars; and since those who bear the burden of war are unlikely to start it lightly, republics tend to peace.[65] But this democratic argument for peace is limited by the fact that self-ruling peoples can be quite enthusiastic about wars that promise imperial greatness, as shown by the Athenians in antiquity and Britain, France, and the United States in the latter half of the nineteenth century. Hence, it is really the spread of *liberal* thinking during the last two centuries that has led to peace. Liberal states imbued with the "spirit of commerce" prefer peace, because wars are costly and greater gains are made by free trade.[66] More significantly, since liberals assume individuals to be prior to political society, they apply the principle of respect for persons not only to the members of their own society, but also to foreigners and their governments–insofar as the former are enlightened and the latter representative. In short, liberal states respect the autonomy of other liberal states. From both of these reasons, constitutional republics will form a pacific federation that forbids war among its members and protects them from nonliberal powers.[67] And as more peoples recognize that respect for persons ought to govern political life, this federation will expand until–after many reversals–it encompasses humanity as a whole.

Although Kant's thought is somewhat utopian, it nonetheless helps to account for the most remarkable fact that there have been no wars among truly liberal states since the first three–England, France, the United States–began to coexist and the upheavals that created the latter two had subsided around 1815. While other causes, such as being allied for geopolitical reasons, may explain some of this peace, it seems clear that war has become nearly unthinkable among Western states in large part because they take respect for rights as their highest principle and pursue prosperity by productive enterprise and trade–rather than seeking to exalt God and fatherland by martial deeds or pursuing wealth by plunder, as had been the norm for millenia.

Insofar as this epochal change from a conflict-prone past to a rights-based future is real, Machiavelli's account of foreign affairs as a violent and endless struggle for domination must be challenged on the most fundamental grounds. Just as in domestic politics, the decline of unjust violence in foreign affairs suggests that Machiavelli was wrong when he assumed that the habituation of human beings to a lawful life can only be temporary because their first nature is inherently bad, requiring the repeated use of necessary evil to hold them in check.

Conclusion

It is on two grounds that Machiavelli's doctrine of necessary evil is fundamentally mistaken. First, it exaggerates the effectiveness of unjust force and fraud. Since political order rests at least as much on justice as on coercion, clever wickedness carries the seeds of its own destruction, especially in the long run. Foreign security rests more reliably on deterrence and balancing power than preventive war and imperial domination, particularly in modern times; indeed, among liberal states anarchy may be giving way to a pacific union.

Second, insofar as force and fraud remain necessary, they can be subsumed under the allowance that absolutist morality makes for their use against against transgressors. For instance, martial law can be justly declared when anarchy threatens a generally good order, making it permissible to detain and even execute without trial those who violate emergency regulations, such as curfews, prohibition of assembly, etc. Further, it may be right to bribe already corrupt pulic officials if so doing is the only way to make justice prevail, as Lincoln did when he used patronage to secure passage of the Amendment abolishing slavery in the House of Representatives.[68] Indeed, it can be argued that torture may be used on those who are known to have intentionally put innocent lives at risk and withhold the information that alone can save them, as, for instance, when terrorists refuse to reveal the whereabouts of the bomb they planted.[69] Thus, as Jacques Maritain concluded, "many rules of political life, which the pessimists of Machiavellianism usurp to the benefit of immorality, are in reality ethically grounded," so that, "in the last analysis, Political Ethics is able to absorb and digest all the elements of truth contained in Machiavelli."[70]

The chasm between political necessity and traditional morality that Machiavelli believed he had discovered is therefore an illusion. He created this illusion because he overestimated the effectiveness of unjust means and, like many cynics, had a naive notion of morality as something that needs to be removed from practical life in order to remain pure. But morality properly understood is practical in its very essence and thus quite capable of guiding political men through difficult situations. In Aristotelian terms, the virtue of prudence (*phronesis*) requires the agent not only to grasp concrete particulars, but also to use cleverness in finding the means that realize the good life (and thus promote justice, moderation, and the other virtues).[71] And since attaining political ends without doing harm is often more difficult than resorting to straightforward violence and deception, the truly prudent man needs to be a good deal smarter than a Machiavellian prince. Put differently, a true founder like Moses, who created a society that greatly advanced civilization, was far wiser than someone like Machiavelli could ever understand.

Notes

1. Jeremy Bentham, *A Fragment of Government* [1776], ed. J. H. Burns and H. L. A. Hart (Cambridge: Cambridge University Press, 1988), 3.

2. Hermann Rauschning, *Gespräche mit Hitler* (Zürich, 1940), 249 ff, mt, cited in Theodor Schieder, "Niccolò Machiavelli: Epilog zu einem Jubiläumsjahr," *Historische Zeitschrift* 210, no. 2 (April 1970): 265-94, at 291.

3. Cf. Friedrich Mehmel, "Machiavelli und die Antike," in *Antike und Abendland: Beiträge zum Verständnis der Griechen und Römer und ihres Nachlebens,* ed. Bruno Snell, vol. 3 (Hamburg: Marion von Schröder, 1948), 151-86, esp. 159, 164-70, 180-83.

4. On the relation between Machiavelli and Livy, see also J. H. Whitfield, "Machiavelli's Use of Livy," in *Livy,* ed. T. A. Dorey (London: Routledge Kegan Paul, 1971), 73-96; Alain Michel, "Machiavel lecteur de Tite-Live:

Entre l'optimism de Ciceron et le pessimisme de Tacite," in *Machiavelli attuale/Machiavel actuel,* ed. Georges Barthouil (Ravenna: Longo, 1982), 139-48.

5. Livy, *The Early History of Rome,* trans. Aubrey de Sélincourt (London: Penguin Books, 1960), I.7, I.13-14; cf. D.I.9.1-2.

6. See Livy, *Rome and Italy,* trans. Betty Radice (London: Penguin Books, 1982), IX.4-15.

7.See Sallust, *The War With Catiline,* in *Sallust,* trans. J. C. Rolfe, Loeb Classical Library 116 (Cambridge, Mass.: Harvard University Press, 1985), 1-129, at VII, cf. VI, VIII-X. On the relation between Machiavelli and Sallust, see also Patricia J. Osmond, "Sallust and Machiavelli: From Civic Humanism to Political Prudence," *Journal of Medieval and Renaissance Studies* 23, no. 3 (fall 1993): 407-38.

8. See Sallust, *War With Catiline,* XXXI; D.III.6.19.

9. See P.XVIII.69; Cicero, *On Duties.* trans. Walter Miller, Loeb Classical Library 30 (Cambridge, Mass.: Harvard University Press, 1913), I.xi.34, I.xiii.41, I.xlv.159, II.iii.9, III.iv.19, III.vii.34viii.36. On the relation between Machiavelli and Cicero, see also Leslie J. Walker, "Notes," in *The Discourses of Niccolò Machiavelli,* trans. Leslie J. Walker, vol. II (New Haven: Yale University Press, 1950), 277-79; Marcia L. Colish, "Cicero's *De Officiis* and Machiavelli's *Prince," Sixteenth Century Journal* 9, no. 4 (winter 1978): 81-93; J. H. Hexter, "Claude de Seyssel and Normal Politics in the Age of Machiavelli," in *Art, Science, and History in the Renaissance,* ed. Charles H. Singleton (Baltimore: Johns Hopkins University Press, 1967), 389-415, esp. 392-94.

10. See J. G. A. Pocock, *The Machiavellian Moment: Florentine Political Thought and the Atlantic Republican Tradition* (Princeton: Princeton University Press, 1975), vii, 3, 49-80; Quentin Skinner, *The Foundations of Modern Political Thought,* vol. 1, *The Renaissance* (Cambridge: Cambridge University Press, 1978), 69-128, 152-80; Maurizio Viroli, *From Politics to Reason of State: The Acquisition and Transformation of the Language of Politics 1250-1600* (Cambridge: Cambridge University Press, 1992a), 71-125.

11. Cf. D.I.Pr.2.

12. For a recent interpretation that credits Machiavelli with having sought to create a wholly new way of political life, see Vickie B. Sullivan, *Machiavelli's Three Romes: Religion, Human Liberty, and Politics Reformed* (DeKalb: Northern Illinois University Press, 1996), esp. 124-39.

13. Cf. FH.IV.14

14. Indeed, Machiavelli speaks of "perpetual honor" (D.I.10.1; cf. D.I.27.1-2), but assumes on the other hand that the "variation of sects and languages, together with the accident of floods or plagues, eliminates the memories of things" every few thousand years (D.II.5.T).

15. Thucydides, *History of the Peloponnesian War,* trans. Rex Warner (London: Penguin Books, 1954), II.41-44.

16. Aristotle, *Nicomachean Ethics,* trans. Terence Irwin (Indianapolis: Hackett, 1985), 1097b-1098a, 1102a, 1140a-b, 1144a-1145a.

17. Aristotle, *Nicomachean Ethics,* 1099a, 1115a-1117b. This should not be taken to mean that Aristotle advocates the cultivation of the virtues because they are inherently enjoyable; rather, we ought to pursue them for the sake of doing what is right, and, in so doing, will find that pleasure supervenes.

18. Cf. Aristotle, *Nicomachean Ethics,* 1095b.

19. Jean-Jacques Rousseau, *Discourse on the Origin and Foundations of Inequality Among Men,* in *The Basic Political Writings,* trans. Donald A. Cress (Indianapolis: Hackett Classics, 1987), 23-109, at 81.

20. Aristotle, *Nicomachean Ethics,* 1100b.

21. For interpretations of Machiavelli that center on autonomy, see Neal Wood, "Machiavelli's Humanism of Action," in *The Political Calculus,* ed. Anthony Parel (Toronto: University of Toronto Press, 1972), 33-57; Hannah F. Pitkin, *Fortune Is a Woman: Gender and Politics in the Thought of Niccolò Machiavelli* (Berkeley, Calif.: University of California Press, 1984); Vickie B. Sullivan, "Human Autonomy in Niccolò Machiavelli's *Discourses on Livy*" (Ph.D. diss., University of Chicago, 1990).

22. Cf. P.VII.32-33, XIX.73; D.I.2.7, 3.T, 3.2, 4.1-2, 5.4, 7.1, 8.1, 13.1, 17.1, 18.2-3, 18.5, 25, 33.1, 33.5, 34.1-2, 34.4, 35.T, 35, 37.1, 39.2, 40.T, 40.1-5, 40.7, 41, 44.1, 47.1-2, 49.1, 49.3, 50; D.II.29.1; D.III.1.2, 15.1, 25, 28, 30.1, 33.1, 34.4.

23. See Giannozzo Manetti, *On the Dignity of Man* [ca. 1420-30], trans. Bernard Murchland, in *Two Views of Man* (New York: Frederick Ungar, 1966), 61-103; Giovanni Pico della Mirandola, *Oration on the Dignity of Man* [1486], trans. Elizabeth Livermoore Forbes, in *The Renaissance Philosophy of Man,* ed. Ernst Cassirer, Paul Oskar Kristeller, and John Herman Randall, Jr. (Chicago: University of Chicago Press, 1948), 223-54.

On the humanist idea of autonomy, see also Ernst Cassirer, "Freiheit und Notwedigkeit in der Philosophie der Renaissance," chap. in *Individuum und Kosmos in der Philosophie der Renaissance* (Darmstadt: Wissenschaftliche Buchgesellschaft, 1963), 77-129; Skinner, *The Foundations of Modern Political Thought,* 88-101; Antonino Poppi, "Fate, Fortune, Providence and Human Freedom," in *The Cambridge History of Renaissance Philosophy,* ed. Charles B. Schmitt (Cambridge: Cambridge University Press, 1988), 641-67; Jill Kraye, "Moral Philosophy," in *The Cambridge History of Renaissance Philosophy,* ed. Charles B. Schmitt (Cambridge: Cambridge University Press, 1988), 303-86, at 306-16.

24. See Kurt Kluxen, *Politik und menschliche Existenz bei Machiavelli: Dargestellt am Begriff der Necessità* (Stuttgart: W. Kohlhammer, 1967), 21-22; Herfried Münkler, *Machiavelli: Die Begründung des politischen Denkens der Neuzeit aus der Krise der Republik Florenz* (Frankfurt: Europäische Verlagsanstalt, 1982), 246-50.

25. In addition to the works cited in note 23, see Lorenzo Valla, *Dialogue on Free Will* [1483], trans. Charles Edward Trinkaus, Jr., in *The Renaissance Philosophy of Man,* ed. Ernst Cassirer, Paul Oskar Kristeller, and John Herman Randall, Jr. (Chicago: University of Chicago Press, 1948), 155-82.

26. Thomas Hobbes, *Leviathan: With Selected Variants from the Latin*

Edition of 1688 [1651], ed. Edwin Curley (Indianapolis: Hackett 1994), XIV.2.

27. Hobbes, *Leviathan,* A Review and Conclusion.8; cf. XVIII.20, XX.18, XXI.21, A Review and Conclusion.17.

28. Georg W. F. Hegel, *The Philosophy of History* [ca. 1822], trans. J. Sibree (Buffalo, New York: Prometheus Books, 1991), 32.

29. Hegel, *Philosophy of History,* 67.

30. Hegel, *Philosophy of History,* 21.

31. Donagan, *Theory of Morality,* 185.

32. Donagan, *Theory of Morality,* 185.

33. Thus, it has been shown that Hobbes's construction of a social contract among individuals in the state of nature is logically flawed; see Jean Hampton, *Hobbes and the Social Contract Tradition* (Cambridge: Cambridge University Press, 1986).

34. William Graham Sumner, *Folkways: A Study of the Sociological Importance of Usages, Manners, Customs, Mores, and Morals* (New York: Dover Publications, 1906), 12-18.

35. Gary R. Johnson, "Kin Selection, Socialization, and Patriotism: An Integrating Theory," *Politics and the Life Sciences,* vol. 4, no. 2 (February 1986): 127-40.

36. Immanuel Kant, "Perpetual Peace: A Philosophical Sketch" [1795], in *Political Writings,* 2nd ed., ed. Hans Reiss, trans. H. B. Nisbet (Cambridge: Cambridge University Press, 1991), 93-130, at 104, 102, 98.

37. Immanuel Kant, *The Metaphysics of Morals* [1797], in *Political Writings,* 2nd ed., ed. Hans Reiss, trans. H. B. Nisbet (Cambridge: Cambridge University Press, 1991), 131-75, at 137-38; cf. 162, 173. Cf. Kant, "Perpetual Peace," 117.

38. Kant, "Perpetual Peace," 104.

39. Immanuel Kant, "Idea for a Universal History with a Cosmopolitan Purpose" [1784], in *Political Writings,* 2nd ed., ed. Hans Reiss, trans. H. B. Nisbet (Cambridge: Cambridge University Press, 1991), 41-53, at 45-46.

40. Aristotle, *The Politics,* trans. Carnes Lord (Chicago: University of Chicago Press, 1984), 1252a-b.

41. Aristotle, *Nicomachean Ethics,* 1155a, 1159b-1160a, 1170b-1171a; Aristotle, *Politics,* 1326a-1327a.

42. See P.VII.29-30; P.XVII.65-66; "Mission to the Duke of Valentinois," in W.III.141-280, at 257, 259.

43. Kant, "Idea for a Universal History," 42. Cf. Immanuel Kant, "The Contest of Faculties" [1798], in *Political Writings,* 2nd ed., ed. Hans Reiss, trans. H. B. Nisbet (Cambridge: Cambridge University Press, 1991), 176-90, at 181.

44. Kant, "Contest of Faculties," 184.

45. Kant, "What Is Enlightenment?" [1784], in *Political Writings,* 2nd ed., ed. Hans Reiss, trans. H. B. Nisbet (Cambridge: Cambridge University Press, 1991), 54-60, at 59.

46. Kant, "Perpetual Peace," 121 n, cf. 118. *"Causae non causae"* probably means "apparent reasons are no legal reasons," or, in Kant's more suitable

German, *"Scheingründe sind keine Rechtsgründe."*

47. Kant, "Contest of Faculties," 188.

48. See Kant, "Perpetual Peace," 103; Kant, "Contest of Faculties," 183; Michael Walzer, *Just and Unjust Wars: A Moral Argument with Historical Illustrations* (New York: Basic Books, 1977), 11-12, 19-20.

49. *La cagione dell' ordinanza, dove la si truovi, et quel che bisogni fare* [The reason for the ordinance, where it is found, and what needs to be done], in TO.37-40, at 37-38, mt. Cf. *Allocuzione fatta ad un magistrato* [Address given to a magistrate], in TO.36-37, at 36; *Provvisione prima per le fanterie, del 6 dicembre 1506* [First provision for the infantry, from 6th December 1506], in TO.40-47, at 40.

50. D.I.19.3.

51. David Hume, *Political Essays* [1741] (Cambridge: Cambridge University Press, 1994), 16.

52. Cf. P.XXII.93.

53. Jacques Maritain, "The End of Machiavellianism," *Review of Politics* 4 (January 1942): 1-33, at 9.

54. Thomas Aquinas, *Summa Theologiae,* trans. Fathers of the English Dominican Province, 3 vols (New York: Benziger Brothers, 1947), Pt. II-II, Q. 64, A. 6.

55. Cf. Donagan, *Theory of Morality,* 183.

56. Cf. Maritain, "End of Machiavellianism," 26-27.

57. In contrast, waging *preemptive* war is justified on the grounds that the opponent has decided to commit an aggression and that it is imminent. On the moral status of preventive and preemptive war, see Walzer, *Just and Unjust Wars,* ch. 5.

58. Cf. Richard Rosecrance, *The Rise of the Trading State: Commerce and Conquest in the Modern World* (New York: Basic Books, 1986), 139.

59. See W.III–IV.

60. See Garrett Mattingly*, Renaissance Diplomacy* (Boston: Houghton Mifflin, 1971), chs. 13-16.

61. See Ludwig Dehio, *The Precarious Balance,* trans. Charles Fullman (New York: Knopf, 1962).

62. Carl von Clausewitz, *On War* [1832]*,* trans. Col. J. J. Graham (London: Penguin Classics, 1968), 118, 160, 163, 164-67, 270, 296, 369.

63. Thucydides, *Peloponnesian War,* V.105, II.65.

64. See D.III.25.

65. Kant, "Perpetual Peace," 100, 114; Immanuel Kant, "On the Common Saying: 'This May be True in Theory, but it does not Apply in Practice'" [1793], in *Political Writings,* 2nd ed., ed. Hans Reiss, trans. H. B. Nisbet (Cambridge: Cambridge University Press, 1991), 61-92, at 91. For an empirical corroboration of Kant's argument, see Michael W. Doyle, "Kant, Liberal Legacies and Foreign Affairs," *Philosophy and Public Affairs* 12, no. 3 (summer 1983): 205-35; Michael W. Doyle, "Kant, Liberal Legacies and Foreign Affairs, Part 2," *Philosophy and Public Affairs* 12, no. 4 (autumn 1983): 323-53.

66. Kant, "Idea for a Universal History," 50-51; Kant, "Theory and

Practice," 90.

67. Kant, "Perpetual Peace," 104-05; Kant, *Metaphysics of Morals,* 165; Kant, "Contest of Faculties," 188.

68. Donagan, *Theory of Morality,* 186-87.

69. Donagan, *Theory of Morality,* 187-88.

70. Maritain, "End of Machiavellianism," 5, 28.

71. Aristotle, *Nicomachean Ethics,* 1141b10-1142b35, 1144a21-37.

Bibliography

Adcock, F. E. *Roman Political Ideas and Practice.* Ann Arbor: University of Michigan Press, 1979.

Albertini, Rudolf von. *Das Florentinische Staatsbewußtsein im Übergang von der Republik zum Prinzipat.* Bern: Francke, 1955.

Alunno, Francesco. *La Fabrica del Mondo.* Vinegia, 1548.

Anglo, Sidney. *Machiavelli: A Dissection.* London: Victor Gollancz, 1969.

Aquinas, Thomas. *Aquinas On Being and Essence.* Translated by Joseph Bobik. Notre Dame, Ind.: University of Notre Dame Press, 1965.

——. *Summa Theologiae.* Translated by the Fathers of the English Dominican Province. 3 vols. New York: Benziger Brothers, 1947.

Aristotle. *Aristotle's Metaphysics.* Translated by Hippocrates G. Apostle. Grinell, Iowa: Peripatetic Press, 1966.

——. *Nicomachean Ethics.* Translated by Terence Irwin. Indianapolis: Hackett, 1985.

——. *The Politics.* Translated by Carnes Lord. Chicago: University of Chicago Press, 1984.

Ascoli, Albert Russell, and Victoria Kahn, "Introduction." In *Machiavelli and the Discourse of Literature,* 1-15. Ithaca, New York: Cornell University Press, 1993.

Augustine. *Political Writings.* Translated by Michael W. Tkacz and Douglas Kries. Indianapolis: Hackett, 1994.

Austin, J. L. "A Plea for Excuses." In *Philosophical Papers,* ed. J. O. Urmson and G. J. Warnock, 123-52. Oxford: Oxford University Press, 1961.

Bacon, Francis. *Of the Advancement of Learning* [1605]. London: Oxford University Press, 1906.

Ball, Terence, and Richard Dagger. *Political Ideologies and the Democratic Ideal.* New York: Harper-Collins, 1991.

Baricelli, Gian Piero. "Rereading 'The Prince': Philosophical Themes in Machiavelli." *Italian Quarterly* 13, no. 52 (spring–summer 1970): 43-62.

Baron, Hans. *The Crisis of the Early Italian Renaissance: Civic Humanism and Republican Liberty in an Age of Classicism and Tyranny.* 2nd ed. Princeton: Princeton University Press, 1966.
——. "Machiavelli: The Republican Citizen and the Author of 'The Prince.'" *English Historical Review* 76 (April 1961): 217-53.
Bentham, Jeremy. *A Fragment of Government* [1776]. Edited by J. H. Burns and H. L. A. Hart. Cambridge: Cambridge University Press, 1988.
Berki, R. N. "Machiavellism: A Philosophical Defense." *Ethics* 81, no. 2 (January 1971): 107-27.
Berlin, Isaiah. "The Originality of Machiavelli" [1953]. In *Studies On Machiavelli,* ed. Myron P. Gilmore, 147-206. Florence: Sansoni, 1972.
Bluhm, William T. *Theories of the Political System: Classics of Political Thought and Modern Political Analysis.* 3rd ed. Englewood Cliffs: Prentice-Hall, 1978.
Bock, Gisela. "Civil Discord in Machiavelli's *Istorie Fiorentine.*" In *Machiavelli and Republicanism,* ed. Gisela Bock, Quentin Skinner, and Maurizio Viroli, 181-201. Cambridge: Cambridge University Press, 1990.
Bodin, Jean. *Methodus ad facilem historiarum cognitionem* [1556]. Paris: P. Mesnard, 1951.
Bonadeo, Alfredo. "The Role of the 'Grandi' in the Political World of Machiavelli." *Studies in the Renaissance* 16 (1969): 9-30.
——. "The Role of the People in the Works and Times of Machiavelli." *Bibliothèque d'Humanisme et Renaissance* 32, no. 2 (1970): 351-77.
Büchner, Karl. "Altrömische und Horazische virtus." In *Römische Wertbegriffe,* ed. Hans Oppermann, 376-401. Wege der Forschung, vol. 34. Darmstadt: Wissenschaftliche Buchgesellschaft, 1967.
Burckhardt, Jacob. *The Civilization of the Renaissance in Italy* [1860]. Translated by S. G. C. Middlemore. New York: Modern Library, 1954.
Butterfield, Herbert. *The Statecraft of Machiavelli.* London: G. Bell, 1940.
Cassirer, Ernst. "Freiheit und Notwendigkeit in der Philosophie der Renaissance." Chapter 3 of *Individuum und Kosmos in der Philosophie der Renaissance.* Darmstadt: Wissenschaftliche Buchgesellschaft, 1963.
——. *The Myth of the State.* New Haven: Yale University Press, 1946.
Chabod, Federico. *Machiavelli and the Renaissance.* Translated by David Moore. New York: Harper & Row, 1958.
Chiapelli, Fredi. *Studi sul linguaggio di Machiavelli.* Florence: Le Monnier, 1952.
Cicero. *Brutus.* Translated by G. L. Hendrickson. Loeb Classical Library 342. Cambridge, Mass.: Harvard University Press, 1971.
——. *De Amicitia.* Translated by W. A. Falconer. Loeb Classical Library 154. Cambridge, Mass.: Harvard University Press, 1923.
——. *De Finibus Bonorum et Malorum.* Translated by H. Rackham. Loeb Classical Library 40. Cambridge, Mass.: Harvard University Press, 1914.
——. *De Inventione.* Translated by H. M. Hubbell. Loeb Classical Library 386. Cambridge, Mass.: Harvard University Press, 1949.
——. *De Legibus.* Translated by C. W. Keyes. Loeb Classical Library 213.

Cambridge, Mass.: Harvard University Press, 1928.

———. *De Oratore.* Translated by E. W. Sutton and H. Rackham. Loeb Classical Library 348-349. Cambridge, Mass.: Harvard University Press, 1942.

———. *De Partitione Oratoria.* Translated by H. Rackham. Loeb Classical Library 349. Cambridge, Mass.: Harvard University Press, 1942.

———. *De Re Publica.* Translated by C. W. Keyes. Loeb Classical Library 213. Cambridge, Mass.: Harvard University Press, 1928.

———. *On Duties.* Translated by Walter Miller. Loeb Classical Library 30. Cambridge, Mass.: Harvard University Press, 1913.

Clark, Richard C. "Machiavelli: Bibliographical Spectrum." *Review of National Literatures* 1, no. 1 (spring 1970): 93-135.

Clausewitz, Carl von. *On War* [1832]. Translated by Col. J. J. Graham. London: Penguin Classics, 1968.

Cochrane, Eric W. "Machiavelli: 1940-1960." *Journal of Modern History* 33, no. 2 (June 1961): 113-36.

Colish, Marcia L. "Cicero's *De Officiis* and Machiavelli's *Prince.*" *Sixteenth Century Journal* 9, no. 4 (winter 1978): 81-93.

———. "The Idea of Liberty in Machiavelli." *Journal of the History of Ideas* 32, no. 3 (July-September 1971): 323-50.

Copenhaver, Brian P. "Astrology and Magic." In *The Cambridge History of Renaissance Philosophy,* ed. Charles B. Schmitt, 264-300. Cambridge: Cambridge University Press, 1988.

Croce, Benedetto. "Machiavelli and Vico" [1924]. In *Poetry, History: An Anthology of Essays by Benedetto Croce,* trans. Cecil Sprigge, 665-60. London: Oxford University Press, 1966.

Curtius, Ludwig. "Virtus und Constantia." In *Römische Wertbegriffe,* ed. Hans Oppermann, 370-75. Wege der Forschung, vol. 34. Darmstadt: Wissenschaftliche Buchgesellschaft, 1967.

De Grazia, Sebastian. *Machiavelli in Hell.* New York: Random House, 1994.

Dehio, Ludwig. *The Precarious Balance.* Translated by Charles Fullman. New York: Knopf, 1962.

De Vries, Hans. *Essai sur la terminologie constitutionelle chez Machiavel ("Il Principe").* 'S-Gravenhage, Netherlands: Uitgeverij Excelsior, 1957.

Donagan, Alan. *The Theory of Morality.* Chicago: University of Chicago Press, 1977.

Donaldson, Peter S. *Machiavelli and Mystery of State.* Cambridge: Cambridge University Press, 1988.

Doyle, Michael W. "Kant, Liberal Legacies and Foreign Affairs." *Philosophy and Public Affairs* 12, no. 3 (summer 1983): 205-35.

———. "Kant, Liberal Legacies and Foreign Affairs, Part 2." *Philosophy and Public Affairs* 12, no. 4 (autumn 1983): 323-53.

Earl, D. C. *The Moral and Political Tradition of Rome.* Ithaca: Cornell University Press, 1967.

Flanagan, Thomas. "The Concept of *Fortuna* in Machiavelli." In *The Political Calculus,* ed. Anthony Parel, 127-56. Toronto: University of Toronto

Press, 1972.

Fleisher, Martin. "A Passion for Politics: The Vital Core of the World of Machiavelli." In *Machiavelli and the Nature of Political Thought,* ed. Martin Fleisher, 114-47. New York: Atheneum, 1972.

Forde, Steven. "Varieties of Realism: Thucydides and Machiavelli." *Journal of Politics* 54, no. 2 (May 1992): 372-93.

Friedrich, Carl J. *Constitutional Reason of State.* Providence, R.I.: Brown University Press, 1957.

Funke, Gerhard. *Gewohnheit.* Archiv für Begriffsgeschichte, vol. 3. Edited by Erich Rothacker. Bonn: H. Bouvier, 1961.

Garin, Eugenio. *Italian Humanism, Philosophy and Civic Life in the Renaissance.* Translated by Peter Munz. New York: Harper & Row, 1965.

Garver, Eugene. *Machiavelli and the History of Prudence.* Madison, Wisc.: University of Wisconsin Press, 1987.

Gauthier, David P. *Practical Reasoning: The Structure and Foundations of Prudential and Moral Arguments and their Exemplification in Discourse.* Oxford: Oxford University Press, 1963.

Geerken, John H. "Homer's Image of the Hero in Machiavelli: A Comparison of *arete* and *virtù.*" *Italian Quarterly* 14 (1970): 45-90.

——. "Machiavelli Studies Since 1969." *Journal of the History of Ideas* 37, no. 2 (April-June 1976): 351-68.

Gentillet, Innocent. *Anti-Machiavel* [1576]. Edited by C. Edward Rathé. Geneva: Librairie Droz, 1968.

Germino, Dante. "Machiavelli's Thoughts on the Psyche and Society." In *The Political Calculus,* ed. Anthony Parel, 59-82. Toronto: University of Toronto Press, 1972.

Gilbert, Felix. "The Humanist Concept of the Prince and *The Prince* of Machiavelli." Journal of Modern History 11, no. 4 (December 1939): 449-83.

——. *Machiavelli and Guicciardini: Politics and History in Sixteenth Century Florence.* New York: Norton, 1984 [1965].

——. "On Machiavelli's Idea of *virtù.*" *Renaissance News* 4 (1951): 53-56.

——. "Machiavelli's 'Istorie Fiorentine': An Essay in Interpretation." In *Studies on Machiavelli,* ed. Myron P. Gilmore, 75-99. Florence: Sansoni, 1972.

——. "Machiavellism." In *Dictionary of the History of Ideas,* ed. Philip P. Wiener, 116-26. New York: Scribner's Sons, 1973.

——. "Machiavelli: The Renaissance of the Art of War." In *Makers of Modern Strategy from Machiavelli to the Nuclear Age,* ed. Peter Paret, 11-31. Princeton: Princeton University Press, 1986.

Guicciardini, Francesco. *Maxims and Reflections of a Renaissance Statesman* [1512-30]. Translated by Mario Domandi. New York: Harper Torchbooks, 1965.

——. *Ricordi* [1528-30]. Florence: R. Spongano, 1951.

Guillemin, Bernard. "Machiavel, lecteur d'Aristote." In *Platon et Aristote à la renaissance: XVIe Colloque International de Tours, De Petrarque à*

Descartes, vol. XXXII, 163-73. Paris: Librairie Philosophique J. Vrin, 1976.

Hampton, Jean. *Hobbes and the Social Contract Tradition.* Cambridge: Cambridge University Press, 1986.

Hancock, Graham. *Fingerprints of the Gods.* New York: Crown Trade Paperbacks, 1995.

Hardin, Russell. *Collective Action.* Baltimore: Johns Hopkins University Press, 1982.

Harvey, E. Ruth. *The Inward Wits: Psychological Theory in the Middle Ages and the Renaissance.* London: Warburg Institute, 1975.

Hegel, Georg W. F. *The Philosophy of History* [ca. 1822]. Translated by J. Sibree. Buffalo, New York: Prometheus Books, 1991.

Herz, John. "Idealist Internationalism and the Security Dilemma." *World Politics* 2, no. 2 (January 1950): 157-80.

Hexter, J. H. "Claude de Seyssel and Normal Politics in the Age of Machiavelli." In *Art, Science, and History in the Renaissance,* ed. Charles H. Singleton, 389-415. Baltimore: Johns Hopkins University Press, 1967.

———. "*Il principe* and *lo stato.*" In *Studies in the Renaissance,* ed. M. A. Shaaber, vol. 4, 113-38. New York: Renaissance Society of America, 1958.

Hobbes, Thomas. *Leviathan: With Selected Variants from the Latin Edition of 1688* [1651]. Edited by Edwin Curley. Indianapolis: Hackett 1994.

Hulliung, Mark. *Citizen Machiavelli.* Princeton: Princeton University Press, 1983.

Hume, David. *Political Essays* [1741]. Edited by Knud Haakonssen. Cambridge: Cambridge University Press, 1994.

Huovinen, Lauri. *Das Bild vom Menschen im politischen Denken Niccolò Machiavellis.* Annales Academiae Scientiarum Fennicae, ser. B, tom. 74.2. Helsinki: Finnische Akademie der Wissenschaften, 1951.

Ingegno, Alfonso. "The New Philosophy of Nature." In *The Cambridge History of Renaissance Philosophy,* ed. Charles B. Schmitt, 236-63. Cambridge: Cambridge University Press, 1988.

Ingersoll, David E. "The Constant Prince: Private Interests and Public Goals in Machiavelli." *Western Political Quarterly* 21, no. 4 (December 1968): 588-96.

Jervis, Robert. "Deterrence, the Spiral Model, and the Intentions of the Adversary." Chap. 3 of *Perception and Misperception in International Politics.* Princeton: Princeton University Press, 1976.

Johnson, Gary R. "Kin Selection, Socialization, and Patriotism: An Integrating Theory." *Politics and the Life Sciences,* vol. 4, no. 2 (February 1986): 127-40.

Kahn, Victoria. "Habermas, Machiavelli, and the Humanist Critique of Ideology." *PMLA* 105 (1990): 464-76.

———. *Machiavellian Rhetoric: From the Counter-Reformation to Milton.* Princeton: Princeton University Press, 1994.

Kant, Immanuel. *Groundwork of the Metaphysics of Morals* [1785]. Translated by H. J. Patton. New York: Harper Torchbooks, 1964.

——. *Political Writings.* 2nd ed. Edited by Hans Reiss. Translated by H. B. Nisbet. Cambridge: Cambridge University Press, 1991.

Kelley, Donald R. "The Theory of History." In *The Cambridge History of Renaissance Philosophy,* ed. Charles B. Schmitt and Quentin Skinner, 746-61. Cambridge: Cambridge University Press, 1988.

Kemp, Simon. *Medieval Psychology.* New York: Greenwood Press, 1990.

Kessler, Eckhart. "The Intellective Soul." In *The Cambridge History of Renaissance Philosophy,* ed. Charles B. Schmitt, 485-534. Cambridge: Cambridge University Press, 1988.

Kluxen, Kurt. *Politik und menschliche Existenz bei Machiavelli: Dargestellt am Begriff der Necessità.* Stuttgart: W. Kohlhammer, 1967.

Knoche, Ulrich. "Der römische Ruhmesgedanke" [1937]. In *Römische Wertbegriffe,* ed. Hans Oppermann, 420-45. Wege der Forschung, vol. 34. Darmstadt: Wissenschaftliche Buchgesellschaft, 1967.

Kontos, Alexis. "Success and Knowledge in Machiavelli." In *The Political Calculus,* ed. Anthony Parel, 83-100. Toronto: University of Toronto Press, 1972.

Kraye, Jill. "Moral Philosophy." In *The Cambridge History of Renaissance Philosophy,* ed. Charles B. Schmitt, 303-86. Cambridge: Cambridge University Press, 1988.

Kristeller, Paul Oskar. "Humanism." In *The Cambridge History of Renaissance Philosophy,* ed. Charles B. Schmitt and Quentin Skinner, 113-37. Cambridge: Cambridge University Press, 1988.

——. *Renaissance Thought: The Classic, Scholastic, and Humanistic Strains.* New York: Harper Torchbooks, 1961.

Krüger, Paul, and Theodor Mommsen, eds. *Corpus iuris civilis.* Vol 1. 17th ed. Hildesheim: Weidmann, 1963.

Landi, Ernesto. "The Political Philosophy of Machiavelli." *History Today* 14, no. 7 (July 1964): 550-55.

Lida de Malkiel, Maria Rosa. *L'idée de la gloire dans la tradition occidentale: Antiquité, moyen-age occidental, Castille* [1952]. Translated by Sylvia Roubaud. Paris: C. Klincksieck, 1968.

Livy. *The Early History of Rome: Books I–V of* The History of Rome from its Foundation. Translated by Aubrey de Sélincourt. London: Penguin Books, 1960.

——. *Rome and Italy: Books VI–X of* The History of Rome from its Foundation. Translated by Betty Radice. London: Penguin Books, 1982.

——. *Rome and the Mediterranean: Books XXXI–XLV of* The History of Rome from its Foundation. Translated by Henry Bettenson. London: Penguin Books, 1976.

Luciani, Vincent. "Bacon and Machiavelli." *Italica* 24, no.1 (March 1947): 26-41.

Machiavelli, Niccolò. *The Chief Works and Others.* Translated by Allan Gilbert. Durham: Duke University Press, 1958.

——. *A Dialogue on Language.* In *The Literary Works of Machiavelli,* ed. and trans. J. R. Hale, 174-90. London: Oxford University Press, 1961.

———. *Discourses on Livy.* Translated by Harvey C. Mansfield and Nathan Tarcov. Chicago: University of Chicago Press, 1996.

———. *Florentine Histories.* Translated by Laura F. Banfield and Harvey C. Mansfield, Jr. Princeton: Princeton University Press, 1988.

———. *The Historical, Political, and Diplomatic Writings of Niccolò Machiavelli.* Translated by Christian E. Detmold. Boston: Houghton, Mifflin, 1891.

———. *The Prince.* Translated by Harvey C. Mansfield, Jr. Chicago: University of Chicago Press, 1985.

———. *Tutte le Opere* [Complete works]. Edited by Mario Martelli. Florence: Sansoni, 1992.

MacIntyre, Alasdair. *After Virtue: A Study in Moral Theory.* 2nd ed. Notre Dame, Ind.: University of Notre Dame Press, 1984.

Manetti, Giannozzo. *On the Dignity of Man* [ca. 1420-30]. Translated by Bernard Murchland. In *Two Views of Man,* 61-103. New York: Frederick Ungar, 1966.

Mansfield, Harvey C., Jr. *Machiavelli's New Modes and Orders: A Study of the Discourses on Livy.* Ithaca: Cornell University Press, 1979.

———. "Machiavelli's Political Science." *American Political Science Review* 75, no. 2 (June 1981): 293-305.

———. "Machiavelli's Virtue." Chapter 1 of *Machiavelli's Virtue.* Chicago: University of Chicago Press, 1996.

———. "On the Impersonality of the Modern State: A Comment on Machiavelli's Use of *stato.*" *American Political Science Review* 77, no. 4 (December 1983): 849-57.

———. "Necessity in the Beginnings of Cities." In *The Political Calculus,* ed. Anthony Parel, 101-25. Toronto: University of Toronto Press, 1972.

———. "Party & Sect in Machiavelli's *Florentine Histories.*" In *Machiavelli and the Nature of Political Thought,* ed. Martin Fleisher, 209-75. New York: Atheneum, 1972.

———. "Translators' Introduction." In Niccolò Machiavelli, *Florentine Histories,* trans. Laura F. Banfield and Harvey C. Mansfield, Jr., vii-xv. Princeton: Princeton University Press, 1988.

Mansfield, Harvey C., and Nathan Tarcov. "Introduction." In Niccolò Machiavelli, *Discourses on Livy.* Translated by Harvey C. Mansfield and Nathan Tarcov, xvii-xliv. Chicago: University of Chicago Press, 1996.

Maritain, Jacques. "The End of Machiavellianism." *Review of Politics* 4 (January 1942): 1-33.

Mattingly, Garrett. *Renaissance Diplomacy.* Boston: Houghton Mifflin, 1971.

Mayer, Eduard Wilhelm. *Machiavellis Geschichtsauffassung und sein Begriff virtù: Studien zu seiner Historik.* Munich: R. Oldenbourg, 1912.

McCanles, Michael. *The Discourse of* Il Principe. Malibu, Calif.: Undena, 1983.

McCormick, John P. "Preparation and Response Regarding the Political Exception: Machiavelli's *accidenti* and the Mixed Regime." Paper presented at the 88th Annual Meeting of the American Political Science

Association, Chicago, September 3-6, 1992.

Mearsheimer, John J. *Conventional Deterrence.* Ithaca: Cornell University Press, 1983.

Mehmel, Friedrich. "Machiavelli und die Antike." In *Antike und Abendland: Beiträge zum Verständnis der Griechen und Römer und ihres Nachlebens,* ed. Bruno Snell, vol. 3, 151-86. Hamburg: Marion von Schröder, 1948.

Meinecke, Friedrich. *Machiavellism: The Doctrine of Raison d'Etat and Its Place in Modern History* [1924]. Translated by Douglas Scott. Boulder: Westview Press, 1984.

Michel, Alain. "Machiavel lecteur de Tite-Live: Entre l'optimism de Ciceron et le pessimisme de Tacite." In *Machiavelli attuale/Machiavel actuel,* ed. Georges Barthouil, 139-48. Ravenna: Longo, 1982.

Minogue, K. R. "Theatricality and Politics: Machiavelli's Concept of Fantasia." In *The Morality of Politics,* ed. Bhikhu Parekh and R. N. Berki, 148-63. London: Allen & Unwin, 1972.

Mommsen, Theodor. *Römisches Staatsrecht* [1888]. 4th ed. Tübingen: Wissenschaftliche Buchgemeinschaft, 1952.

Münkler, Herfried. *Machiavelli: Die Begründung des politischen Denkens der Neuzeit aus der Krise der Republik Florenz.* Frankfurt: Europäische Verlagsanstalt, 1982.

Nicolet, Claude. *The World of the Citizen in Republican Rome.* Translated by P. S. Falla. Berkeley, Calif.: University of California Press, 1980.

Nietzsche, Friedrich. *The Birth of Tragedy and The Case of Wagner* [1872, 1888]. Translated by Walter Kaufmann. New York: Random House, 1967.

Olschki, Leonardo. *Machiavelli the Scientist.* Berkeley, Calif.: Gillick, 1945.

Olsen, Mancur. *The Logic of Collective Action: Public Goods and the Theory of Groups.* Cambridge, Mass.: Harvard University Press, 1965.

Orr, Robert. "The Time Motif in Machiavelli." In *Machiavelli and the Nature of Political Thought,* ed. Martin Fleisher, 185-208. New York: Atheneum, 1972.

Osmond, Patricia J. "Sallust and Machiavelli: From Civic Humanism to Political Prudence." *Journal of Medieval and Renaissance Studies* 23, no. 3 (fall 1993): 407-38.

Pagel, Walter. "Medieval and Renaissance Contributions to Knowledge of the Brain and Its Functions." In *The History and Philosophy of Knowledge of the Brain and its Functions: An Anglo-American Symposium, London, July 15th-17th, 1957,* 95-114. Amsterdam: B.M. Israël, 1973.

Palmer, Michael. "Machiavellian *virtù* and Thucydidean *arete*: Traditional Virtue and Political Wisdom in Thucydides." *Review of Politics* 51, no. 3 (summer 1989): 365-85.

Parel, Anthony J. "Introduction: Machiavelli's Method and His Interpreters." In *The Political Calculus,* ed. Anthony Parel, 3-32. Toronto: University of Toronto Press, 1972.

———. "Machiavelli *Minore.*" In *The Political Calculus,* ed. Anthony Parel, 179-208. Toronto: University of Toronto Press, 1972.

———. "Machiavelli On Justice." *Machiavelli Studies* I (1987): 65-81.

———. *The Machiavellian Cosmos.* New Haven: Yale University Press, 1992.
Park, Katherine. "The Organic Soul." In *The Cambridge History of Renaissance Philosophy,* ed. Charles B. Schmitt, 464-84. Cambridge: Cambridge University Press, 1988.
Parkinson, G. H. R. "Ethics and Politics in Machiavelli." *Philosophical Quarterly* 5, no. 18 (January 1955): 37-44.
Pennington, K. "Law, Legislative Authority and Theories of Government, 1150-1300." In *The Cambridge History of Medieval Political Thought c. 350-c. 1450,* ed. J. H. Burns, 424-53. Cambridge: Cambridge University Press, 1988.
Pergamino, Giacomo. *Il Memoriale della Lingua Italiana.* Venice: Gio. Battista Ciotti, 1617.
Petrarca, Francesco. *The Ascent of Mont Ventoux* [1336]. Translated by Hans Nachod. In *The Renaissance Philosophy of Man,* ed. Ernst Cassirer, Paul Oskar Kristeller, and John Herman Randall, Jr., 36-46. Chicago: University of Chicago Press, 1948.
Philipp, Günther B. "Zur Problematik des römischen Ruhmesgedankens." *Gymnasium: Zeitschrift für Kultur der Antike und humanistische Bildung* 62, no. 1 (1955): 51-82.
Pico della Mirandola, Giovanni. *Oration on the Dignity of Man* [1486]. Translated by Elizabeth Livermoore Forbes. In *The Renaissance Philosophy of Man,* ed. Ernst Cassirer, Paul Oskar Kristeller, and John Herman Randall, Jr., 223-54. Chicago: University of Chicago Press, 1948.
Pico della Mirandola, Gianfrancesco. *On the Imagination* [1501]. Translated by Harry Caplan. New Haven: Yale University Press, 1930.
Pitkin, Hannah F. *Fortune Is a Woman: Gender and Politics in the Thought of Niccolò Machiavelli.* Berkeley, Calif.: University of California Press, 1984.
Plamenatz, John. "In Search of Machiavellian *Virtù.*" In *The Political Calculus,* ed. Anthony Parel, 157-78. Toronto: University of Toronto Press, 1972.
Plato. *Plato's Republic.* Translated by Allan Bloom. 2nd ed. New York: Basic Books, 1991.
———. *The Laws of Plato.* Translated by Thomas L. Pangle. Chicago: University of Chicago Press, 1980.
———. *Gorgias.* Translated by Donald J. Zeyl. Indianapolis: Hackett, 1987.
Pocock, J. G. A. "Custom & Grace, Form & Matter: An Approach to Machiavelli's Concept of Innovation." In *Machiavelli and the Nature of Political Thought,* ed. Martin Fleisher, 153-74. New York: Atheneum, 1972.
———. *The Machiavellian Moment: Florentine Political Thought and the Atlantic Republican Tradition.* Princeton: Princeton University Press, 1975.
Pole, Reginald Cardinal. *Apologia Reginaldi Poli ad Carolum V. Caesarem* [1539]. In *Epistolarum Reginaldi Poli S. R. E. Cardinalis et aliorum ad ipsum collectio,* ed. Angelo M. Quirini, vol. I, 66-172. Brescia, 1744-57. Reprinted Farnborough, England: Gregg Press, 1967.
Polybius. *The Rise of the Roman Empire.* Translated by Ian Scott-Kilvert.

London: Penguin Classics, 1979.

Popkin, Richard H. "Theories of Knowledge." In *The Cambridge History of Renaissance Philosophy,* ed. Charles B. Schmitt and Quentin Skinner, 668-84. Cambridge: Cambridge University Press, 1988.

Poppi, Antonino. "Fate, Fortune, Providence and Human Freedom." In *The Cambridge History of Renaissance Philosophy,* ed. Charles B. Schmitt, 641-67. Cambridge: Cambridge University Press, 1988.

Posen, Barry R. *The Sources of Military Doctrine: France, Britain, and Germany Between the World Wars.* Ithaca: Cornell University Press, 1984.

Post, Gaines. *Studies in Medieval Legal Thought: Public Law and the State, 1100-1322.* Princeton: Princeton University Press, 1964.

Prezzolini, Giuseppe. "The Christian Roots of Machiavelli's Moral Pessimism." *Review of National Literatures* 1, no. 1 (spring 1970): 26-37.

———. *Machiavelli.* Translated by Gioconda Savini. New York: Farrar, Straus & Giroux, 1967.

Price, Russell. "*Ambizione* in Machiavelli's Thought." *History of Political Thought* 3, no. 3 (November 1982): 383-445.

———. "The Senses of *Virtù* in Machiavelli." *European Studies Review* 3, no. 4 (October 1973): 315-45.

———. "The Theme of *Gloria* in Machiavelli." *Renaissance Quarterly* 30, no. 4 (winter 1977): 588-631.

Rahe, Paul A. *Republics Ancient and Modern.* Vol I, *The Ancien Régime in Classical Greece.* Chapel Hill: University of North Carolina Press, 1994.

Reinhardt, Karl. "Thukydides und Machiavelli" [1943]. In *Vermächtnis der Antike: Gesammelte Essays zur Philosophie und Geschichtsschreibung,* ed. Carl Becker, 2nd ed, 184-218. Göttingen: Vandenhoeck & Ruprecht, 1966.

Renaudet, Augustin. *Machiavel.* Paris: Gallimard, 1942.

Ridolfi, Roberto. *The Life of Niccolò Machiavelli.* Translated by Cecil Grayson. Chicago: University of Chicago Press, 1963.

Ritter, Gerhard. "Machiavelli und der Ursprung des modernen Nationalismus." In *Das sittliche Problem der Macht: Fünf Essays,* 40-90. Bern: A. Francke, 1948.

Rosecrance, Richard. *The Rise of the Trading State: Commerce and Conquest in the Modern World.* New York: Basic Books, 1986.

Rousseau, Jean-Jacques. *Discourse on the Origin and Foundations of Inequality Among Men.* In *The Basic Political Writings,* trans. Donald A. Cress, 23-109. Indianapolis: Hackett, 1987.

Ruffo-Fiore, Silvia. "Machiavelli and Reinhold Niebuhr: Politics and Christian Pragmatism." *Machiavelli Studies* I (1987): 127-36.

Sallust. *The War With Catiline.* In *Sallust.* Translated by J. C. Rolfe. Loeb Classical Library 116, 1-129. Cambridge, Mass.: Harvard University Press, 1985.

Santi, Victor A. "'Fama' e 'laude' distinte da 'gloria' in Machiavelli." *Forum Italicum* 12, no. 2 (summer 1978): 206-15.

Sasso, Gennaro. *Niccolò Machiavelli: Geschichte seines politischen Denkens* [1953]. Translated by Werner Klesse and Stefan Burger. Stuttgart: W.

Kohlhammer, 1965.

Schieder, Theodor. "Niccolò Machiavelli: Epilog zu einem Jubiläumsjahr." *Historische Zeitschrift* 210, no. 2 (April 1970): 265-94.

Simon, Yves R. *Practical Knowledge.* New York: Fordham University Press, 1991.

Snyder, Glenn H. "Deterrence and Defense." In *The Use of Force,* ed. Robert J. Art and Kenneth N. Waltz, 2nd ed., 123-41. Lanham, Md.: University Press of America, 1983.

Skinner, Quentin. *The Foundations of Modern Political Thought.* Vol. 1, *The Renaissance.* Cambridge: Cambridge University Press, 1978.

———. *Machiavelli.* New York: Hill and Wang, 1981.

———. "Machiavelli's *Discorsi* and the Pre-humanist Origins of Republican Ideas." In *Machiavelli and Republicanism,* ed. Gisela Bock, Quentin Skinner, and Maurizio Viroli, 121-41 (Cambridge: Cambridge University Press, 1990a).

———. "Meaning and Understanding in the History of Ideas." *History and Theory* 8, no. 1 (1969): 3-53.

———. "The Republican Ideal of Political Liberty." In *Machiavelli and Republicanism,* ed. Gisela Bock, Quentin Skinner, and Maurizio Viroli, 293-309. Cambridge: Cambridge University Press, 1990b.

Spackman, Barbara. "Politics on the Warpath: Machiavelli's *Art of War.*" In *Machiavelli and the Discourse of Literature,* ed. Albert Russell Ascoli and Victoria Kahn, 179-94. Ithaca: Cornell University Press, 1993.

Stein, P. G. "Roman Law." In *The Cambridge History of Medieval Political Thought c. 350-c. 1450,* ed. J. H. Burns, 37-47. Cambridge: Cambridge University Press, 1988.

Sternberger, Dolf. "Machiavellis Principe und der Begriff des Politischen." In *Herrschaft und Vereinbarung,* vol. 3 of *Schriften,* 31-111. Frankfurt am Main: Insel Verlag, 1980.

Strauss, Leo. "Machiavelli and Classical Literature." *Review of National Literatures* 1, no. 1 (spring 1970): 7-25.

———. *Natural Right and History.* Chicago: University of Chicago Press, 1950.

———. "Niccolò Machiavelli: 1469–1527." In *History of Political Philosophy,* ed. Leo Strauss and Joseph Cropsey, 3rd ed., 296-317. Chicago: University of Chicago Press, 1987.

———. *Thoughts on Machiavelli.* Chicago: University of Chicago Press, 1958.

———. *On Tyranny.* Chicago: University of Chicago Press, 1975.

Struever, Nancy S. *Theory as Practice: Ethical Inquiry in the Renaissance.* Chicago: University of Chicago Press, 1992.

Sullivan, Vickie B. "Human Autonomy in Niccolò Machiavelli's *Discourses on Livy.*" Ph.D. diss., University of Chicago, 1990.

———. "Machiavelli's Momentary 'Machiavellian Moment': A Reconsideration of Pocock's Treatment of the *Discourses.*" *Political Theory* 20, no. 2 (May): 309-18.

———. *Machiavelli's Three Romes: Religion, Human Liberty, and Politics Reformed.* De Kalb, Ill.: Northern Illinois University Press, 1996.

Sumner, William Graham. *Folkways: A Study of the Sociological Importance of Usages, Manners, Customs, Mores, and Morals.* New York: Dover Publications, 1906.

Tarcov, Nathan. "Quentin Skinner's Method and Machiavelli's *Prince.*" *Ethics* 92 (July 1982): 692-709.

Thucydides. *History of the Peloponnesian War.* Translated by Rex Warner. London: Penguin Books, 1954.

Tommasini, Oreste. *La vita e gli scritti di Machiavelli nello loro relazione col machiavellismo.* Vol. 2. Rome: E. Loescher, 1911.

Treitschke, Heinrich von. *Politics* [1897]. Translated by Blanche Dugdale and Torben de Bille. New York: Macmillan, 1916.

Valla, Lorenzo. *Dialogue on Free Will* [1483]. Translated by Charles Edward Trinkaus, Jr. In *The Renaissance Philosophy of Man,* ed. Ernst Cassirer, Paul Oskar Kristeller, and John Herman Randall, Jr., 155-82. Chicago: University of Chicago Press, 1948.

Vickers, Brian. "Rhetoric and Poetics." In *The Cambridge History of Renaissance Philosophy,* ed. Charles B. Schmitt and Quentin Skinner, 715-45. Cambridge: Cambridge University Press, 1988.

Villari, Pasquale. *The Life and Times of Niccolò Machiavelli.* New ed. Translated by Linda Villari. London: T. Fisher Unwin, 1892.

Viroli, Maurizio. *From Politics to Reason of State: The Acquisition and Transformation of the Language of Politics 1250-1600.* Cambridge: Cambridge University Press, 1992a.

——. *Machiavelli.* Oxford: Oxford University Press, 1998.

——. "Machiavelli and the Republican Idea of Politics." In *Machiavelli and Republicanism,* ed. Gisela Bock, Quentin Skinner, and Maurizio Viroli, 143-72. Cambridge: Cambridge University Press, 1990.

——. "The Revolution in the Concept of Politics." *Political Theory* 20, no. 3 (August 1992b): 473-95.

Walker, Leslie J. "Introduction by the Translator." In *The Discourses of Niccolò Machiavelli,* trans. Leslie J. Walker, vol. I, 1-164. New Haven: Yale University Press, 1950.

——. "Notes." In *The Discourses of Niccolò Machiavelli,* trans. Leslie J. Walker, vol. II. New Haven: Yale University Press, 1950.

Walt, Stephen M. *The Origins of Alliances.* Ithaca: Cornell University Press, 1987.

Waltz, Kenneth. *Theory of International Politics.* New York: Random House, 1979.

Walzer, Michael. "Political Action: The Problem of Dirty Hands." *Philosophy and Public Affairs* 2, no. 2 (winter 1973): 160-80.

——. *Just and Unjust Wars: A Moral Argument with Historical Illustrations.* New York: Basic Books, 1977.

Weber, Max. *Politics As a Vocation* [1921]. In *From Max Weber: Essays in Sociology,* trans. H. H. Gerth and C. Wright Mills, 77-128. NewYork: Oxford University Press, 1946.

Weinstein, Donald. "Machiavelli and Savonarola." In *Studies on Machiavelli,* ed. Myron P. Gilmore, 253-64. Florence: Sansoni, 1972.

Whitfield, J. H. "The Anatomy of Virtue." In *Machiavelli,* 92-105. New York: Russell & Russell, 1947.

——. *Discourses On Machiavelli.* Cambridge: W. Heffer & Sons, 1969.

——. "Machiavelli's Use of Livy." In *Livy,* ed. T. A. Dorey, 73-96. London: Routledge Kegan Paul, 1971.

——. "On Machiavelli's Use of *Ordini.*" *Italian Studies* 10 (1955): 19-39.

——. "The Politics of Machiavelli." *Modern Language Review* 50 (1955): 433-43.

Wilson, Ronald C. *Ancient Republicanism: Its Struggle for Liberty Against Corruption.* New York: P. Lang, 1989.

Wolin, Sheldon S. "Machiavelli: Politics and the Economy of Violence." Chapter 7 of *Politics and Vision: Continuity and Innovation in Western Political Thought.* Boston: Little Brown, 1960.

Wood, Neal. "Machiavelli's Concept of *Virtù* Reconsidered." *Political Studies* 15, no. 2 (June 1967): 159-72.

——. "Machiavelli's Humanism of Action." In *The Political Calculus,* ed. Anthony Parel, 33-57. Toronto: University of Toronto Press, 1972.

——. "The Value of Asocial Sociability: Contributions of Machiavelli, Sidney and Montesquieu." In *Machiavelli and the Nature of Political Thought,* ed. Martin Fleisher, 282-307. New York: Atheneum.

Woollam, D. H. M. "Concepts of the Brain and Its Functions in Classical Antiquity." In *The History and Philosophy of Knowledge of the Brain and Its Functions: An Anglo-American Symposium, London, July 15th-1th, 1957,* 5-18 (Amsterdam: B.M. Israël, 1973).

Zeitlin, Irving M. *Plato's Vision: The Classical Origins of Social & Political Thought* (Englewood Cliffs, N.J.: Prentice Hall, 1993).

Zuckert, Michael P. "Appropriation and Understanding in the History of Political Philosophy: On Quentin Skinner's Method," *Interpretation* 13 (1985): 403-24.

Index

About the Author

Markus Fischer has taught political theory at Dartmouth College, Trinity College, and Oglethorpe University. He is currently a Fellow at the John F. Kennedy School of Government at Harvard University.